HOME
FRONT

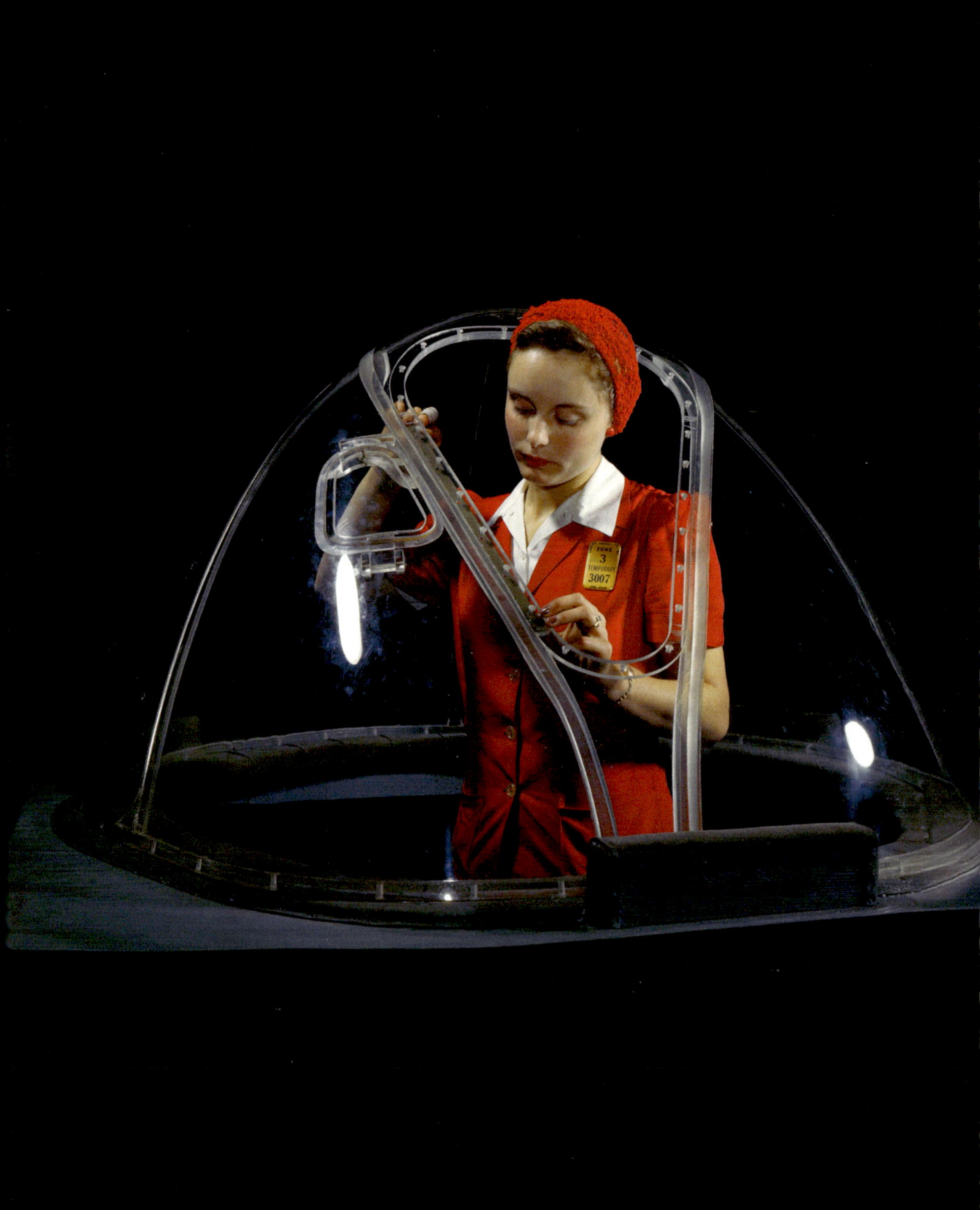

HOME FRONT

ALFRED T. PALMER'S WWII PHOTOGRAPHY

MARY M. CRONIN AND BRUCE BERMAN

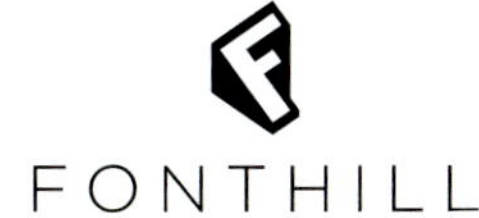

FONTHILL

First published in Great Britain in 2025 by
Fonthill
An imprint of
Pen & Sword Books Ltd
Yorkshire – Philadelphia
www.fonthill.media

ISBN 978-1-62545-103-3

A CIP catalogue record for this book
is available from the British Library.

Typeset in Sabon LT 10/13
Typeset by Fonthill
Printed and bound in the UK by 4Edge Limited, Essex SS5 4AD

The Publisher's authorised representative in the EU for product safety is Authorised Rep Compliance Ltd., Ground Floor, 71 Lower Baggot Street, Dublin D02 P593, Ireland.
www.arccompliance.com

For a complete list of Pen & Sword titles please contact
PEN & SWORD BOOKS LIMITED
47 Church Street, Barnsley, South Yorkshire, S70 2AS, England
E-mail: enquiries@pen-and-sword.co.uk
Website: www.pen-and-sword.co.uk

Or
PEN AND SWORD BOOKS
1950 Lawrence Rd, Havertown, PA 19083, USA
E-mail: Uspen-and-sword@casematepublishers.com
Website: www.penandswordbooks.com

FOREWORD

"MY FATHER"

A young man was standing on the Long Beach, California, pier where the big ships came and went every day. He was gazing out over the Pacific Ocean and daydreaming of being on that ocean to discover all that was past the shore on which he was standing. Nearby, the port captain was watching him. The young man wandered over and asked him if he could have a job on one of those big ships. The port captain said, "Get lost kid."

The next day, the young man was on the pier again gazing out to sea. The ships continued to go in and out of the harbor. The young man again asked the port captain if he could have a job on one of those big ships and again was told to get lost. Somehow, in this young man's mind there was a job for him on one of those ships, and he was undaunted. After several days of telling the kid to go away, the port captain lost his patience and told him to show up at 5:30 the next morning and he could get on a ship. This was said grudgingly just to get rid of this pesky, determined kid.

The young man packed a rucksack with a few belongings and his camera, said goodbye to his ma, and arrived at the pier early the next morning. After signing some papers, he was directed to board the *SS President Monroe*, a Dollar Steamship Lines vessel bound for the Orient. He knew that the excitement he felt inside him would have to be subdued in order to conform to being the lowest member of the crew.

The year was 1925. The young man was eighteen years old, and this was the beginning of Alfred Thompson Palmer's life on the sea. The young man was my father, Alfred T. Palmer. He went on to have a career as a photographer at sea and on land. He took twenty-three trips around the world, most as chief photographer for various shipping lines, and also produced thousands of photographs at home in America. I knew him as a man who knew what his dreams were made of, and he had the tenacity and skills to make them a reality—his camera was his tool to this reality.

He married Alexa Hulse on Christmas Eve in 1929 in Long Beach, California. Alexa had a vision that if she married this handsome young man, she would travel the world by his side, living the romance that was his. It did not happen that way, though, and she remained homebound raising three children with a part-time husband. She lived through his letters when he was away for long periods of time. But he was a good writer and explained through words the work that he was doing and how much he missed his family.

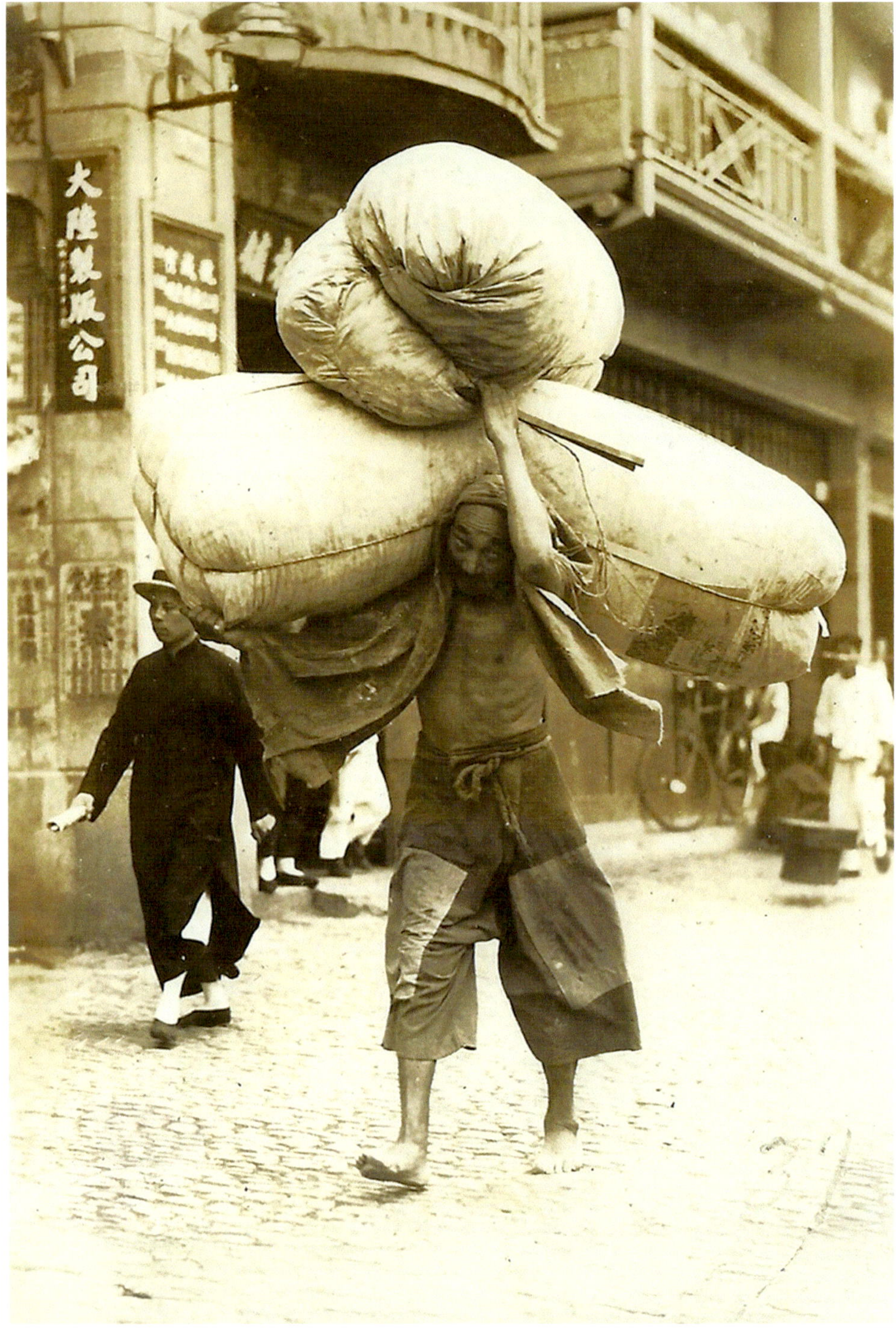

Heavily laden worker in China, undated (1920s or 1930s). (*A. T. Palmer Collection, privately held*)

My father was a true artist, creating vast canvases from the world he traveled through. When I think of how he captured what he was seeing, I find it unbelievable that he was able to communicate his reality through the lens of the camera he was using. The Graflex camera had a tall bellows that had a piece of ground glass at the bottom with the image perceived upside down! I remember, as a tiny child, bending over and looking down though that bellows, not having any idea about what he saw though it.

He also made documentary films for Standard Vacuum Oil Company, Bank of America, and American President Lines and was able to take his family on a trip around the world as his work party in 1956—before Southeast Asia exploded into war, a conflict that changed that part of the world forever. I was sixteen and my brother, Don, was seventeen. This trip lasted a year, and we traveled mostly by ship to Hawaii; Japan; the Philippines; Hong Kong, Macao, and Kowloon, China; Singapore; Thailand; Cambodia; Vietnam; Ceylon (Sri Lanka); India; Cape Town, South Africa; and through the Panama Canal to San Francisco.

As a teenager, I looked at the world as a place teeming with cultures unknown to me, and I learned that not everyone was like my fellow countrymen—that people live their lives with habits and traditions that can be centuries old. The influences of colonization and infiltration have had their effect on these traditions, but in so many places—like the farms of India, where I threw seed in the field with a young farm girl—the influences did not mean much. Speaking their language was not always necessary because we could enter into their world with friendly gestures and smiles. I came home with a new perspective on how we live in America and how we can be tolerant of other people and their ways of life.

My job on this trip was to manage and keep tabs on our stuff—133 pieces of various gear: camera equipment, suitcases, and boxes of things we picked up along the way. Each one was numbered and noted in a notebook—no computers or tablets. When everything was unloaded off a ship or a truck, I would count each one and make sure they were all accounted for. Especially the camera equipment, which included not only cameras, but lights and lighting gear, electric cords and plugs, film, and recording machines. Everything was heavy and bulky.

We spent day after day tramping around with a movie camera on us—walking, climbing, standing—everything dad wanted to shoot. Sometimes we were inclined to whine but were stopped by the view, the scenery, the heat, the people, the camera aimed at us—and soon we got used to it and stopped complaining. Light was most important to him. We were in India, driving to Agra and the Taj Mahal. The driver of our 1950s Chevy was reckless and could barely handle the rickety vehicle, which had no shocks. The roads were very bumpy. There would be a sign that said "dip," and the road would dump into a ditch, and we would bounce. The driver could not find the Taj Mahal. At one point he stopped and there it was, across the river. By now dad was feeling a loss because the light was going, and he would not be able to get the film shots that he wanted.

My father began his adventure into unknown territory when he was young. He did not make a big deal out of being American—he just participated and was involved in other cultures. And because of his camera—which many people had never seen nor heard of in the 1920s—he was able to be a part of what they did in their daily lives.

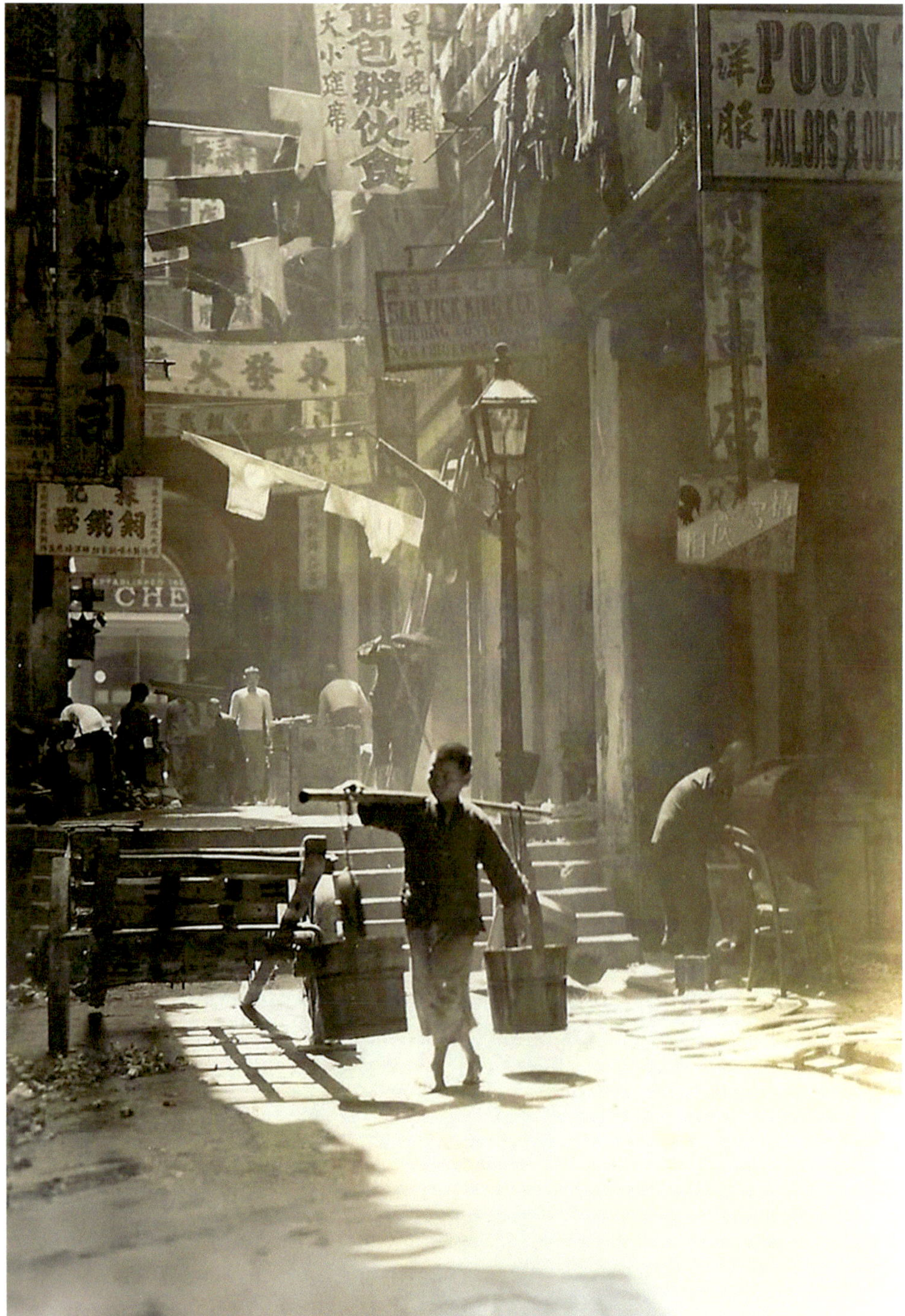

Boy worker, China street scene, undated (1920s or 1930s). (*A. T. Palmer Collection, privately held*)

They would gather around—fascinated—and the result was what he wanted on film.

The cameras that I used on our world trip in 1956 were a Stereo and a Polaroid. In Bali, I took a Polaroid picture of an elderly couple and presented it to them. They were astounded, having never seen an image of themselves.

Alfred made twenty-three trips around the world on American ships, using his cameras, his artistic eye, and his technical expertise to capture images of indigenous cultures on every continent. These photographs are important as testimony to a world gone by, left behind as it were, to be replaced by the enormity of modern technology and often the neutralization of those cultures.

As a staff photographer for *National Geographic* magazine, he suggested that they make films, and since they ignored the idea, he quit and went on to make documentary and travel films on his own and for American companies and for world governments. His thousands of photographs have been preserved and catalogued by his daughter. His world film library is housed at the Mystic Seaport Museum in Connecticut. These images are a valuable part of twentieth-century history to be used by educational facilities, corporations, news media, libraries, and by personal collectors worldwide. They are irreplaceable original images of humanity that document an era of extraordinary activity and diversification.

Julia Palmer Gennert

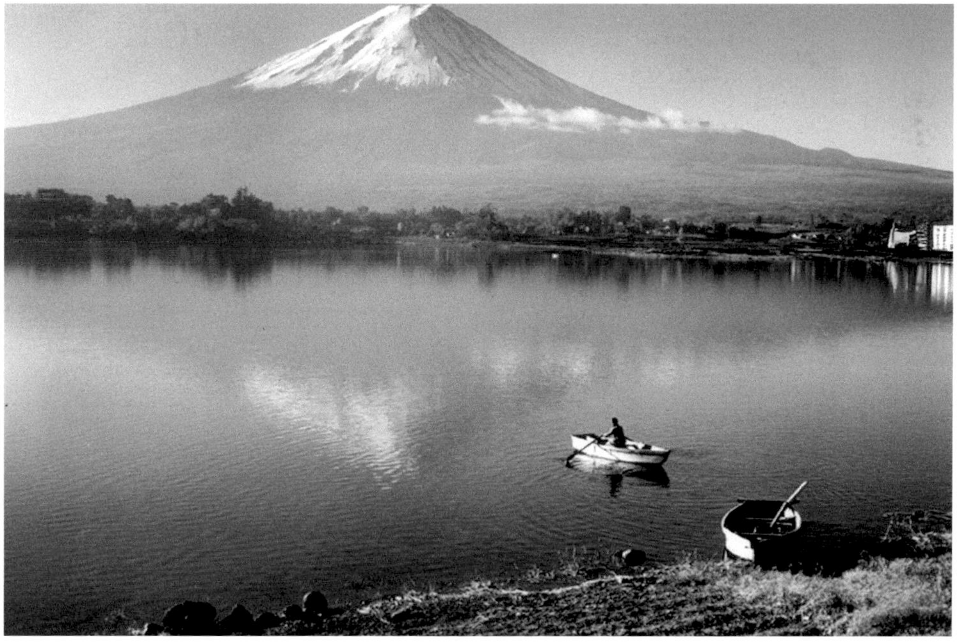

Mt. Fuji, Japan, with lake in foreground, undated. (*A. T. Palmer Collection, privately held*)

ACKNOWLEDGMENTS

The authors would like to thank Julia Palmer Gennert, Alfred T. Palmer's daughter and the keeper of his archives, for her willingness to open those archives—and her home—to us. She has shared a wealth of primary source material, much of which went into this book. We would also like to thank her son, Tim Gennert, for his support of this project.

Professor Katrina J. Quinn of the Department of Strategic Communication and Media at Slippery Rock University of Pennsylvania, and Crompton 'Hub' Burton, a historian extraordinaire who recently retired from his position as internal communications manager in the Office of Human Resources for the University of Maine System, Augusta, Maine, also have our deepest appreciation. Both scholars carefully proofread drafts of the manuscript and made suggestions that have improved the final book greatly.

Several individuals at our institution—New Mexico State University—also have our gratitude. The terrific interlibrary loan staff at the Zuhl Library helped us obtain numerous books and scholarly journal articles that our own university did not own. And Professor Darren Phillips, our colleague in the Department of Journalism and Media Studies, helped digitize some of the images that the Palmer family loaned to us.

Finally, Mary M. Cronin would like to thank her husband, Keith, and her adult daughter, Emily, for their patience as this manuscript was researched and written. Emily also read the book and made excellent suggestions that helped improve the manuscript.

CONTENTS

A WORD ABOUT THE PHOTOGRAPHS

All of Alfred T. Palmer's color photographs were shot on Kodachrome film, which was considered to be the premier color film of the film era. Almost all the images were produced from a 4" × 5" Speed Graphic or 5" × 7" Graflex camera.

The photographs that appear in this book were made from the Library of Congress' straight scans. Scans are not reproductions. Time and age have slightly changed the film stock over the past eighty-plus years. In fact, they are informed approximations.

To bring Palmer's work back to what it looked like to him, at the time, preparing them for this publication, required interpretation. One needed to be familiar with the characteristics inherent to that film's pallet. Every effort was made to honor Palmer's work to make the images as he would have viewed them, were he himself producing this book.

Bruce Berman

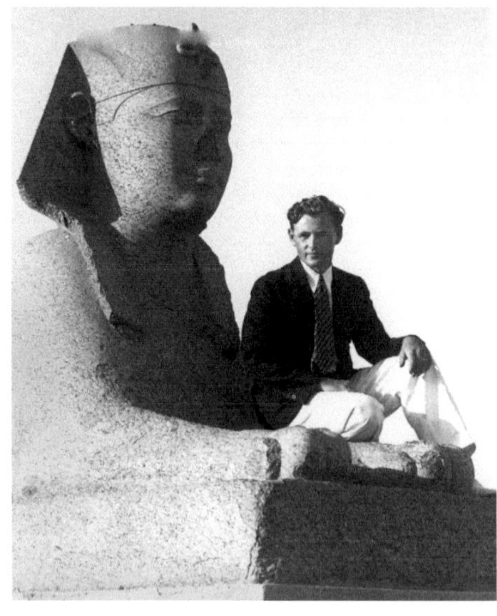

Alfred T. Palmer in Egypt, 1920s.
(*A. T. Palmer Collection, privately held*)

INTRODUCTION

"GET OUT THERE AND DO THE JOB!"

The principal battleground of this war is not the South Pacific. It is not the Middle East. It is not England, or Norway, or the Russian Steppes. It is American opinion.

Archibald MacLeish, poet, Librarian of Congress, Director of the Office of Facts and Figures, and Assistant Director of the Office of War Information

As Americans prepared for—and then entered—World War II, the nation was awash in propaganda. Posters, billboards, traveling exhibitions, advertisements, newspaper and magazine articles, motion pictures, and leaflets created by federal agencies and private businesses exhorted individuals to serve their country, either in uniform or in critical wartime jobs, including defense plant work. Members of the public also were encouraged to purchase war bonds, to conserve much-needed raw materials, and to accept such home front annoyances as the rationing of essentials, including food and gasoline, as part of their patriotic duty. The collective message was a clear one: the United States could not defend itself against foreign enemies unless all citizens recognized their obligations to their nation and followed through by doing what was expected of them.

Armed with his Graflex, Speed Graphic, and Contax rangefinder cameras, Alfred T. Palmer (1906–1993) shot many of the iconic images that illustrated the federal government's patriotic appeals. One photograph from his portfolio became the centerpiece of a tremendously popular 1942 War Production Board poster. Encouraging Americans to "Keep the Home Fires Burning" and engage in "More Production," the poster featured a shirtless foundry worker who served as the physical embodiment of the nation's wartime strength. Glistening with sweat, his muscles are clearly defined as he shovels coal into an immense furnace.[1]

Palmer, a self-employed commercial photographer who specialized in maritime imagery, was hired in May 1940 on a contract basis by Robert Horton, who was then serving as the director of public relations for the U.S. Maritime Commission, and Admiral Emory Land, chairman of the commission, to make 'glamorous' photographs—and a short motion picture—of ship construction, an effort that

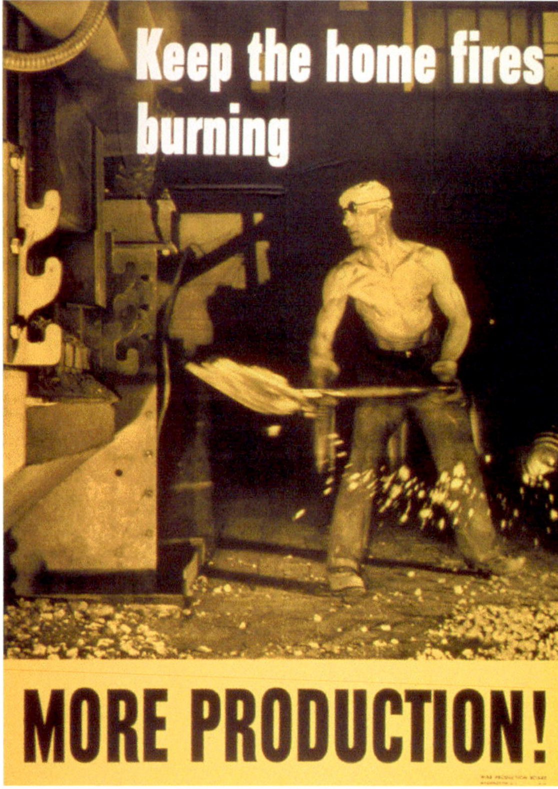

"Keep the Home Fires Burning—More Production" poster. Created for the United States War Production Board, 1942. The photograph was taken at the Allegheny Ludlum Steel Corporation in Brackenridge, Pennsylvania. (*National Archives*)

was part of the country's pre-war defense buildup. The images were used to help explain and justify why the government was embarking on the expensive endeavor.[2]

A month later, Horton took a parallel position with the Division of Information for the National Defense Advisory Commission (which was housed within the newly formed Office for Emergency Management) and brought his photographer with him. By employing Palmer, Horton sought to establish a picture file of feature photographs. Those images were given to newspaper and magazine editors to illustrate defense stories. The photographs also were used to illustrate the federal government's defense campaigns, including worker recruitment.[3] Horton knew that visual images, including photographs, could help shape the public's perceptions.[4]

Horton and Palmer worked together on and off throughout the war years at several agencies, including the Office for Emergency Management, the Office of War Information, and the U.S. Maritime Commission.[5] Horton's public relations unit, the Division of Information, was relocated several times as President Franklin D. Roosevelt established new wartime information agencies and dissolved others.

Initially, Horton's Division of Information provided the press with information and photographs on the defense buildup that occurred prior to America's involvement in World War II. After the United States entered the conflict following the Japanese attack on Pearl Harbor on December 7, 1941, Horton's staff provided the press with information concerning war activities on the home front and abroad. Although Horton, a former journalist, preferred to provide information to the public, rather than propaganda, both the Office for Emergency Management and the Office of War Information engaged in what has been called "agitative" propaganda—that is, the creation of information that is packaged to "rouse" a target audience toward some form of significant change, whether that be in behaviors, attitudes, or beliefs.[6]

Horton's dedication to the use of information notwithstanding, officials at federal defense information and propaganda agencies largely used what has been called "White" propaganda—that is, propaganda that comes from an identifiable source and tends to be accurate, although the information may not give all sides of the story. This approach is in sharp contrast to so-called "Black" propaganda. This latter form involves concealing the source of the information or crediting the information "to a false authority." Such propaganda involves spreading lies, deceptions, and fabrications. Used by Nazi Germany's propaganda minister Joseph Goebbels, "Black" propaganda involves "all types of creative deceit."[7]

A BATTLE OF POLITICAL WILLS

President Roosevelt's political maneuvering also was a factor in Palmer's employment as a government photographer. The eighteen months before the United States entered World War II were marked by political tensions and seemingly endless and emotional debate about America's role in the world, including the issue of whether to help supply the nation's European allies with military armaments.[8] The president knew that the political neutrality and isolationist policies developed during the 1920s and 1930s—to which he paid lip service as the price of getting re-elected—had to be abandoned. The nation's European allies needed help standing up against Nazi Germany's military might. Then, too, Roosevelt also believed that the German threat to America's democratic system was equally concerning. A battle of political wills set in among the president, conservative members of Congress who supported an isolationist approach to foreign policy, and prominent anti-war public figures, including beloved aviation hero Charles A. Lindbergh, Jr. That infighting made the task of war preparation far more difficult. The neutrality debate and the issue of whether the nation should come to the aid of Great Britain and France, and even enter the war itself, "spilled over" into the press, as well as into the country's main streets, schools, and businesses.[9]

Back in Washington, D.C., the president, who hated to lose a political battle, and was at times cautious in the face of criticism from conservatives, proposed what he viewed as a viable strategy to defend the nation from potential German aggression: the United States would vastly expand its armed forces (in terms of

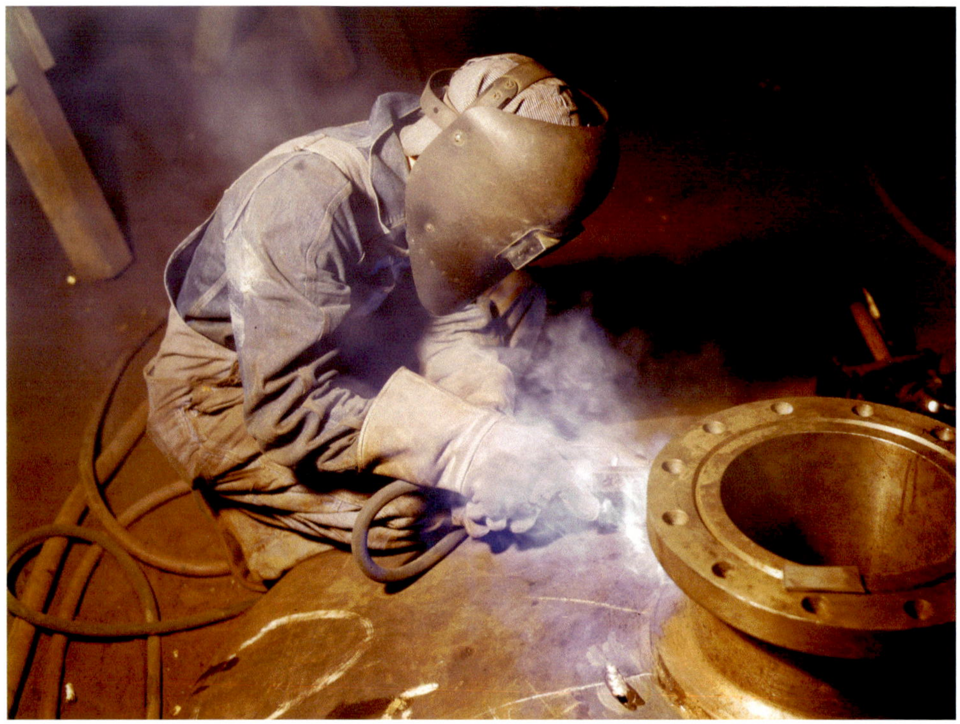

Welder making boilers for a ship, Combustion Engineering Co., Chattanooga, Tennessee, June 1942. (*Library of Congress*)

both men and materials) to protect the country against possible external threats.[10] This national defense strategy necessitated a surge in the industrial production of military materials, a tactic which put depression-weary Americans back to work.

Roosevelt needed public opinion on his side to accomplish his policy goals and to prepare Americans for the war he knew would come. The president used his radio addresses, including a May 26, 1940, talk on national defense, as a means of reaching the public directly to educate citizens on the dangers of European fascism. But he knew that his radio talks were only one means of persuading the American people. Roosevelt also recognized that a new commitment to government-initiated propaganda was necessary to sway public opinion in his favor as well.

Initially, the president wavered in his beliefs about the use of propaganda, remembering the near-hysteria and fear that the Committee on Public Information—the first federally-sanctioned government propaganda unit—had created among citizens during World War I. Yet, Roosevelt knew that Americans had to be more than just informed about the conflicts in Europe and Asia. The public also had to be convinced that German, Italian, and Japanese expansionist aggression was a direct threat to the United States and its democratic system. And those citizens had to be motivated to act in their own defense and the defense of their nation.[11]

A "STRATEGY OF TRUTH"

The directors of the information agencies that Roosevelt established settled on what became known as a "strategy of truth" as a means of persuading the public to embrace the president's foreign and domestic policy goals. Grounded in both logic and emotion, the approach was based on the assumption that if the public was presented with the facts about the Axis powers' threats to the nation, citizens would take the appropriate steps to protect their country. Thus, the Office for Emergency Management's Division of Information under Horton initially sought to present "the plain, unvarnished truth." That approach would change during the autumn months of 1941, much to Horton's dismay. Persuasive communication increasingly came to the fore to help boost civilian morale and encourage citizens to shake off their complacency toward defense preparations. Federal propaganda activities would expand with the creation of the Office of War Information on June 13, 1942, and the hiring of advertising executives at that agency—individuals who used the techniques from their occupation to sell the war to the public.[12]

Photography became a crucial, persuasive tool in both the informational and propaganda arsenals, for it provided a means of visually presenting the truth that the Roosevelt administration envisioned. The need to move the public toward acceptance of the president's interventionist foreign policy while also maintaining morale at home necessitated that the truth presented by federal officials and government agencies be one-sided. In the eighteen months before the attack on Pearl Harbor plunged the United States into war, Palmer was tasked by Horton

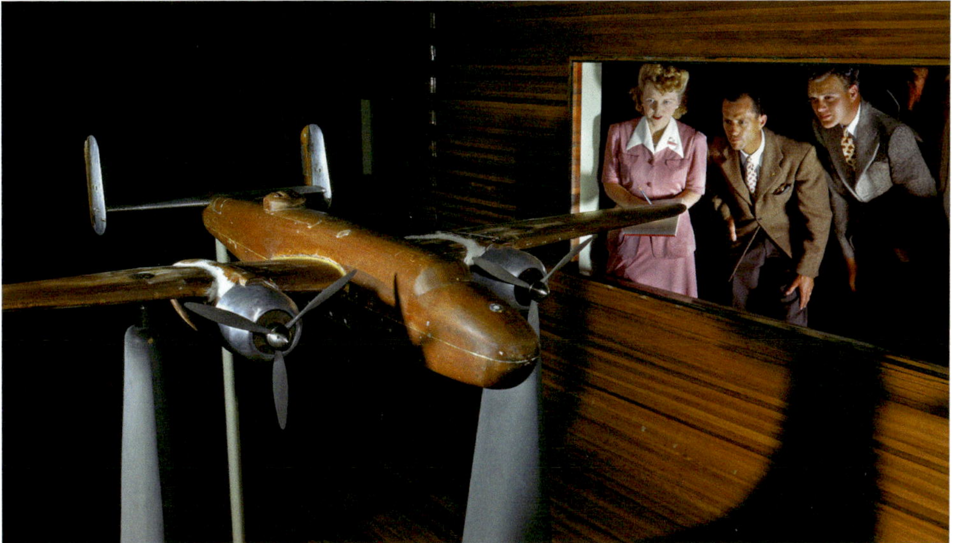

Members of the experimental staff at the North American Aviation, Inc., plant, observe wind tunnel tests on an accurate scale model of the B-25 ("Billy Mitchell") bomber, Inglewood, California, October 1942. (*Library of Congress*)

with showing the public how their tax dollars were being spent. But those photographs also were meant to boost citizens' morale and convince the public that the president's defense plans for the nation were necessary and correct. Shot in both black-and-white and color, Palmer's images attempted to achieve those various purposes by portraying a confident, strong, and unified nation readying itself for defense.

The photographs also were meant to help persuade citizens to serve their nation in jobs that many individuals had not previously held. When the civilian labor pool began dwindling as men went off to war in 1942 and 1943, women—especially white middle-class women who had not previously worked outside of their homes—became a key target of government propaganda campaigns since the continued production of war materials was crucial for victory.

The campaign initially proved a difficult sell for federal officials. A poll undertaken by the American Institute of Public Opinion in December 1942 revealed that 54 percent of middle-class men were opposed to their wives working in factories, despite the ongoing war. Such labor was broadly perceived by the middle classes as not quite respectable; men were expected to be the breadwinners in the family.[13] An Office of War Information document acknowledged as much. The report stressed that for the "Womanpower" information campaign to be a success, federal propaganda efforts not only had to convince men that their wives

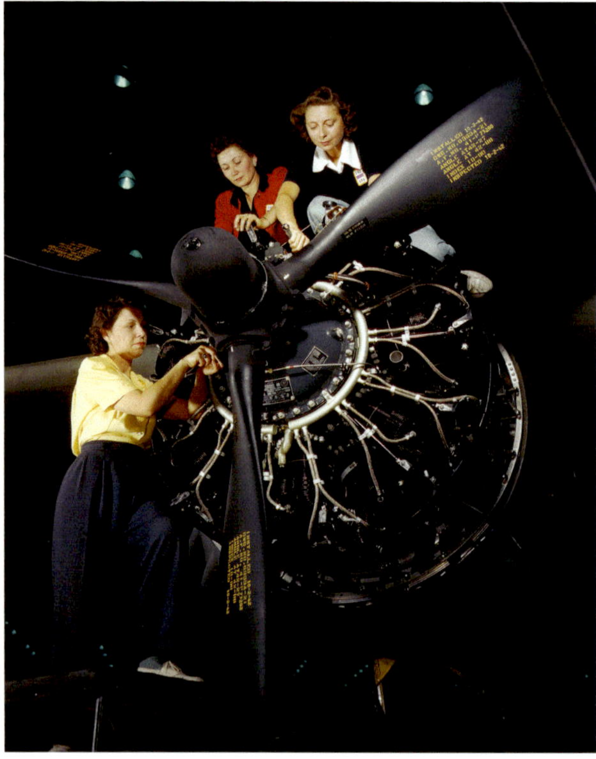

The careful hands of women are trained in precise aircraft engine installation duties at Douglas Aircraft Company, Long Beach, California, October 1942. (*Library of Congress*)

were needed as factory laborers, but the campaign's materials also had to cajole women into accepting that it was their duty to take such jobs.[14]

Federal officials later expanded this campaign to include minority women, particularly African Americans.[15] Palmer's photographs were an important tool used to encourage middle-class women to undertake temporary jobs in once-unthinkable industries. The photographer helped normalize such work by representing women laborers as patriotic, dignified, and, importantly, feminine, and attractive despite their temporary foray into occupations previously pursued by men.[16]

FIGHTING PUBLIC APATHY WITH PATRIOTIC IMAGES

Palmer's home front war work led him to crisscross the country from 1940 to 1945, taking still photographs and making documentary films. "Get out there and do the job!" were his orders from Horton.[17] He did so, and his short features and full-length motion pictures were shown in cinemas across the nation, while his still photographs appeared in a variety of media both at home and abroad.

Palmer did not undertake his job solely for the steady paycheck that it offered. Fifteen years of international travel as a commercial photographer for cruise ship lines exposed Palmer to the world's cultures and political systems. His worldliness led him to disagree with the isolationist sentiment that was embraced by much of the public and many members of Congress. Palmer thought that mindset was

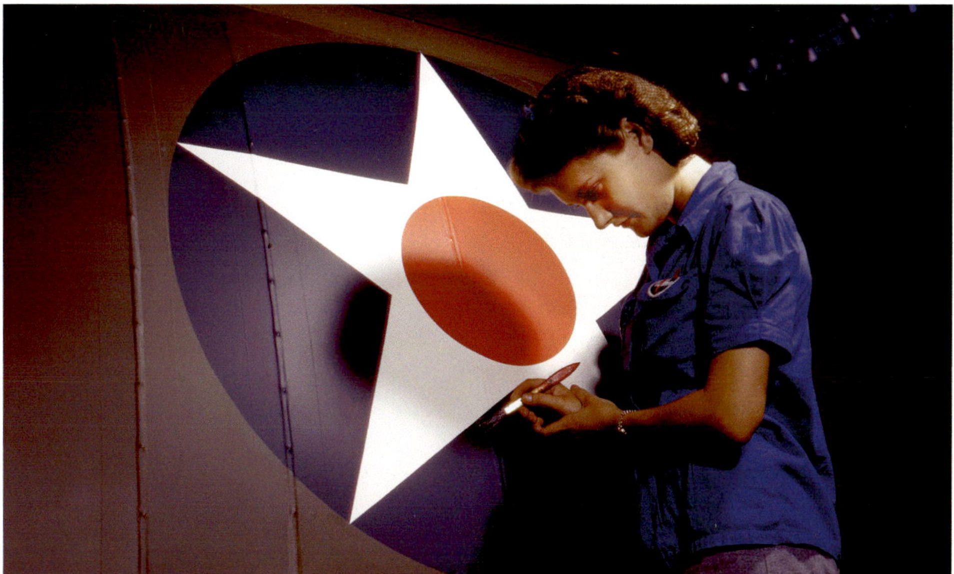

A candid view of one of the women workers touching up the U.S. Army Air Force's insignia on the side of the fuselage of a Vengeance dive bomber manufactured at Vultee's Nashville, Tennessee, division, February 1943. (*Library of Congress*)

short-sighted and harmful to the nation's interests given German, Italian, and Japanese aggression. He had witnessed the latter nation's bombing of Shanghai first-hand in August 1937 while working as photographer aboard the *President Pierce*, a cruise ship owned by the Dollar Steamship Lines, as it sailed up the Huangpu River to pick up American refugees. That experience contributed to his conviction that there was an imminent need to awaken his fellow citizens to the dangers of the Axis powers and their totalitarian political beliefs.[18]

Despite his years of globetrotting and his fascination with other cultures, particularly Asian ones, Palmer was deeply patriotic and believed in the American dream. He strongly supported his nation's democratic system and way of life. According to historian Jeanie Cooper Carson, one of the few individuals to interview Palmer at length before his death, the photographer was convinced that with hard work, most individuals could thrive under a democratic system and ultimately live comfortable lives.[19]

As America's involvement in World War II approached, Palmer believed that geography gave many of the nation's citizens a false sense of security. Most individuals kept themselves informed about the ongoing war in Europe and Japanese aggression in Asia via newspapers and radio news. They were aware of Japan's expansion of its navy, as well as that nation's military incursions into China during the 1930s, but those actions seemed distant, as did the need to help America's allies. "These things were overseas," Palmer said, recalling the public's overall apathy toward engaging in global conflict. "The attitude was, 'So what!'" The public, he said, was not motivated to return to armed conflict. The devastation caused by World War I was a recent and very raw memory for many Americans, and a key reason for the rise of isolationist and non-interventionist federal policies in the two decades prior to World War II. "When I think of the horrible things that came out of World War I, millions and millions of people killed, smashed, their whole lives gone and ruined—what did it all amount to, really?" Palmer stated, explaining the thinking of many Americans. The result of World War I was clear to Palmer, however. The conflict "created a Hitler," he stated.[20]

Public apathy remained a concern even after the Japanese attack on Pearl Harbor on December 7, 1941. Two months after the U.S. entered the war, the editors of *Time* magazine questioned whether the public was "Smug, Slothful, [or] Asleep." The article that accompanied the seemingly dramatic headline included warnings from a wide variety of political and military leaders, including Eleanor Roosevelt, interventionist members of the U.S. Congress, and broadcast journalist Edward R. Murrow (who had been covering the war in Europe for CBS radio), that the public had not fully awakened to the wartime responsibilities ahead of them. Murrow, in particular, had tried via his broadcasts from London to remove the sense of distance between Great Britain and America, while also attempting to allay his listeners' suspicions that the English did not have the will to fight.[21] The broadcaster, who was back in the United States for a brief lecture tour in late 1941, was quoted in the *Time* article as saying that Americans "still viewed the war as a spectacle." He voiced the concerns that many interventionists held when he encouraged Americans to realize their place in world affairs and become the leaders that they were meant to be:

Some of us are reluctant to accept the greatness that has been thrust upon us, but we have no choice.... Had you been with me for the last month wandering about our country, you would agree that we are prepared to make ... sacrifices, but you might feel, as I do, that we do not fully appreciate the need for speed, that we do not quite understand that if we delay too long in winning the victory we will inherit nothing but a cold, starving embittered world.[22]

William Batt, director of materials for the War Production Board, issued an equally frank assessment in the same *Time* article regarding the potential consequences of Americans' slow response to the global conflict. "Not since the days of the Revolution have we had much of a chance to lose a war," he said. "We have a chance to lose this one."[23]

In the mind of at least some government officials, therefore, the need for persuasive propaganda—both visual and written—was urgent, even though those officials could not always agree on the strategies, tactics, or messaging necessary for that propaganda to succeed.[24] Despite this ongoing disagreement, Palmer provided those officials with a steady stream of photographs that represented a consistent vision of a nation preparing for—and then entering—the war. The photographer stressed positive imagery—spiritual and material strength— believing that negative images, including the depictions of poverty taken by the Farm Security Administration (FSA) photographers during the 1930s, should not be published during wartime.[25]

Given his beliefs, Palmer's America, as seen through his camera lens, looked industrially strong and orderly, replete with competent, hard-working, and patriotic citizens who were dedicated to a common cause. Far from seeming rattled or dismayed as the German, Italian, and Japanese militaries made rapid geographic strikes into other nations, the subjects of Palmer's images appear confident, upbeat, and bright. Any private thoughts of despair at the nation's return to global war were never depicted. Instead, Palmer's photographs demonstrated a home front whose citizens had rallied behind the president and were up to the task of protecting their nation's democratic system and way of life.

Privately, however, the photographer was dismayed when the social reality did not match his confident, idealized images. Americans could not win the war unless they came together. In an April 1942 letter to his wife from Detroit, Michigan, Palmer voiced his concerns about labor unrest that slowed or halted the production of much needed military equipment, including planes, jeeps, and tanks that were being produced by the Ford Motor Company:

I can't help thinking that most of the country is going to go to the bow-wows [i.e., dogs] when this war is over and the billions in cash is stopped flowing into and out of people's pockets. Today there is a strike on at the Willow Run Bomber plant. There was a riot at River Rouge [i.e., the Ford Motor Company plant] the other day.... It seems to me that when there is so much trouble now—with so much money dripping all over the place—that when the time comes to stop war production—our good old

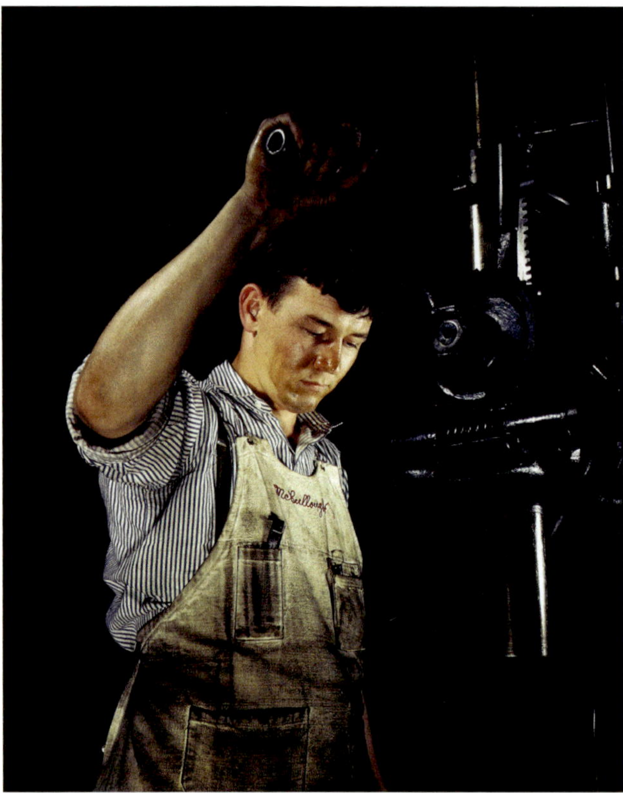

Drill press operator,
Allegheny Ludlum Steel Corp,
Brackenridge, Pennsylvania.
(*Library of Congress*)

U.S.A. is going to have one big headache. Because people have become so careless, and greedy, and excited.[26]

Soldiers awaiting their orders to be shipped overseas also were angered by the labor strikes. One U.S. Army Air Corps pilot admitted that he would 'just as soon shoot down one of those strikers' as shoot down Japanese soldiers.' The unnamed pilot viewed the strikers as detriments to victory. 'They're doing just as much to lose the war for us,' he added.[27]

While Palmer's images never depicted any of the nation's labor unrest, production problems, or racial strife that occurred during the war years, the psychological reasoning behind the photographs shifted after the United States entered the war. In the period between May 1940 and early December 1941, federal officials engaged in propaganda creation had been tasked with convincing the nation's citizens of the need to abandon isolationist sentiment in favor of protecting the country by supporting America's allies against the Axis powers. But following America's entrance into the war, Palmer's photographs were used to depict both the nation's industrial might and its citizens' unity against their enemies. The objective now was to keep the public motivated toward the twin goals of winning the war and seeing democracy triumph over fascism.[28]

CREATING VISUAL PROPAGANDA ARCHETYPES

Although Palmer used both black-and-white and color film throughout the war years, his use of color film, especially when photographing soldiers engaged in training and factory workers producing much-needed military supplies, can be considered as much a psychological tactic as was his selection of often attractive-looking subjects and the care he took in lighting them. Kodachrome film was a relatively new product, having been on the market only since 1936 for still photography cameras.[29] Palmer's color images subconsciously reinforced the idea that the United States was a modern, vibrant nation, one that laid claim to a bright and colorful future as an industrial powerhouse and as a shining beacon of democracy.

The photographer's subjects, which included defense plant workers, soldiers engaged in training, and civilians in a variety of occupations, frequently were not identified by name. They—like the coal shoveler portrayed on the poster—served as necessary propaganda archetypes: heroic, patriotic Americans doing their duty unfailingly and without complaint. While most of the images portrayed white Americans, Palmer also photographed African Americans contributing to the war effort, and, to a much lesser extent, captured images of Native Americans and Chinese Americans. Hispanic soldiers and workers either were not photographed or were not identified by ethnicity if they were photographed. Most of Palmer's

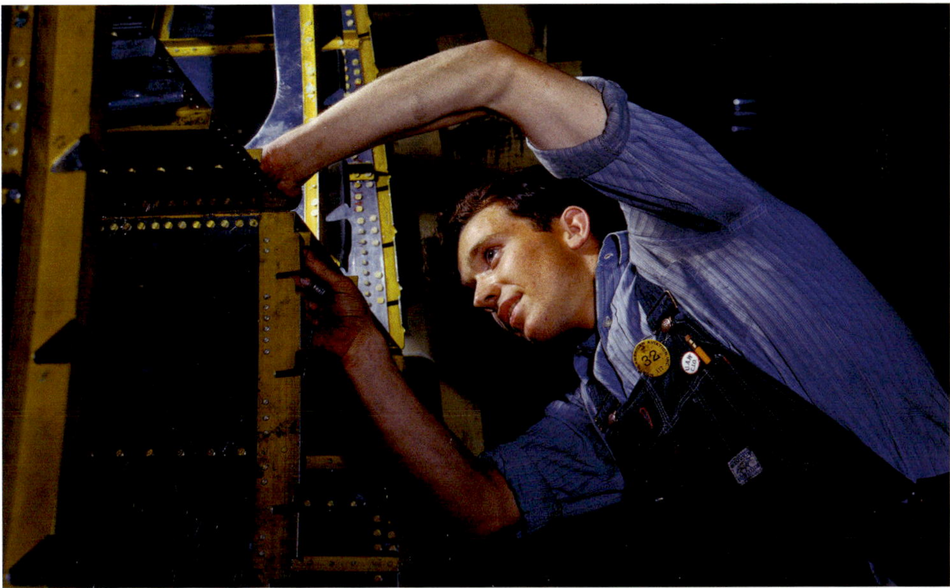

A wing brace assembly for a B-25 bomber is prepared for the assembly line of an aircraft plant, North American Aviation, Inc., Inglewood, California, October 1942. With plenty of speed, a 1,700-mile cruising range, and a ceiling of 25,000 feet, it has performed as a medium bomber and as an escort plane. (*Library of Congress*)

minority subjects were photographed after June 1942. Their inclusion in federal propaganda campaigns reflected changes in the nation's wartime workforce. With more than three million men in uniform by 1942, managers at factories, foundries, and other essential wartime industries increasingly sought women and minorities as temporary replacement workers.[30] While Palmer was conscious of the political and social climate of the era, his humanistic impulses led him to portray his subjects with dignity, regardless of gender, race, class, or religion.

The subject of race—and the promotion of the contributions of minority workers and soldiers—was a contentious topic for government propagandists to explore and exploit. Federal officials trod carefully in their promotion of ethnic minorities' wartime contributions, caught between the concerns of conservative politicians and white citizens who were not ready to accept racial equality, and the interests of minority citizens themselves, especially African Americans, who wanted and needed to see their accomplishments on the battlefields and in the factories acknowledged. As historians Jinx Coleman Broussard and John Maxwell Hamilton have stated, African Americans faced an "intense struggle" at home for recognition and inclusion in American society, as well as equal rights. "Blacks, who even had to fight for the right to fight, sought a double victory, one that vanquished fascism abroad *and* affirmed their claim on civil rights at home."[31]

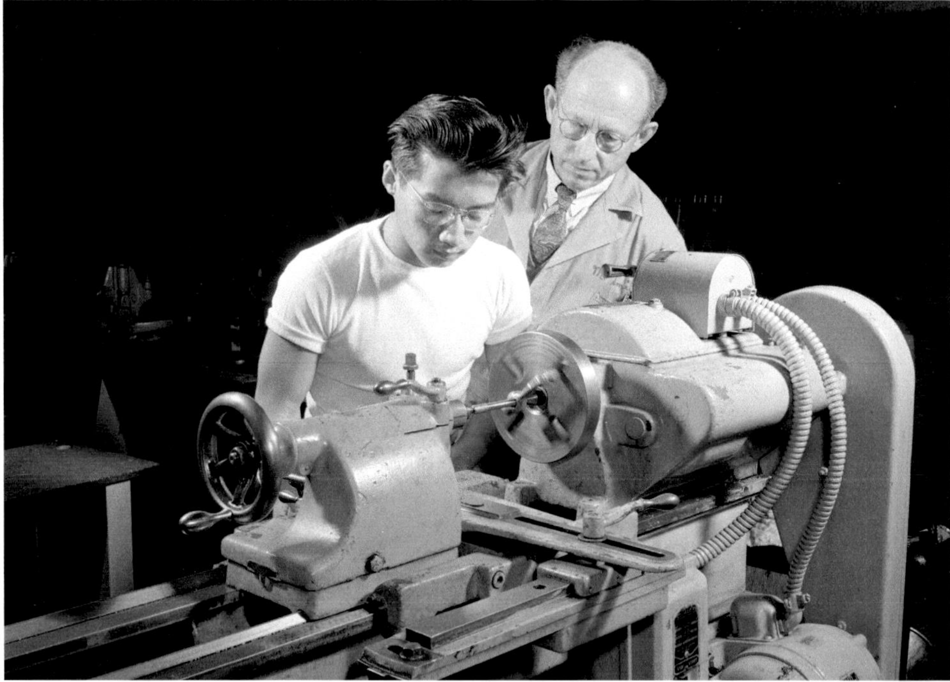

High school Victory Corps. Polytechnic High School, Los Angeles, California, teaches its students trades which fit them to help in the war program. This Chinese student is learning to operate a lathe, September–October 1942. (*Library of Congress*)

The end result was that many members of Congress were openly hostile to the materials produced by the Office of War Information, as well as the agency itself, perceiving it as a soap box for Roosevelt's New Deal policies. By 1943, Congress would tighten the purse strings at the agency, which led many employees, including Palmer, to depart.[32]

A VISUAL INNOVATOR

Palmer's name is not widely known today; however, between 1940 and 1945, he was a prolific home front photographer, responsible for taking more than 8,000 images in his role as chief photographer (or as a photographer) for several federal agencies, including the National Defense Advisory Commission (which was part of the Office for Emergency Management), the Office of War Information, the War Production Board, the War Shipping Administration, and the U.S. Maritime Commission.[33] More than 5,100 of his images are housed in the Library of Congress. Those photographs, which were used in a wide variety of propaganda media, also were distributed by government agencies free of charge to the press. Publications across the nation—including major metropolitan dailies such as the *New York Herald Tribune*, ethnic newspapers, including the *Jewish Daily Forward*, a variety of magazines, in-house publications (including those issued by the American Legion and Bell Telephone), and scientific and technical journals—reproduced Palmer's images.

His output was prodigious, which reflects the fact that Palmer worked steadily throughout the war years. But it is the quality of his work, particularly his color photography, which makes him worthy of appreciation and study. That Palmer served as a home front photographer tasked with taking the images needed to illustrate the federal government's wartime propaganda should not relegate him to continuing obscurity, nor should the nature of his work nor his client—the federal government—negate the quality of his work. Indeed, the present volume seeks to reintroduce Alfred T. Palmer's photography to the public while assessing his wartime output. The authors contend that Palmer's innovations with color photography and lighting, as well as his artistic impulses, make him worthy of being remembered and studied with the same respect and attention that has been given to other photographers of the era, including combat photographers.

Although Palmer engaged in commercial photography work for the U.S. government, his work is notable for its experimentation with new methods of electronic light as well as his use of color film for aesthetic purposes—innovations that the advertising industry began to adopt in the decade before the war. In fact, Palmer's most important contribution to the war effort may have been his masterful use of color film. The images that he produced were among the finest of his career.

One of the few photographers to embrace color film during the 1940s, he understood how to use color effectively at a time when only a few other photographers, including some who worked for the FSA, were using Kodachrome. Yet, those photographers, including Jack Delano, who shot color images of Chicago's train yards, and Russell Lee, who produced a notable color documentary project on dust bowl migrants who settled in Pie Town, New Mexico, mostly used Kodachrome in the same way they shot black-and-white film, meaning they relied on existing light, which often resulted in color images that were muddy. Some of these early adopters (or experimenters) with color film did not yet understand the powerful emotional appeal that images could have when the photographer incorporated color, an aesthetic that can be called "the language of color." While black-and-white photography speaks to intellect, color imagery speaks to emotions and became a valuable visual tool in selling the war to the public.

With experience making motion pictures for the cruise ship industry—an ancillary field that required knowledge of lighting—Palmer knew that color film had to be saturated. Electronic flash or flood lights would produce the powerful, sharp, clean imagery that government officials needed for their propaganda materials. Strobe lights were relatively new at the time, but Palmer knew they would allow a photographer to use faster shutter speeds to freeze action, which weaker continuous tungsten lighting could not do. Palmer predominantly used flood lights for his lighted images, which made his work appear crisp and clear.[34]

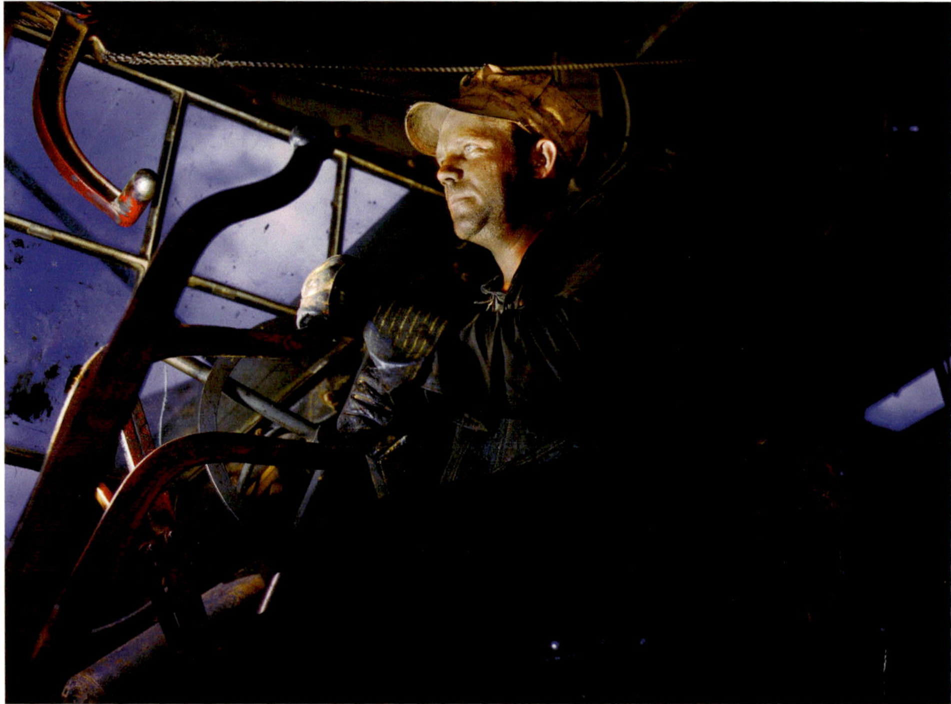

Crane operator at TVA's Douglas Dam, Tennessee, June 1942. (*Library of Congress*)

The technique created additional depth because he could use smaller apertures (i.e., f-stops). The lighting also helped heighten the photographs' color and contrast, which made his work attention grabbing and sharply focused. Palmer was an innovator, and these innovations of color, strobe, and razor-sharp clarity launched a new aesthetic in photography decades before the use of color photography and studio strobe became a standard in 1960s commercial and editorial photography.

Many photographers working during the 1930s and 1940s had derided the use of color in photography, especially in documentary work, seeing it as a passing fad or as a gimmick. Walker Evans, for example, denounced color film in no uncertain terms, stating, 'Color tends to corrupt photography, and absolute color corrupts it absolutely. There are four simple words for the matter, which must be whispered: Color photography is vulgar.'[35]

Despite some pushback, color imagery increasingly was embraced by advertising executives and magazine editors beginning in the 1920s. Improvements in printing presses (including the development of offset printing in the early 1900s, which allowed for crisper, sharper image reproduction), paper technology, and inks made color printing both viable and affordable. Color proved a boon to advertising executives and manufacturers who used it as a unique selling point in an era that saw the rise of mass-produced goods. Indeed, color became part of the so-called "triumph of style" in the 1920s—a decade in which a tremendous range of merchandise became available to consumers. Corporations also used other details, including unique lines and shapes attributed to the Modernist movement, to help differentiate many products, including kitchen appliances and bathroom fixtures, which were otherwise similar in function.[36]

Palmer's embrace of color along with his masterful use of lighting produced images that were noted for their rich contrast, sharp clarity of focus, and an emphasis on red and yellow—colors that Kodachrome film was particularly strong in reproducing. For example, Palmer's photograph of eighteen-year-old Phyllis Ann Marxson Clark, at the Douglas Aircraft Plant in Long Beach, California, emphasized Clark's red blouse and cap, as well as the little detail of the yellow ID badge. The contrast demonstrates that Palmer's work boldly manifested the "language of color," a language formerly recognized by Renaissance and Dutch painters of a distant past.

The striking image was used in an OWI poster as part of the government's "Womanpower" campaign, which began in late 1942 to encourage married women and mothers who did not have young children to take jobs in factories that produced war materials or to join the women's military auxiliary units.[37]

Palmer's color work predates similar work by other twentieth-century photographers—including Pete Turner, Ernest Haas, and Jay Maisel, all of whom brought color imagery into vogue—by several decades. The curators at the Museum of Modern Art in New York City also helped bring color photography into respectability by staging an exhibit of Memphis, Tennessee, photographer William Eggleston's photographs in 1976. While members of the art world hailed Eggleston's "inimitable, colour-saturated" photographs and stated that

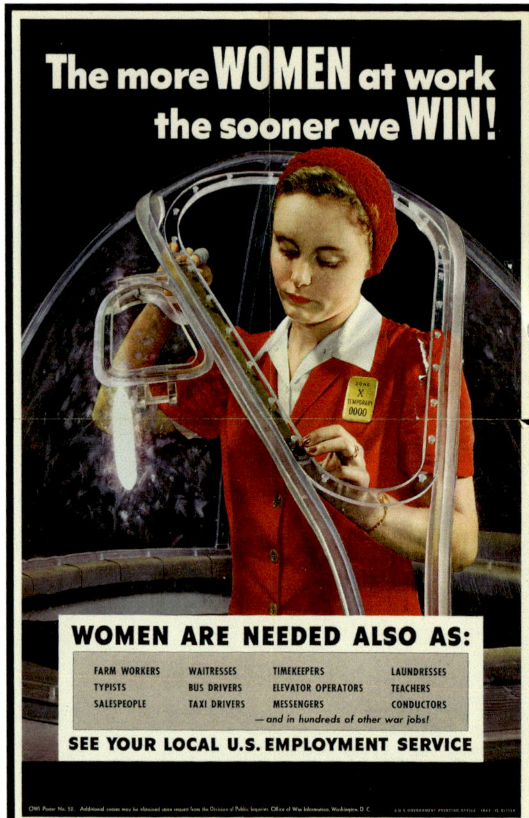

"The more women at work the sooner we win! See your local U.S. Employment Service." Office of War Information poster, 1943. (*Library of Congress*)

the photographer had "an uncanny ability to find beauty and something extraordinary" in everyday objects and people, such praise ignores Palmer's place in creating equally artistic, color-saturated imagery of wartime workers and the materials they produced a full three decades earlier.[38]

AN ERA OF PROFOUND VISUAL CHANGE

Unfortunately for modern viewers interested in Palmer's wartime work, the photographer made few comments during interviews or in writing concerning artistic influences on his work. A self-taught photographer, Palmer appears to have developed his skills and improved his commercial work largely based on comments from clients.[39] But he undoubtedly was influenced by imagery that he viewed in popular magazines and advertisements. Palmer came of age and began his career during an era marked by widespread and profound changes in the arts, including graphic arts and photography. Several European immigrants, many of whom were fleeing rising totalitarianism during the 1930s, helped modernize graphic design in American publishing while serving as editors, photographers, and art directors. They brought with them a broad range of new visual aesthetic ideas, including Bauhaus, constructivism, futurism, surrealism, and modernism that did more than revolutionize magazine design; collectively, Leslie Camhi states, they transformed "visual culture at large."[40]

Fashion magazines were at the forefront of the change in visual aesthetics that began occurring during the 1930s, however, similar changes in visual design quickly spread to other magazine genres, including picture magazines like *Life*. Even technical journals were visually reconceived and refreshed. The broad circulation of American and European fashion and pictorial magazines made them influential since they were seen by millions of readers. Some of the European immigrant editors and art designers, including Russian émigré Alexey Brodovitch, the noted art director for *Harper's Bazaar*, and Ukrainian Alexander Liberman at *Vogue*, expanded their influence by conducting design workshops that influenced a generation of twentieth-century photographers and artists, including New York street photographer Garry Winogrand, *Vogue* magazine photographer Irving Penn, Diane Arbus, known for her portraits of people on the fringes of society, and fashion and portrait photographer Richard Avedon.[41]

Palmer's wartime work broadly reflects thematic aspects of several aesthetics then in vogue, including modernism, Bauhaus, and precisionism, however, most of his images were not shot in the actual style of these popular aesthetics. Instead, Palmer, like other commercial photographers and photojournalists of the time, embraced a style of photography that became popular in the late 1920s called straight photography, an aesthetic free from darkroom manipulation and known for its sharp focus and detail. That style was popularized and promoted by a diverse group of West Coast photographers, including Imogen Cunningham, Ansel Adams, and Edward Weston, who in 1932 formed Group f/64, described as "an informal association of like-minded photographers." The members "disavowed" an artistic, darkroom manipulated aesthetic termed pictorialism, which was popular in the early twentieth century, in favor of straight photography, promoting the latter by hosting exhibitions of the members' work, as well as images from like-minded photographers. As Susan Ehrens states: "The overall concern throughout was an emphasis on the integrity of the photographic process, its objectivity and capacity for individual expression." Members of Group f/64 recorded life as they saw it, creating photographs that were free from darkroom manipulation. Although Group f/64 was relatively short-lived, it had an outsized influence. Several of the FSA photographers, as well as Alfred Palmer, found the aesthetic style of straight photography useful to their work, whether artistic, commercial, or focused on social documentation.[42]

Like his fellow wartime photographers Margaret Bourke-White and Andreas Feininger, Palmer also appeared drawn to the Precisionist aesthetic that developed in the first decade of the twentieth century and came of age in the 1920s and 1930s. That movement, a strand of American modernism, explored the machine age by highlighting the geometric shapes and strong lines inherent in industry and industrial products. The aesthetic was a useful one for World

War II-era photographers who were tasked with visually representing American manufacturing might. Indeed, many of the photographs produced by Palmer, Bourke-White, and Feininger made strong use of geometric forms and often were shot using dramatic angles to heighten the viewer's sense of American industrial superiority. Their photographs, in the broadest aesthetic sense, paralleled the work of artists Charles Sheeler and Elsie Driggs, whose paintings explored representations of industrial structures, including smokestacks, steel mills, and power plants, during a period of rapid industrial growth throughout the nation.[43]

Several wartime photographers also found aspects of the Bauhaus aesthetic useful in their work during the 1940s, because the movement also emphasized the beauty of industrial forms. As Carson states, the popularity of machine aesthetic imagery came to the fore in the 1920s and was widely reproduced by magazine editors during a period when those editors—and much of the public—expressed faith in the "efficiency and leadership of American industry and in the inevitability of progress through technology." Such faith, she adds, "had waned considerably during the Depression, [however] the mobilization effort of the early 1940s called for confidence akin to that of the heady days of 1920s prosperity." As a result, the modernist, machine aesthetic saw a resurgence of popularity during wartime.[44]

While the federal government and the branches of the armed forces collectively employed thousands of photographers who took images for propaganda purposes, Palmer's positions with the nation's key wartime propaganda agencies led his work to be widely distributed, seen by millions of Americans and Europeans.[45] Yet his name also was not widely known to the public during the 1940s. The nature of Palmer's government employment meant that when his work was published, the images often were credited to the agencies to which he worked, rather than to the photographer himself.

A DEEP VISUAL SKILL SET

Horton knew he had the right photographer for the job of promoting pre-war home front defense preparations when he hired Palmer. Palmer, like Horton, not only supported the defense buildup, but the photographer also agreed with many federal officials on the need to use photographs, motion pictures, and other visuals for propaganda purposes.[46] Then, too, Palmer had some industrial manufacturing knowledge gained from high school classes in the industrial arts, as well as fifteen years of commercial photography experience. The photographer also had several years of motion picture-making experience (this latter work done for shipping lines), knowledge that he would use throughout the war to make several short subject films as well as full-length motion pictures for a variety of federal agencies.

Palmer's photography career began in the mid-1920s. He did freelance work for shipping lines and sold images to magazines and newspapers of exotic locations around the globe while serving in the Merchant Marine. Beginning as

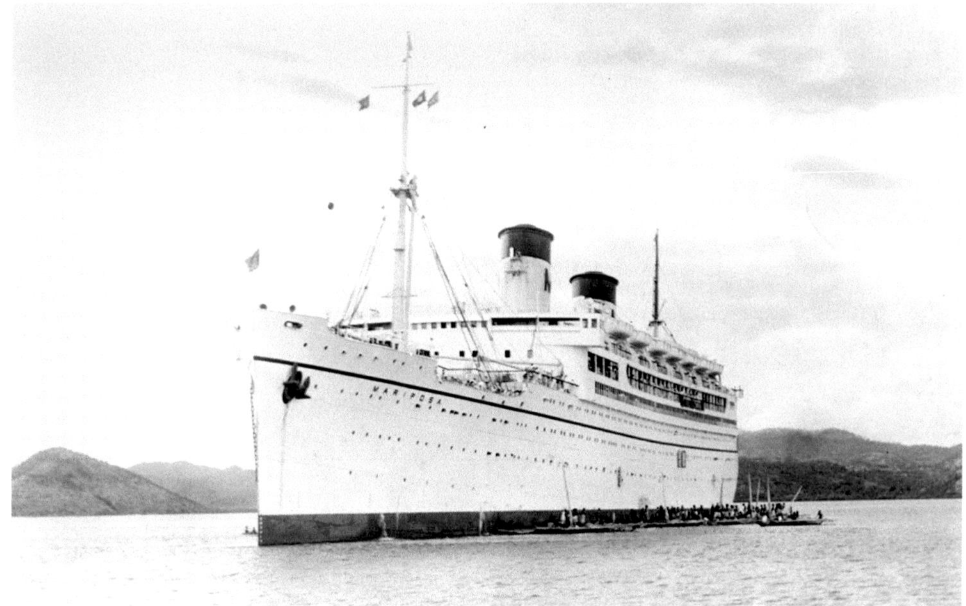

The Matson liner SS *Mariposa* anchored in Pago Pago Harbor, Samoa, 1932. Photographed by Alfred T. Palmer. (*Library of Congress*)

a cadet in 1925, then, later, while serving as a quartermaster or as an assistant purser, Palmer pursued photography during his free time, capturing all aspects of shipboard existence, including the tasks and working conditions of the crew as well as the culture of cruise ship life. Some of the images were taken to document shipboard life, while other images were used in promotional materials, including advertisements and brochures, by the shipping lines. And at shipping executives' request, he also took images of ship construction. The work helped the young photographer hone his craft. Palmer learned to style the photographs he took for maritime companies to obtain the most glamorous look possible of products, places, and people. He made frequent use of this glamour aesthetic during the early 1940s when making propaganda photographs for the U.S. government.

Palmer's Merchant Marine experiences also helped make him worldly. His travels from 1925 to 1931 took him to Asian nations, South Pacific islands, South American countries, Australia, Egypt, and various European nations. Once ashore, he spent much of his time capturing images of the people and the architecture of port communities.

When ashore back home in the United States, Palmer also shot jobs for West Coast advertising agencies from his studio in Berkeley, California, during the 1920s and 1930s. But he remained best known for his maritime work, as well as for his images of people and places throughout the world.[47] These latter images captured the pre-war lives of average people, including rickshaw drivers, Geishas, temple workers, pearl divers, fishermen, and children on the street. Often working

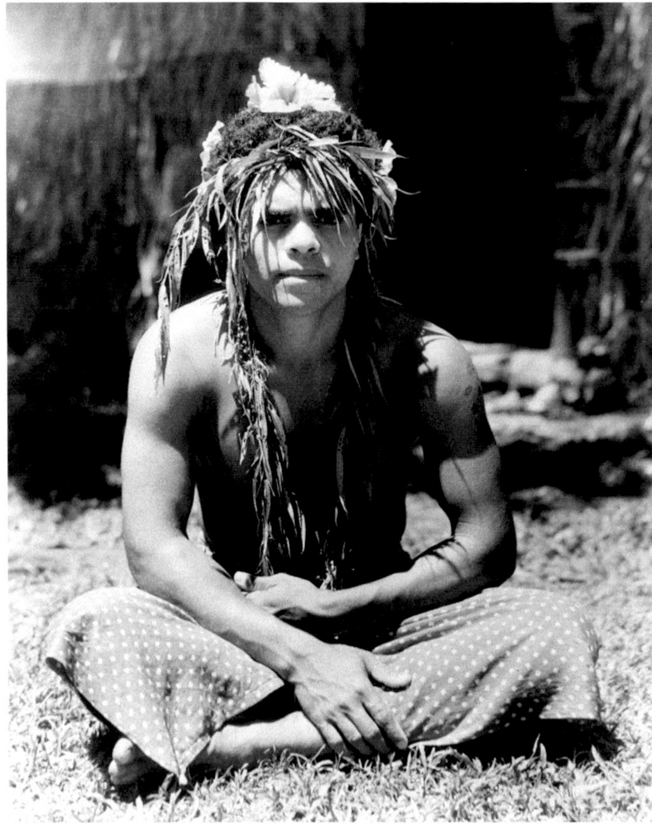

Native of Rarotonga,
Cook Islands, 1930s.
Photographed by
Alfred T. Palmer.
(*Library of Congress*)

from the vantage point of the unobtrusive photographer, Palmer captured many subjects unaware.

Once Palmer left the Merchant Marine in 1931 to pursue photography as a full-time occupation, his main, pre-war income was derived from his work as an official photographer for various passenger lines. He made additional money—as well as valuable media industry contacts—by selling photographs of international locales to magazines and newspapers including *Life, National Geographic,* and *Travel.* By the early 1930s, Palmer had expanded into filmmaking, initially making promotional films for cruise ship lines that advertising executives could use to sell the romance of travel to the public. One of Palmer's earliest filmmaking jobs occurred while he was on a cruise ship—but the work was not for the ship's parent company. Instead, Palmer shot footage of Robert Ripley, the creator of the *Believe It or Not* comic strip panels and radio show. Palmer encountered the celebrity on the Matson Line's SS *Mariposa* in 1932. Ripley needed film taken of him in both New Zealand and Indonesia, which Palmer shot when the ship arrived in those locations. That footage was later used in Vitaphone short subject films that were produced by Warner Brothers and were shown at movie theaters before the main feature.[48]

PORTRAYING INDUSTRIAL STRENGTH AND AGRICULTURAL PLENTY

Palmer's commercial photography background coupled with a basic interest in and knowledge of industrial design, as well as his reverence for artistic beauty, allowed the photographer to produce images for wartime propaganda purposes that advertised the strength of a nation. Attractive, well-dressed defense plant workers were depicted turning out an endless arsenal of tanks, ships, planes, blimps, bombs, and vehicles before returning home each day to comfortable, middle-class housing in communities that boasted well-stocked grocery stores, clean, orderly schools, and an array of entertainment options, including baseball games.

While Palmer's work was largely meant for a domestic audience, Office of War Information officials used some of the idealized images of defense plant workers for their European propaganda campaigns. Palmer's photographs appeared in international magazines and on posters, however, the agency also used some of the images on leaflets dropped over France and the Netherlands prior to the United States' involvement in the war. The leaflets, which were part of a psychological campaign to build morale in Europe, announced that "America was at work to help." Although the photographer did not design the leaflets or even help choose the photographs that were used, Palmer believed that the propaganda was highly important, stating that the leaflets reminded people in "occupied Europe ... that they were not alone."[49]

Other images, especially ones taken for American consumption, portrayed the United States as a prosperous country, one which had thrown off the economic woes brought on by the Great Depression. Palmer's photographs of the nation's rural areas reflected a similar horn-of-plenty approach that was necessitated by wartime propaganda demands. Gone were the images of impoverished rural regions previously depicted by the FSA photographers. Those photographs, which included ragged, hardworking sharecroppers and beaten down, but determined dust bowl migrants making their way to the promised land of California, were replaced by Palmer's more positive images of the nation: glistening wheat fields, fat Wyoming cattle, proud Texas farmers astride modern tractors, and overstuffed hay wagons. By wielding his camera, Palmer brought a visual weapon to America's arsenal—one that depicted an idealized nation to its citizens and to the world to counter Nazi propaganda. It was a portrait of a country transformed into an economically wealthy, socially coherent, energetic nation, a middle-class America worth preserving and defending.

The implicit psychological and emotional appeals inherent in Palmer's visual depiction of the nation in many ways paralleled those of illustrator and painter Norman Rockwell. During a period of international upheaval and national stress, both men adopted a subjective visual aesthetic meant to rally the public by revealing the nature of the American character, a theme that previously was depicted by the FSA photographers under the direction of Roy Stryker.[50]

Palmer's photographs, like Rockwell's illustrations, were meant to focus the public's emotions by portraying a united and determined nation whose citizens were again willing to face predatory enemies. The propaganda work was necessary. Both men labored during a socially volatile era. As the United States began emerging from the economic woes of the Great Depression, industrialists who were once again selling cars and other durable goods in the early months of 1940 initially expressed reluctance to convert their factories over to military production. Society continued to be wrought by persistent racial and class inequalities and prejudices. Food rationing (once the war began) caused grumbling; severe housing shortages (brought on by massive population shifts to booming industrial communities for defense jobs) made life difficult for workers, raised sanitation concerns, and threatened urban upheaval. And growing fear of enemies at home led 120,000 Japanese Americans to be rounded up and interned in rural prison camps.[51]

REDISCOVERING A RESPECTED TALENT

Despite Palmer's extensive photography work during World War II and a subsequent, decades-long career as both a commercial photographer and, increasingly, as a filmmaker who shot and produced documentaries and educational motion pictures, both Palmer's name and his work remain largely unknown. Few studies of wartime propaganda even mention him.[52] Some of Palmer's lack of recognition can be attributed to the fact that much of the photographer's work before and after the war may have been published without a photo credit or credited to the government agencies for which he took the photographs. Then, too, in the post-war period, Palmer focused largely on making documentary films, although he did continue to do some commercial photography work. This shift from one visual genre to another did not give him the rich body of work that some photographers possessed. And the commercial nature of that work again often kept his name uncredited in the photographs that he shot for advertising purposes. Yet Palmer's talents were acknowledged and respected throughout his lifetime by other photographers as well as by advertising executives. He was an active commercial photographer and documentary filmmaker whose services were regularly in demand by a variety of clients.

The artistry and quality of Palmer's pre-war and wartime work also drew the attention of members of the artistic community during the 1940s. Some of Palmer's images were displayed in a 1940 "Salon of Photography" exhibit curated by *Fortune* magazine and held at the Rochester (New York) Museum of Arts and Sciences from July through September of that year. The exhibit's seventy photographs (sixty black-and-white and ten color photographs) were taken by photographers whose work had appeared in the magazine. Palmer's work was displayed alongside images taken by Fenno Jacobs, Dmitri Kessel, Ansel Adams, Margaret Bourke-White, Walker Evans, Lewis Hine, and others. The images were selected, according to the brochure, by the magazine's editors based on the

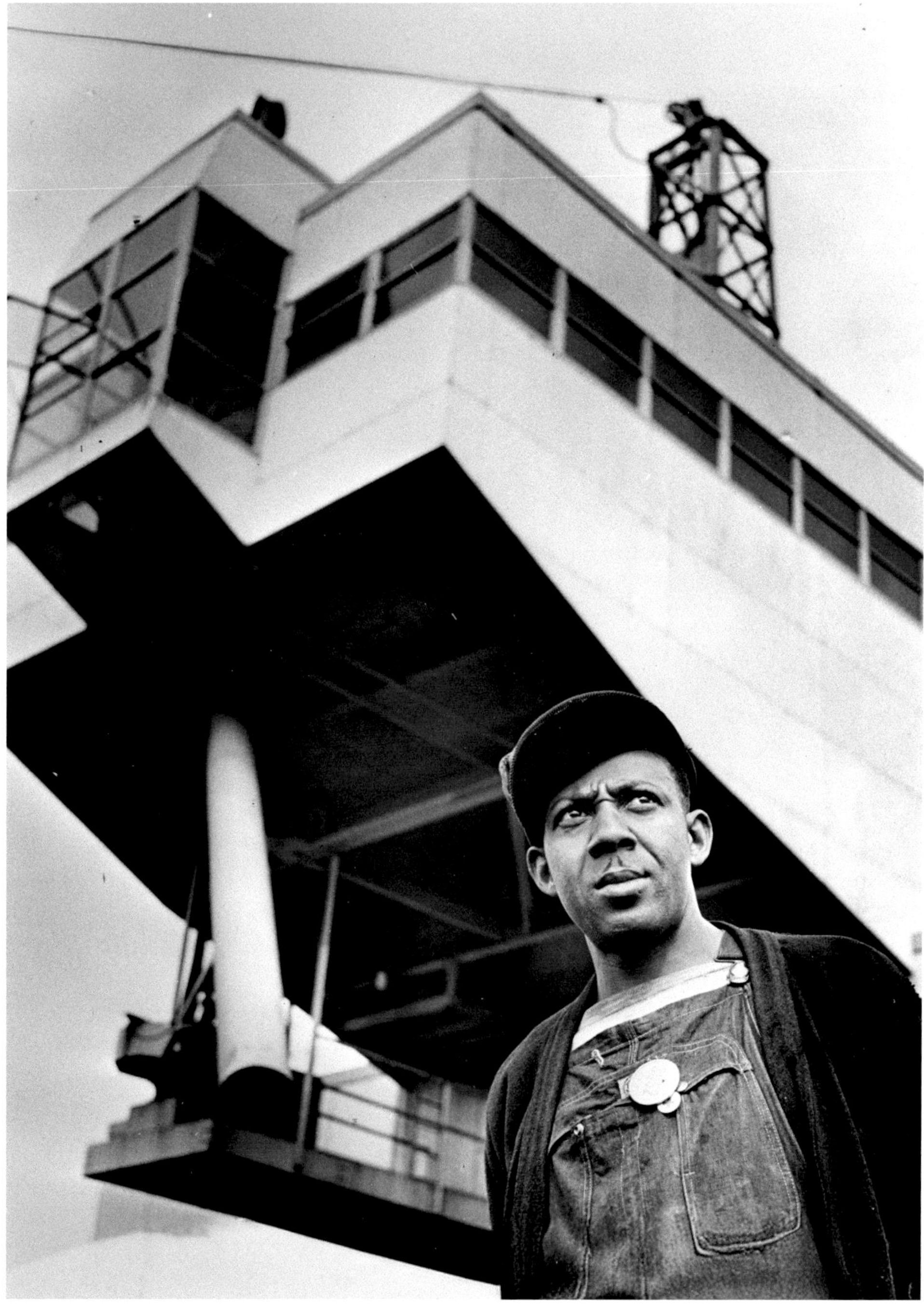

Earl Tulloss is a skilled operator of a dragline capable of moving a fifth of a carload of coal at once, June 1942. He is president of the Hod Carriers' local union at Watts Bar Steam Plant of TVA, and he is active in labor-management campaigns for sale of war bonds, and reduction of absenteeism. (*Library of Congress*)

"individual excellence in prints which, considered as an ensemble, should best illustrate *Fortune*'s use of photography as an integral element in its presentation of U.S. industry."[53]

Palmer's images also were part of five other ensemble photography exhibits during the war years. The first and most prestigious, titled "The Road to Victory," curated by photographer Edward Steichen, opened at New York City's Museum of Modern Art in June 1942, six months after America's entrance into World War II. Propagandistic in nature, the show was created with the intention of convincing "every American to see himself as a vital and indispensable element of victory." Four of Palmer's photographs were featured, all of which depicted individuals engaged in necessary war tasks: a carpenter, a riveter, a military gunner, and a research worker. Following the exhibit's run in New York City, the Office of War Information traveled the exhibit for two years, sending it across the nation and then onto the United Kingdom.[54]

Two other 1942 exhibits, titled "The Arsenal of Democracy" and "The Four Freedoms," were created by the federal government as enormous mobile photo montages approximately 15 feet high and 30 feet long. First displayed in Washington, D.C., near the White House, the billboard-sized exhibits were moved by rail car across the nation and displayed to millions of citizens.[55] Both exhibits drew their titles from Roosevelt's pre-war appeals aimed at persuading Americans (including recalcitrant members of Congress) to support the nation's European allies. In a speech delivered on December 29, 1940, the president called on Americans to turn the nation into an "arsenal of democracy," by building the weapons that Great Britain and other allies needed to fight the German military. Roosevelt, who was a master political strategist, did not call for Americans to go to war to defeat Nazi Germany during his December 1940 speech, but instead appealed to Americans' patriotism and sense of responsibility to help the country's European allies battle fascist forces—an action meant to protect democracy. But the president also included an element of fear in the same speech, warning that a German victory over the English would threaten the safety of the United States.

The second exhibit's title, the "Four Freedoms," was derived from Roosevelt's January 6, 1941, State of the Union address. The president attempted through the speech to nudge Americans emotionally toward involvement in the war. He argued that in supporting his policy of coming to the aid of Great Britain, the public was helping fight for four universal freedoms that all individuals should possess: freedom of speech, freedom of worship, freedom from want, and freedom from fear. The final two exhibits, which took place in 1943, featured images that Palmer had taken of women war workers. The first exhibit opened in April at Philadelphia's Franklin Institute, while the second debuted on Labor Day at New York's Museum of Modern Art.[56]

THE COMMERCIAL *V.* ARTISTIC DIVIDE IN PHOTOGRAPHY

The nature of Palmer's career, which was unapologetically commercial, is a key factor in his lack of recognition among members of the art and photography world. Regardless of the aesthetic quality of their images, the work produced by many commercial photographers is often ignored by scholars, artists, and the public simply because that work, in the broadest sense, is someone else's vision. As photography historian F. Jack Hurley has stated, the photographers who became nationally known throughout the twentieth century "preferred to explore their own inner vision." They did not shoot commercial work on a regular basis (or even at all) and many did not get involved in government work or social documentation as did the FSA photographers. Instead, Hurley says, the past century's best-known photographers focused on their own artistry: "Their search was for abstract beauty. The men [and women] who used cameras as tools for social understanding were left out of the mainstream of salon and magazine photography."[57]

Many artists who were drawn to photography established a divide in the interwar years between art photography and other forms of photography, including fashion photography, commercial photography, and photojournalism, as an elitist means of attempting to protect their reputations.[58] They portrayed themselves as artists for art's sake, and thus viewed themselves as free from the taint of being commercial photographers. Yet other rising stars of twentieth-century photography, including Edward Steichen, Irving Penn, Richard Avedon, and William Klein, bridged the two worlds, bringing a beauty aesthetic to their commercial work while also experimenting with visually inventive techniques.[59]

That divide cut both ways in the first four decades of the twentieth century. Although Steichen is often viewed by art historians as a key figure in promoting photography—including commercial photography—as an art form and for popularizing modernist aesthetics and industrial design as a means of reaching a wide audience, many of the commercial and editorial photographers of the era held dubious opinions of art photographers, considering them limited and effete.[60] They viewed themselves as outside of the art world or ambivalent about their place in it.[61] Like Palmer, they had jobs to do for their clients and they did them. But those commercial photographers often were visually imaginative craftsmen and craftswomen of the first order.

The commercial and propaganda impulses behind Palmer's wartime imagery, therefore, do not negate the photographs' aesthetic quality, nor do they reduce the photographer's talent and vision to topics unworthy of study. On the contrary, Palmer's wartime photographs should be viewed instead as part of the richness and diversity that marked twentieth-century visual culture. Furthermore, many of Palmer's innovations and techniques, not to mention his insight into the power of color, influenced whole generations of photographers. He was a modernist pioneer. Many generations of photographers—whether artistic, commercial, or editorial—have benefited from his foundational work.

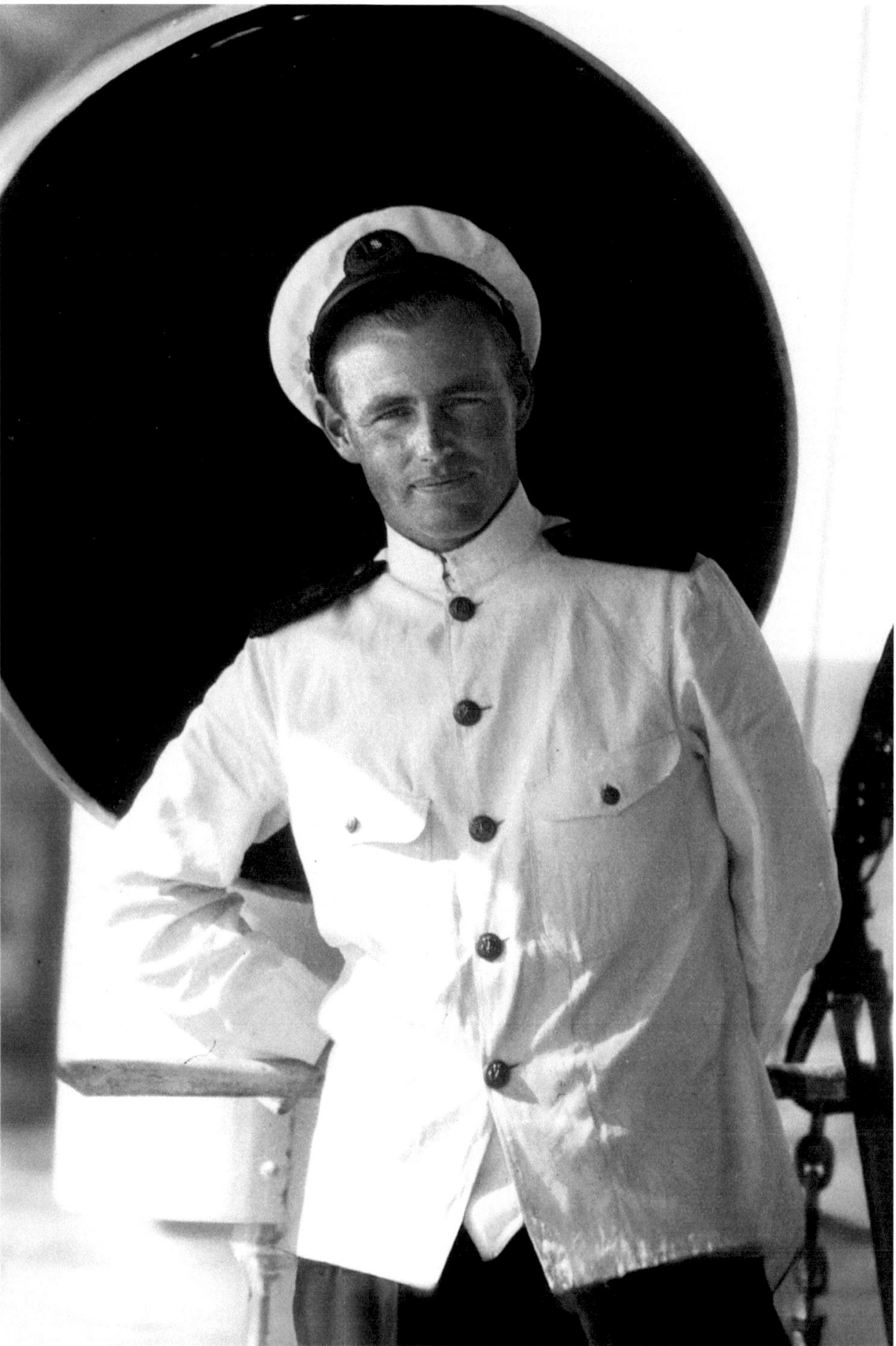

Alfred T. Palmer during his service in the Merchant Marine, undated. (*A. T. Palmer Collection, privately held*)

I
A CAREER INFLUENCED BY THE SEA

To understand Alfred Palmer, his career, and his aesthetic decisions, one needs to begin with the sea. Palmer's upbringing in Long Beach, California, helped influence his world view, shaped his career choices, and, ultimately, set him on the path that led him to obtain the knowledge and have the experiences that turned a young man with a camera into a successful commercial photographer and filmmaker.

Born in San Jose, California, in 1906, Palmer moved to Long Beach with his family after the San Francisco earthquake of April 18, 1906, destroyed their home. Although his parents, Grant and Harriett (Dundas) Palmer, ran a delicatessen in their new hometown, young Alfred had no desire to join the family business. The seaside community's sailors, ships, and shipyard so entranced him that he was determined to have a seafaring life when he became an adult. "Living in Long Beach, not very far from the [Craig] shipyard and the harbor, I could see these big ships coming and going. Naturally, I wanted to be on one of them sometime, and I wanted to go to sea. At least I wanted to travel," Palmer recalled of his childhood.[2] That determination grew when his older brother, Wallace, returned home on leave from the U.S. Navy and shared photographs that he had taken of his ship, the USS *San Diego*, as well as images that he captured of Mexican port communities. Those photographs fired Alfred's imagination and provided an "opening into the world" that intrigued the then-seven-year-old Palmer.[3]

A reintroduction to photography occurred in an unexpected way four years later when Palmer spent part of a summer carrying photographer Ansel Adams's heavy tripod through Yosemite National Park while Palmer's mother worked as the head caterer for Yosemite's Curry Camp, now known as Curry Village. Although the then-fifteen-year-old Adams refused to share many tips on making good photographs, Palmer learned by observing the teen, whom he termed "a genius." Recalling his youthful experience, Palmer said of Adams: "Of course, his real genius came from using an f-64 stop so everything was wire sharp. He used to stand around for hours waiting for the clouds to come in just right."[4] Adams paid Palmer for his services by presenting the youngster with a camera: a Kodak Brownie that cost one dollar. It was little pay for the hard work that Palmer had endured, but the experience proved invaluable.

Palmer soon discovered that his love of the sea and ships was matched by his love of photography. But several more years would pass until Palmer could combine the two. The eleven-year-old returned from his summer trip to a rapidly growing community. America's entry into World War I made Long Beach a busy, crowded, community. The city's shipyard, potash plant, and woolen mills increased production in response to the war. So many new workers arrived in the seaside community seeking wartime jobs that housing soon became an issue.[5] But the newcomers helped Palmer's parents' business thrive. While they were engaged in running their delicatessen on Broadway Avenue, young Alfred and his friends were equally busy a few blocks away, building rafts from discarded wood and paddling around the harbor and near the shipyard, studying the big ships that had come into port. His fascination—and sense of wonder about those ships and their next ports of call—remained even as Palmer entered his teenage years and saw the vessels as he set off each day for high school.[6]

A largely self-taught photographer, Palmer was well-equipped by the time he entered Long Beach Polytechnic High School in 1921. His mother, Harriett, supported her teenage son's growing interest in photography by purchasing a Graflex camera for him. Palmer soon had a darkroom set up at his home, as well. During his junior and senior years of high school, Palmer's equipment saw good use; he spent numerous hours taking images for the student newspaper and the yearbook.[7]

Palmer fulfilled his ambition of a life at sea and began his professional photography career on the day he graduated from high school by shipping out as a cadet—complete with his camera—on the Dollar Steamship Lines' *President Monroe*, a luxury cruise ship that offered round-the-world service.[8] A determined Palmer learned that the ship, which was supposed to be manned with three cadets, had only two. The then-eighteen-year-old approached the captain, telling him that he was ready to become a cadet and added that his bag was packed. The captain found the request irregular since the young man had not formally applied for the position, but he responded by telling Palmer to be on the ship by 11 p.m. to take over the midnight watch.[9]

Although he earned a paltry twenty-five cents per month during his first voyage as a cadet, Palmer saw the world, learned some seamanship, and gained valuable navigation skills, relieving the quartermaster at the wheel when he was not polishing and cleaning the ship. In his free time, Palmer photographed every aspect of the ship and shipboard life. Tight living quarters for cadets meant that Palmer had to find a sympathetic officer on each voyage who was willing to allow the young sailor to stow his camera and other equipment in the officers' quarters.[10] The journey would be the first of twenty-three trips around the world for Palmer, initially as a sailor and later as a full-time photographer.[11]

A summer foray inland to Wyoming's Teton Mountains in 1926 helped the young photographer further hone his craft, including sharpening his darkroom skills.[12] With his shipboard stints in the Merchant Marine lasting approximately three months, a then-nineteen-year-old Palmer obtained work as a lab assistant for Harrison R.

"Hank" Crandall, a painter and fine arts photographer known for his sharp contrast images of soaring Teton vistas, wildflowers, Native Americans, and western life.[13] Crandall's renown grew throughout the 1920s to the point that by 1929, he was designated as the official photographer for Grand Teton National Park.

Palmer left only photographs and no written records from that summer, yet he undoubtedly discussed his passion for photography, including composition issues, with the affable Crandall. The older photographer was well positioned to be a good mentor for Palmer. Crandall had what the young photographer lacked: several years of formal art school training in Los Angeles.[14] Crandall also was well versed in darkroom work, yet he began hiring lab assistants like Palmer, so that he would have more time to roam the countryside taking photographs and painting western scenes.

Even though he was not a regular presence in his own darkroom, Crandall was exacting in what he expected of his lab technicians, which undoubtedly helped polish Palmer's technical skills. The conditions under which Palmer and other lab assistants labored were primitive, however. The young staffers often used a tent as a darkroom and relied on water from nearby creeks to mix the developing chemicals. Regardless of his surroundings, whether in a tent or at Crandall's log cabin studio, Palmer helped create Crandall's fine art prints, which were noted for their "luminous mountains and bright skies," images that were enhanced through careful dodging and burning techniques in the darkroom.[15]

The older photographer may have found a kindred spirit in his young lab assistant during that summer. Crandall had achieved what the teenage Palmer aspired to be: a working photographer who supported himself free of such artistic encumbrances as bosses or superiors to whom he might have to report. And Crandall had no problem spanning two worlds, as a fine arts photographer and painter and as a commercial, graphic artist, as well. Before he became a well-known and well-respected painter and photographer, Crandall supported himself and his young wife by running a sign and cartoon shop in Pocatello, Idaho, in 1921. His cartoons and graphic images soon appeared throughout the Idaho frontier, above storefronts, on roadside billboards, across the sides of airplanes, and in publications.[16]

Crandall had moved to his beloved Teton mountains with his wife, Hilda, in 1922. The couple supported themselves by turning Hank's photographs into postcards, which were sold at the Moran (Wyoming) General Store.[17] A few years later, when Palmer spent his summer as one of Crandall's lab assistants, the older photographer was well established with a homestead located 20 miles from Jackson, Wyoming. Sales of his photographs and postcards not only helped Crandall support a growing family, but they also allowed him to begin construction of his own studio—a tidy 22 by 28-foot log cabin building located on the family homestead.[18]

Like Crandall, the young Palmer clearly cherished his time in Wyoming. Both men were drawn toward beauty and landscape photography. When Palmer was not developing film and printing photographs for Crandall, the photo albums in the hands of his family show that young Alfred was off photographing the soaring Teton mountains, the region's alpine meadows filled with wildflowers, area wildlife, and crystal-clear lakes.

Following his summer in Wyoming, Palmer attempted college, studying archeology at UCLA. He also worked as a photographer for the *Daily Bruin*, the student newspaper. That flirtation with higher education lasted a brief three months. Two dinner meetings with a former Merchant Marine shipmate led Palmer to disenroll, sell his books, and go back to sea, this time employed as a quartermaster, again for the Dollar Steamship Lines. The photographer decided that obtaining a university degree involved taking too many required classes that failed to hold his interest. Then, too, the sea beckoned to him.[19]

Two years later, Palmer still was serving as quartermaster, this time on the Dollar Lines' *President Garfield*. He steered the ship thousands of nautical miles, including through the Suez Canal in Egypt. Life was good for Palmer; his wanderlust was being satiated. "From the beginning, I liked the exotic," Palmer said, reflecting on his lifelong interest in seeing the world. "And of course, everyone likes to travel. I just had the good fortune to follow through with photography as a vehicle."[20]

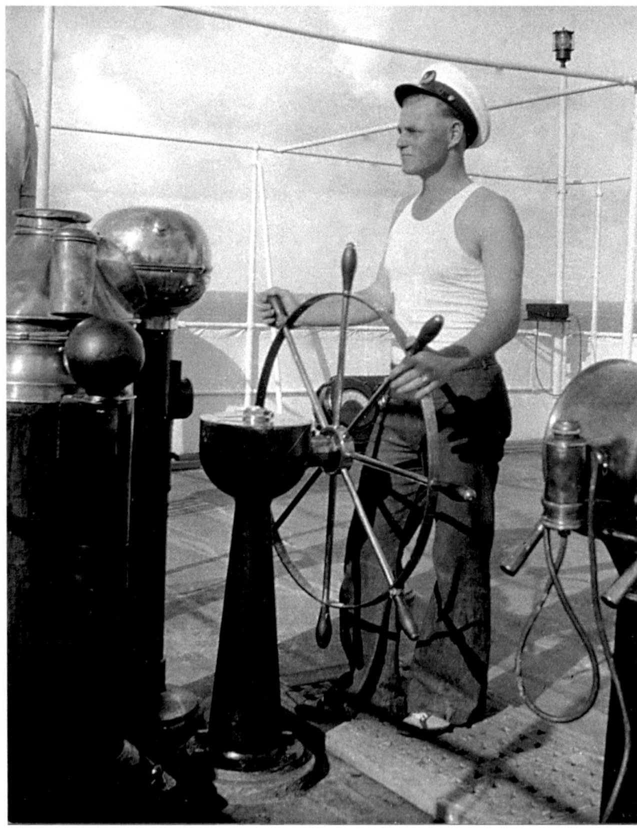

Alfred Palmer in the Merchant Marine, undated (*c.* 1920s). (*A. T. Palmer Collection, privately held*)

A LOVE OF THE SEA AND PHOTOGRAPHY

Although Palmer loved the seafaring life, he always shipped out with two purposes in mind: to see the world and to photograph people and places in distant ports. He relished documenting shipboard life, as well as the lives of the people that he encountered in port cities. His pluck and work ethic brought him to the attention of executives from the Dollar Steamship Lines who had been admiring the images that Palmer sold to their advertising department. By 1931, they made Palmer their official photographer. What the executives did not do, however, was offer Palmer a salary. With the nation in the throes of the Great Depression, Palmer earned his income in part from selling passengers the photos that he had taken of them, and by developing and processing the film (for a fee) that passengers had taken themselves.[21]

His life at sea helped Palmer survive the economically lean years of the 1930s. Married to his high school sweetheart, Alexa Hulse, on Christmas Eve in 1929, the photographer decided to leave his career in the Merchant Marine in 1931 following his promotion as official photographer for the Dollar Steamship Lines. He worked "ashore" full time as a self-employed commercial photographer. But Palmer's wanderlust did not disappear, nor did his longing for ocean travel. His sense of joy at new cultural experiences remained an important component of his life. Palmer enjoyed taking at least one three-month cruise per year during the 1930s to obtain the promotional images that company executives wanted.

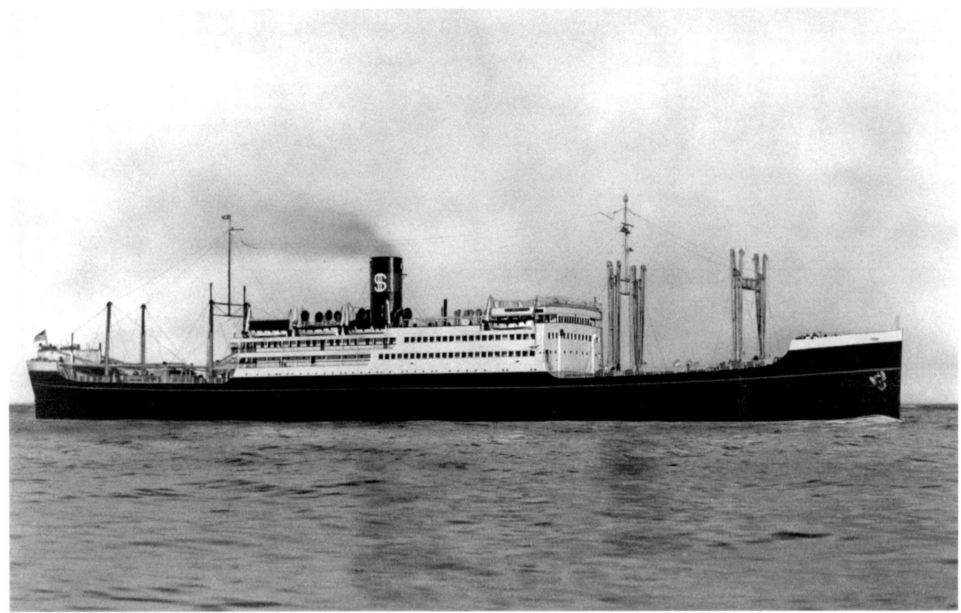

An advertising image of a Dollar Steamship Lines vessel taken by Alfred T. Palmer. Date of photo and location unknown. (*San Francisco Maritime National Historical Park*)

Working for cruise ship lines provided the income that Palmer needed, yet he knew his wife longed to travel with him. Thus, letters home often included placating statements to Alexa that justified his time away from her. For example, one pre-war letter, penned from Suva, Fiji, on February 16, 1932, revealed Alfred's belief that he had a duty to be the family breadwinner. "What the dickens is it that has taken me away from you and [son] Dave? —Just money that's all. I'm making it! I'm making plenty," he acknowledged before including a *mea culpa* of sorts: the money he was earning would not "repay" him for the time he was away from home.[22]

Palmer's images for the Dollar Steamship Lines' advertising campaigns attracted the attention of other cruise ship companies' public relations executives. He soon was taking promotional photographs for several other lines during the 1930s, including the Matson Navigation Company and the Moore-McCormick Lines. The photographer also expanded into filmmaking as a promotional device and made his first film in 1936 for the Dollar Steamship Lines about travel to the Philippines Islands, titled *South to Zamboanga*. That film traced one of the company's cruise ships, the *SS Mayon*, as it traveled for 1,200 nautical miles throughout the Philippines, stopping at various port cities. Sixteen other films would follow for the Dollar Steamship Lines and its successor, American President Lines. Palmer also made motion pictures for other cruise ship lines, including a documentary short film, which saw theatrical release through the *March of Time* series, which depicted the voyage of Moore-McCormick's "Good Neighbor Fleet" as those ships (the *Brazil*, the *Argentina*, and the *Uruguay*) visited South American port cities.[23]

Palmer's tasks were similar, regardless of which cruise ship line employed him. He photographed all aspects of shipboard life and the ships, selling the images to passengers, as well as to the companies' advertising departments. He also maintained the ships' darkroom facilities, oversaw other photography staff, and made assorted prints for sale. Palmer knew that he was fortunate to be employed during a decade that witnessed an 18.26 percent unemployment rate. He was netting approximately $1,000 to $1,300 per three-month voyage from the sale of photographs to passengers, almost as much as the $1,368 average yearly income throughout the 1930s, according to the U.S. Census.[24]

Within a few years, Palmer had established his reputation as an accomplished marine industry photographer.[25] But he envisioned a larger audience beyond the shipping line advertising executives, and a more lucrative plan for his photographic talents. Although commercial radio and motion pictures became popular entertainment choices during the 1920s and 1930s, the public remained voracious consumers of magazines and newspapers.[26] And the editors of those publications needed photographs. Palmer, with a growing portfolio of images taken in exotic locations around the world, was able to provide them. *National Geographic* published several of his images in the 1920s and 1930s, including pictures of Shanghai taken before the Japanese attack on that city, while the first issue of *Life* magazine featured a spread of Palmer's photos taken in Brazil. *Fortune* magazine also published his photographs.[27] During the mid-1940s, during a nine-month break from his government propaganda work, Palmer served as a staff

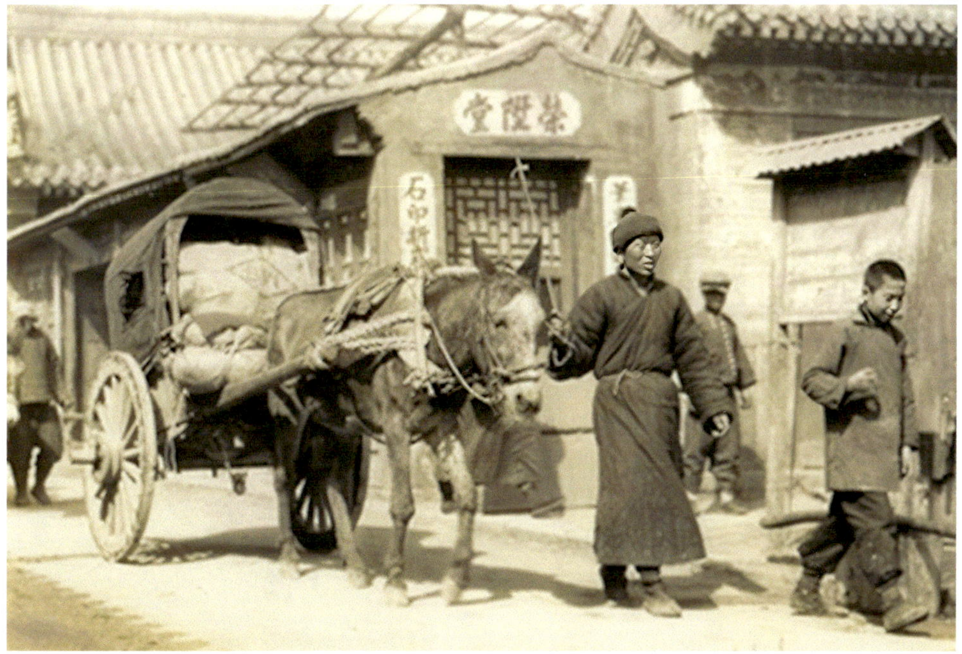

Chinese street scene, undated (1920s or 1930s). (*A. T. Palmer Collection, privately held*)

photographer for *National Geographic*, obtaining the position based on the quality of his earlier freelance work and the contacts that he had made during the previous two decades.[28]

Palmer also developed a solid reputation for his studio work with advertising executives. When not at sea, he undertook jobs for advertising agencies, corporations, newspapers, and magazines. Food companies regularly sought him out to create glamorous images of their products. He became known as a talented technician as well as an accomplished artist whose lighting techniques in the studio helped accentuate the best attributes of the products that he was photographing. Both the United Fruit Company and its rival, the Standard Fruit Company (now known as Dole), employed Palmer to make their produce look as appealing as possible.[29]

THE PHOTOGRAPHER AND THE ADVERTISING INDUSTRY COME OF AGE

Palmer's pre-war jobs provided a wealth of photographic and interpersonal experiences that helped prepare him for his wartime work. He became accustomed to shooting photographs in a variety of locations and under diverse weather conditions. The photographer also did more mundane work for shipping lines, taking "thousands and thousands" of headshots of sailors during the 1920s and 1930s for use on their identity cards.[30]

But capturing beauty became one of Palmer's visual hallmarks. While shipboard and in various ports, he created glamorous images of the ships and their passengers. He took images of those ships while in portside communities, accentuating famous landmarks or landscapes to show where they were. He captured images of one Dollar Steamship Lines' vessel passing under the Golden Gate Bridge in San Francisco and another at anchor in Shanghai, juxtaposed in port with Chinese junks, replete with their curved sails, passing by. Such images provided the visuals advertising executives wanted to sell the romance of travel. The task was once relatively easy, but the economic downturn of the 1930s impacted the cruise ship industry as it did all other businesses.[31]

Palmer's glamour aesthetic was particularly in demand by advertising agencies during the interwar years. Both the photographer and the agencies whose art directors hired him came of age during the 1920s and 1930s. Budgets soared during those two decades as advertisers created innovative campaigns aimed at promoting the goods that a growing number of brand name companies were producing. In doing so, those agencies created a consumer culture in American society. Agency art directors stressed style, beauty, and color as aesthetic selling tools in an era when mass industrial production often led to a level of sameness among competing products. And photography—rather than painting and other forms of illustration—became an increasingly important tool for advertisers in the two decades before World War II. As the 1920s dawned, fewer than 15 percent of illustrated advertisements featured photographs, even though the technology for photographic reproduction had been invented in the early 1880s. Within a decade, almost 80 percent of all advertisements used photographs to illustrate products and services.[32]

Several factors account for this visual shift in advertising design. Technical improvements in paper types, inks, and printing presses, as well as improvements in cameras, lenses, and lighting, allowed the advertising and magazine industries to innovate. Then, too, Eastman-Kodak's introduction of the inexpensive Brownie camera allowed photography to become far more commonplace in American life.

But the triumph of photography as a device in advertising and magazine illustrations during the 1920s and 1930s also can be credited to several photographers, including Edward Steichen, who embraced a modernist aesthetic and served chief photographer for Condé Nast publications from 1923 to 1938, as well as to certain magazine editors, and art directors. These individuals brought bold ideas and modernist aesthetics to advertising and magazine design. Those ideas, which broke with long-standing conventions on design, proved that commercial photography and art were not mutually exclusive fields. Steichen demonstrated through his work for fashion magazines that commercial photography was an excellent medium from which to depict beauty and elegance in both fashion and consumer goods. He used equally innovative ideas in studio lighting to achieve his romantic visuals.[33] Palmer, like other commercial photographers, also produced images for his clients with the attractive aesthetic styling (including lighting innovations) that advertisers and editors expected.

A CAREER IN FULL BLOOM

Palmer's photography jobs often took precedence over family life. Alfred and Alexa postponed their honeymoon and spent the first week of their married life printing one thousand pictures for the Dollar Steamship Lines in a makeshift darkroom in a house in Berkeley, California.[34] The $1,000 that the couple earned for the prints provided much-needed income. With the nation's economic downturn causing growing unemployment, Palmer returned to sea in December 1930, sending his pregnant wife back to Long Beach to live with her parents while he boarded the Dollar Lines' newly launched passenger ship, the *President Hoover*. Executives from the steamship line had hired Palmer to photograph the ship's maiden voyage. He also supervised the cruise ship's darkroom and its photography staff. The journey took the photographer from the Newport News, Virginia, shipyards to New York, then through the Panama Canal to San Francisco. The *Hoover* then ventured across the Pacific to the Philippines, Japan, and China before finally returning to San Francisco.[35]

Palmer had obtained the plum position of photographing the ship's first voyage after pleasing shipping executives with images that he had taken of the ship's construction at the Newport News (Virginia) Shipping and Drydock Company. A commercial photographer from New York had already done the job, but company executives were unsatisfied with the results. The shipping line's advertising manager recommended Palmer for the re-shoot, based on the two men's lengthy professional relationship.[36] The chance to photograph the *President Hoover* along with her sister ship, the *President Coolidge*, while still under construction intrigued Palmer, who soon found himself in Virginia crawling through the ships with his camera in hand. He never turned down physically demanding jobs, a work ethic that served him well during his wartime work.

Prior to Palmer's journey to the Newport News shipyards, Dollar Steamship executives had shared the other photographer's images, all of which were taken with a wide-angle lens. Palmer understood what visuals the executives did—and did not—want for their advertising campaign. The New York photographer, Palmer recalled, "wasn't equipped artistically.... What they [the company executives] wanted was art material for advertising, for release to newspapers, magazines." The wide-angle shots taken by the other man failed to imbue the photographs with the "pizzazz" desired by advertising executives who needed to sell the glamour and allure of ship travel.[37]

In the wealthy years that followed World War I, executives at the steamship line had spent lavishly to construct the *President Hoover*. The ship's launch unfortunately coincided with the start of the Great Depression. Dollar executives wanted—and needed—publicity for their luxury liner, which featured an Art Deco aesthetic on its upper deck, a swimming pool, an elevator, and air conditioning, heating, and telephones in each first-class cabin for those passengers' comfort. Despite the *Hoover*'s luxurious, state-of-the-art facilities, the nation's economic downturn resulted in a maiden voyage that was only half full of the number of passengers that the ship could carry.[38]

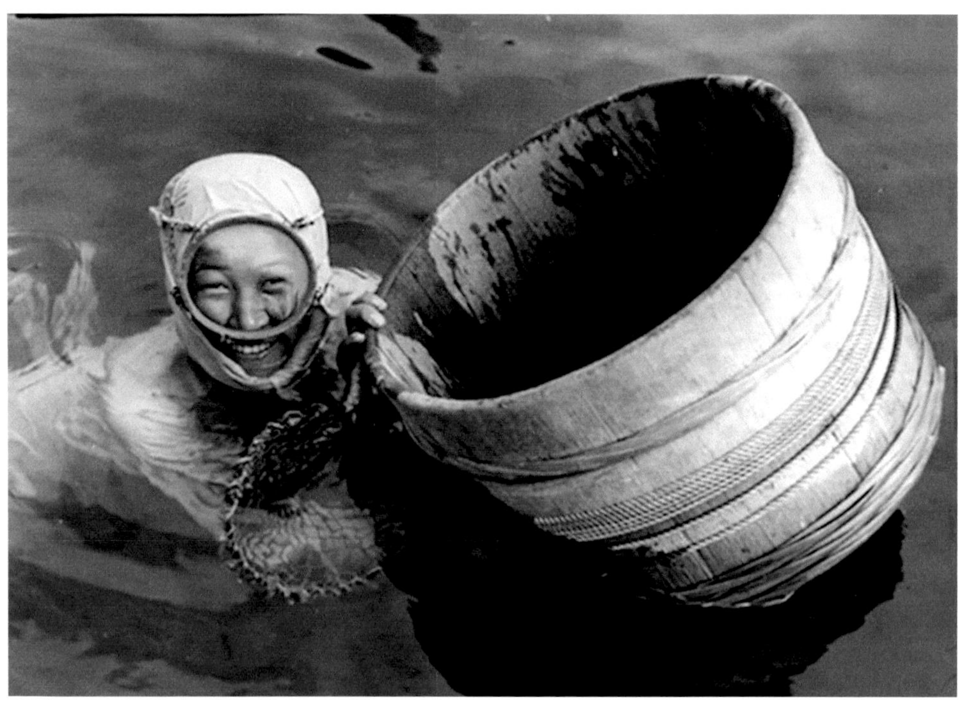

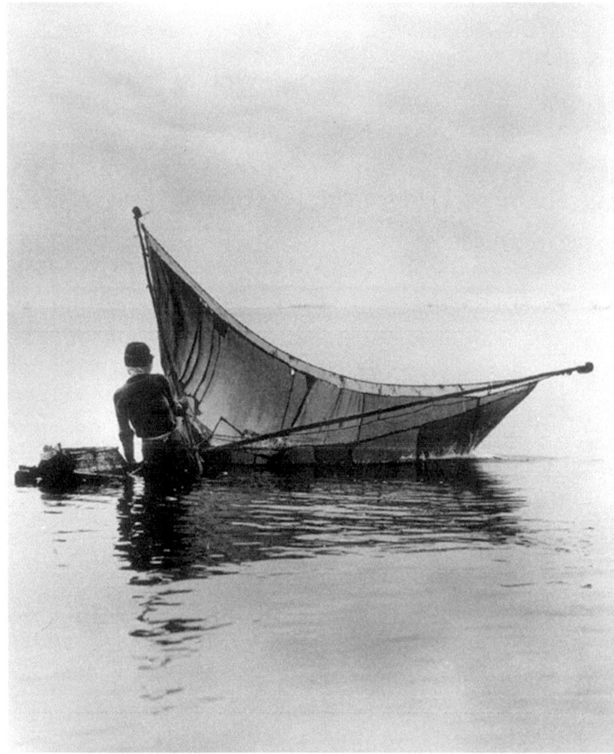

Above: Japanese pearl fisher, undated. (*A. T. Palmer Collection, privately held*)

Left: Japanese fisherman, undated. (*A. T. Palmer Collection, privately held*)

Letters between Alfred and Alexa Palmer reveal some tensions born of the photographer's months-long absences from his wife, but with the birth of their first son, the money Palmer earned helped pay the bills. He continued to sell the photographs that he took in ports of call to any publication that would run them. Even the editors of the local *Long Beach* (California) *Press Telegram* published a selection of the photographer's images in the rotogravure section of the Sunday paper and paid Palmer $10 per page.[39]

Palmer's extensive travel gave him an international perspective that many Americans lacked. He became a global citizen, taking the time to educate himself about other people and their cultures. That understanding of the world around him was important to Palmer, a viewpoint that never wavered throughout his life. "It's essential for the good of all of us to know our world neighbors better," he told a reporter in 1984.[40] But his shipboard photography work during the 1930s also provided Palmer with some pre-war experiences that opened his eyes to growing foreign aggression, experiences that many other American photographers lacked. Palmer witnessed the coming storm of war in Kobe, Japan, in 1937. While walking down a street he came across and photographed "a huge panorama of the Japanese fleet destroying the American fleet in the Pacific." The panorama was a very dramatic one, Palmer recalled: "… our ships were being blown out of the water. A narrator next to the painting explained to citizens what the Japanese were going to do to the Americans."[41]

Soon after, Palmer experienced that aggression firsthand during an August 1937 rescue mission to Shanghai while on board the *President Pierce*. The photographer, who was supposed to be shooting documentary film footage for the ship's parent company, recalled that the *President Pierce* "was the last [American] ship into Shanghai before the Japanese moved in." From his position on the ship, Palmer witnessed the bombing of an electrical plant as well as the bombing of the city's new civic center. "And we were able to get up the Whangpoo River [today known as the Huangpu], up halfway," Palmer recalled. "And the Japanese were bombing us, fore and aft, just to let us know that we weren't supposed to be there." Both the ship and its crew survived the journey, picked up anxious Americans (as well as many Hong Kong residents), and departed.[42]

Soon after the *President Pierce* departed, the captains of the remaining civilian ships in the area refused to come up the river to rescue more civilians. A Chinese air force pilot had mistaken the American civilian steamship *President Hoover*, which was anchored just offshore of Shanghai, for a Japanese war ship and dropped bombs on the *Hoover*. With no one coming to evacuate them, thousands of desperate, frightened Chinese and foreigners of many nationalities were left to fend for themselves in a city under attack.[43]

A RELOCATION TO THE EAST COAST

In 1937, Palmer decided to take a calculated gamble. Despite the ongoing economic uncertainty of the Great Depression, he moved his photography business to New York City. The photographer needed to support his family, but he also wanted to satisfy his continued wanderlust. Japanese aggression in the Pacific halted cruising from the West Coast, a key source of Palmer's income. With his finances tight, the photographer left his family in Berkeley, California, boarded a bus for New York City armed with a portfolio of his cruise ship images, and checked into a cheap hotel upon his arrival in Manhattan.

Like San Francisco, New York was home to numerous shipping lines—but ones that plied Atlantic and Caribbean waters. Palmer knew that one of those companies, the Moore-McCormick Lines, was attempting to put together a new passenger and shipping service to South America. Itching to return to sea as a photographer, Palmer arrived at the Moore-McCormick office unannounced. His timing was perfect, however. The company had no advertising manager or publicist, but the line's vice president, Commodore Robert C. Lee, recognized the value of publicity and hired Palmer after viewing the photographer's portfolio.[44] As he did for the Dollar Steamship Lines, Palmer took still photographs for Moore-McCormick's advertising department and produced several color travelogue films for the company, as well.[45]

Palmer soon opened an office at 90 West Broadway in the Bowling Green section of lower Manhattan, close to where many shipping lines had their headquarters. With the Great Depression grinding on, the task of running his photography business proved itself to be a financial and emotional struggle. Although Palmer offered a diversity of photographic services, including advertising, editorial, and educational photography, the cost of supplies, rent, and an assistant's salary left him short on cash and, at times, questioning his relocation. Trying to convince his wife (and possibly himself) that the move was not a mistake, he noted in an April 27, 1939, letter: "We're making money, but it's taking so much to get this thing started."[46]

In an era when letters, rather than long-distance telephone calls, were the norm for keeping in touch, letter-writing may have been therapeutic for Palmer since he could voice his private concerns to his wife. "I'm getting weary of this seemingly endless struggle," he admitted to Alexa in the same letter. "I work so hard and have so little to show for it. The bank is broke once again," he said in explaining his current financial status. The statement also served as an apology since Palmer was unable to enclose money in the letter. He needed supplies for his business, he explained, then mentioned that executives at the Moore-McCormick Lines owed him $460 for photography work that he had completed, but the company was now paying on a thirty-day plan. "And our gross for the next month will be about 1000.00 So we're pulling out of it. I hope that you'll be able to see your way thru [*sic*]. That's why I suggested that you sell the Olds [i.e., their Oldsmobile car]—if you can get a decent price," he wrote, worried about past-due bills that needed paying. The next morning, in clearly better spirits, he penned an addendum, encouraging Alexa to keep the car, realizing that it would be hard for her to run errands on a bicycle. He closed the letter with a wistful acknowledgement, stating, "It will be a most glorious day when everything is paid for, won't it," before reassuring his wife that he could survive on tins of beans, cheese, milk, and bread until more money flowed into the business.[47]

When finances became too tight, Palmer, who was used to seeking freelance opportunities, interested two photo syndicates in pictures of the nation. The images would serve as a counterpoint of sorts to those taken by the FSA photographers, which were widely reprinted in newspapers, magazines, books, and other forms of print media. Palmer believed that editors wanted positive images of their country to display in their newspapers and magazines for an emotionally exhausted public. So, he took them, capturing the United States' industries, scenic beauty, and its citizens. During June and July 1938, Palmer made the drive home to California from his New York studio, taking photographs of what he termed "the American scene" and selling those images to the Ewing Galloway stock photography company for approximately $1,350. A similar trip from September to December of the same year for another stock photo agency, Armstrong Roberts of Philadelphia, brought in an additional $1,000. The latter project, which was a more detailed look at American life, involved depicting the nation's industrial production, its railroads, agriculture, and its citizens' recreational pastimes.[48]

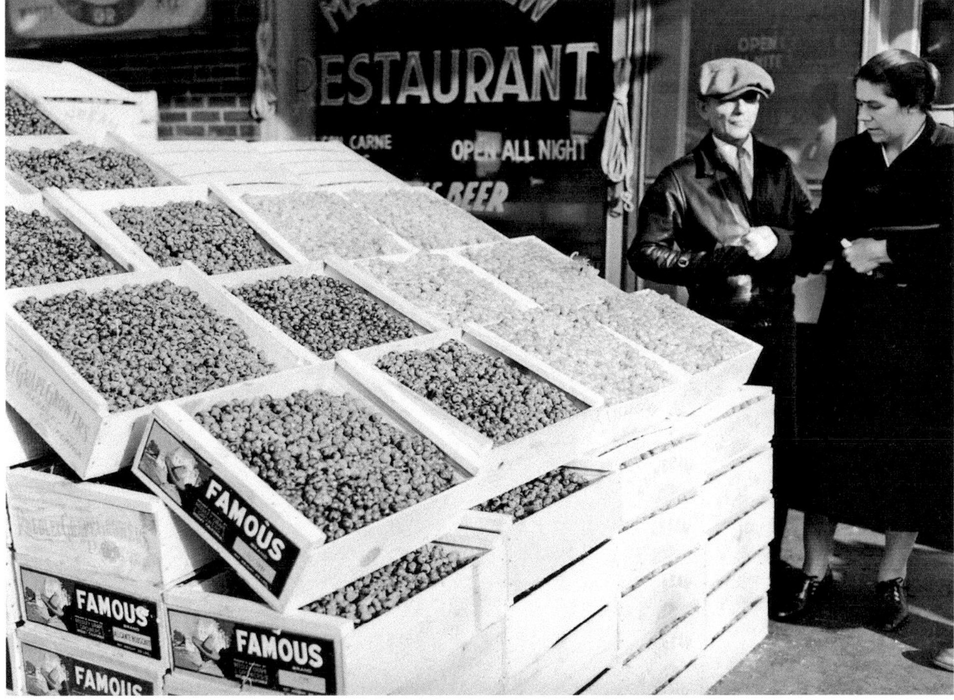

Missouri fruit stand, 1938. (*A. T. Palmer Collection, privately held*)

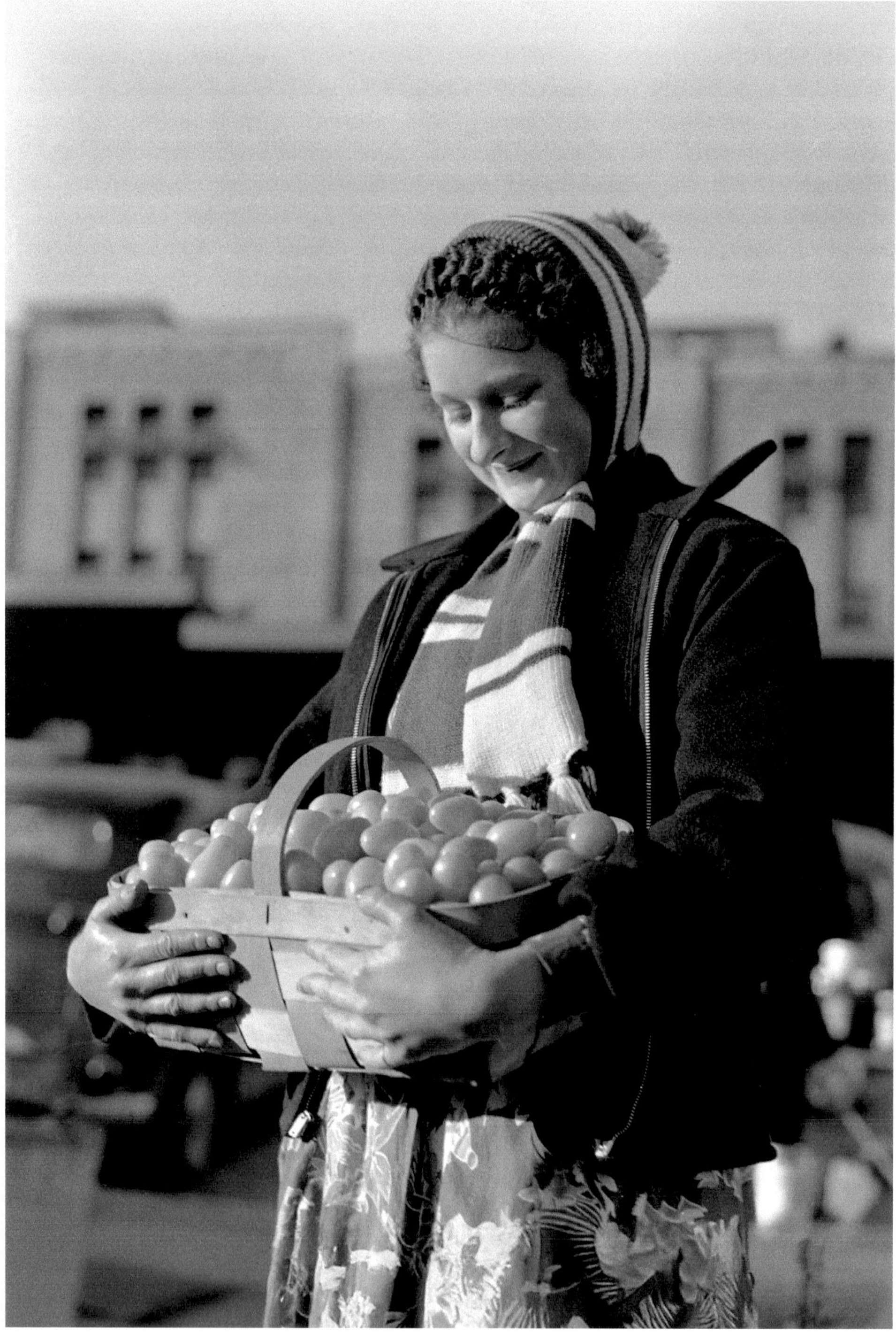

North Dakota farm woman with basket of produce, 1938. (*A. T. Palmer Collection, privately held*)

STRAIGHT PHOTOGRAPHY AS A VISUAL AESTHETIC

In line with other commercial photographers working during the 1930s, Palmer shot his images in a style that has been termed straight photography, a visual aesthetic that was noted for its lack of excessive darkroom manipulation or diffused focus. Those practices were hallmarks of the so-called pictorialists, who produced an artistic style of photography that emulated the painterly arts (especially impressionism) in the early decades of the twentieth century. As Patricia Johnston has stated, advertising executives increasingly embraced photography, especially straight photography, as a visual art form when they discovered photography's "style and elegance" appealed to mass audiences. Then, too, statistical studies revealed that consumers believed photographs were more credible than other forms of illustration in depicting products.[49]

Initially, those executives, like much of the public, were drawn to photography's seeming ability to convey truth and realism. But advertisers soon realized that photographers had the ability to sell glamour and allure via the artistry of their photographs. Images of products portrayed in advertisements appeared accurate; however, the visuals were crafted to provoke an emotional response in consumers during an era when advertising agencies were growing in number. And their budgets soared during the 1920s and 1930s as advertisers helped sell a growing array of mass-produced products that, based on the assembly line process, often were relatively uniform rather than unique. But in an era before clear ethical standards and norms were established, the tactic worked; polls and surveys of consumer behavior proved that photography sold products, which reaffirmed its importance in advertising.[50]

Palmer's status as self-employed commercial photographer meant that he regularly sought new clients. The U.S. Maritime Commission in Washington, D.C., seemed a logical choice, and in early 1940, Palmer contacted Robert W. Horton, the commission's director of the Division of Maritime Promotion and Information. The photographer sent along copies of pictures he had taken on a return trip to the shipyards in Newport News, Virginia, of six new passenger liners being constructed, along with film footage as well. That action—and its timing—proved serendipitous. Horton responded to Palmer's query by saying that the images were "among the most beautiful examples of marine photography which I have ever seen," and in a letter dated April 25, 1940, invited Palmer to come to Washington, D.C., to discuss freelance work possibilities.[51] Two weeks later, on May 10, 1940, the German Blitzkrieg of western Europe began. Nazi troops invaded Belgium, Holland, Luxembourg, and France, while the German Luftwaffe dropped bombs upon Canterbury, England.

Both Horton and Admiral Emory Land, who supervised the Commission, realized that Americans would be unable to stay out of another world war. President Roosevelt knew this, as well.[52] On May 25, 1940, the president signed an administrative order that activated the Office for Emergency Management, the first of a series of agencies and offices that would help coordinate—and promote—the nation's national defense activities. Horton, a former journalist turned public relations practitioner, was selected to head the Office for Emergency Management's Division of Information.[53] The following day, on May 26, the president took to his favorite form of media—radio—to help Americans understand that war was coming and to guide them toward acceptance of that reality. But Roosevelt knew he had to be cautious; public opinion was still largely anti-interventionist.[54] While telling listeners that he hoped to keep the nation out of the war, the president made clear that the creation of a strong military, backed by ships, planes, tanks, and other equipment, was a necessity for national defense. And that defense also included a political move away from isolationism and toward arming American allies.

Following the president's radio address announcing that the U.S. government would be partnering with private businesses by providing the money corporate executives needed to convert, and, in some cases, expand factories to manufacture military equipment, Land and Horton hired Palmer on a contract basis, tasking him with the job of taking photographs and producing motion pictures of the nation's defense preparations, which included ship construction. Palmer's straight photography aesthetic, his understanding of lighting techniques, and his global experiences as a member of the Merchant Marine made the photographer the right individual at the right time to help depict the country's defense-related construction boom.[55]

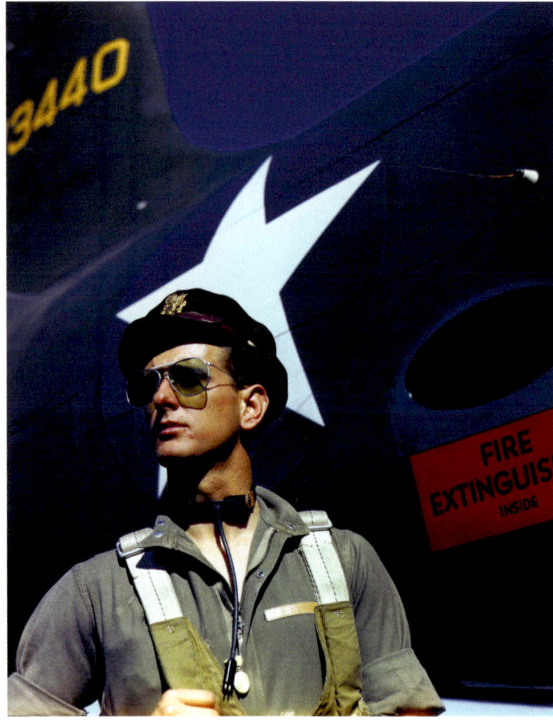

F. W. Hunter, army test pilot, at the Douglas Aircraft Company plant at Long Beach, California, October 1942. (*Library of Congress*)

2

A RETURN TO WAR AND PROPAGANDA

On November 5, 1940, the American public re-elected Franklin D. Roosevelt to an unprecedented third term as president of the United States. But that election—and the promises the president made in the two years before the election—left him mired in a global quandary partly of his own making. European nations had been at war for fourteen months. Led by expansionist leaders, German and Italian forces were sweeping across the continent, extending their military campaigns into the Middle East and, eventually, northern Africa. The Japanese, who had invaded Manchuria in 1931, controlled large swaths of China, were rebuilding their navy, and had seized French Indochina in late September 1940. Soon after his re-election, Roosevelt—who had campaigned on an anti-interventionist platform—had to explain to the public that his longtime support of that policy was coming to an end. He believed that America's democratic system and its citizens' way of life were under threat from fascist enemies.

Persuading the public that the Axis powers were a growing menace to the nation's safety initially proved difficult. Most Americans did not see an immediate threat to their nation.[1] Prior to May 10, 1940, when the Germans launched their Blitzkrieg attack on western Europe, much of the U.S. population was dismissive of Germany's ability to prevail in the conflict; Allied forces numerically outnumbered Adolf Hitler's military. Geography also provided a false sense of security since the nation was separated from both Europe and Asia by vast oceans. And the respect that many Americans had for British naval power led much of the public to overestimate England's ability to protect Atlantic Ocean shipping from German warships and submarines.[2]

Moving citizens toward an acceptance that defensive measures were necessary required both political and communicative finesse. The president knew that he first had to win the support of public opinion before taking action.[3] Roosevelt, therefore, chose to undertake the same persuasive approach that he had employed during the years of the Great Depression—via carefully presented information. The president had promoted his "New Deal" policies by releasing a vast amount of information via press conferences, official speeches, radio addresses, and press releases. Roosevelt made use of many of the media tools that his predecessors had employed, but he did so with greater skill and devotion to detail.[4]

The president and his staff helped sell the administration's policies and accomplishments during the 1930s by using a propaganda technique called card stacking. The method involved marshalling and releasing carefully selected facts that were favorable to the administration's policies and goals, while ignoring other truths. Manipulating information in such a way helped persuade many of the country's citizens that the president's policies were helping pull the nation out of economic distress. As historian Richard W. Steele states, "The strength of this educational effort was its credibility, its factualness, and its dissemination through the medium from which Americans customarily received their political instruction—the daily press."[5]

With the nation once again facing a serious threat—this time from external forces—Roosevelt used this educational strategy as a means of convincing the public that the U.S. needed to become a military powerhouse for the sake of national defense. Crucial to his information strategy throughout his years in office was the president's belief that broad public approval of his policies required that citizens were "fully and sympathetically informed of his efforts."[6] But he also knew that the public would be persuaded only if he tied his goals to Americans' immediate wants and needs. The public, Roosevelt believed, could not be swayed by political ideology or altruistic appeals alone.[7] Protecting the nation by building up the country's national defenses was a sellable strategy during the election year of 1940; sending troops to Europe and Asia to defeat the enemies of democracy was not.

Gaining the support of the press, the public, and members of Congress required a concerted public relations effort since improving and expanding the nation's armed forces required an enormous amount of money and resources. The U.S. military had been neglected during the 1930s as the president and members of Congress focused on domestic concerns. Rapid industrialization had transformed the United States into the world's leading economic power, but as the new decade of the 1940s dawned, the country could not boast of being a global military power. The American military had little in the way of weapons, aircraft, tanks, or ships with which to go to war, should the United States have to enter the conflict. Roosevelt was particularly worried about the military's lack of airplanes. Washington, D.C., analysts believed that the Germans were capable of manufacturing up to 18,000 aircraft per year.[8]

The president was equally concerned about the size of the nation's armed forces. As David Reynolds notes, in 1940, the United States ranked twentieth in terms of military power; the Dutch were ranked nineteenth. Much of the public was unaware that the U.S. Army consisted of only five divisions that totaled a meager 80,000 troops. Those soldiers had minimal accoutrements for warfare, with just 160 pursuit planes and fifty-two heavy bombers. The U.S. Navy was not much stronger. Much of its fleet was based in Hawaii, meant to serve as a deterrent against Japan. That decision left the country's East Coast and Atlantic Ocean largely unprotected. When France fell to Nazi forces in June 1940, Reynolds states that there was "near-panic" in Washington, D.C.[9]

A PERIOD OF DIPLOMATIC AND PSYCHOLOGICAL BATTLES

Roosevelt knew that he had to appeal to the public's emotions as well as to their logic if he were to succeed in accomplishing his defense buildup. To do so, the president established a series of federal agencies, including the Office of Facts and Figures and the Office for Emergency Management, which were tasked with delivering carefully packaged information designed to persuade Americans to set aside their isolationist views.[10] The agencies proved a necessity, even though the president was largely opposed to establishing federal propaganda units. But Roosevelt also knew that a hard sell would not work. Prior to his third term in office, therefore, the president was cautious in his quest to help America's European allies, even as he watched with dismay and alarm as the English and French militaries neared their breaking points. He voiced his concerns publicly but continued to promise non-involvement in the war in the months leading up to his 1940 re-election.[11]

Campaign promises aside, Roosevelt was not isolationist in his thinking. But to win re-election for a third term, the president had to focus on domestic policy objectives and minimize his concerns to the public about the ongoing global crisis.[12] The German Blitzkrieg forced the president to be less complacent in foreign affairs. On May 26, 1940, he again turned to radio to inform the public of the dangers of the Axis powers. But Roosevelt did more than lay out the facts; he built a credible argument against isolationism. With Nazi forces overrunning the European continent, expanding, and improving America's military became a necessity.

The president also faced a delicate diplomatic situation with foreign allies. Under pressure prior to the election to help the British face the Nazi onslaught but facing a predominantly isolationist-leaning Congress, Roosevelt took matters into his own hands. On June 1, 1940, he bypassed the Neutrality Acts (laws that forbid the shipment of weapons and munitions to warring nations, the extension of loans and credit to belligerent nations, and the arming of merchant ships for self-defense) and the U.S. Congress by ordering that "surplus" military equipment be sent to Great Britain over the objections of his military advisors, including his secretary of war, Harry Hines Woodring, who supported a continuation of isolationist foreign policy.[13, 14]

As historian Susan Dunn states, Roosevelt's longstanding public stance of "no political commitments which might entangle us in foreign wars" was at odds with his private awareness during his second term in office that the U.S. might again be plunged into warfare.[15] The president knew that his public promises would not stop the aggressive leaders of Germany, Italy, and Japan. Roosevelt saw the issue clearly. Action was needed. But his hesitancy prior to 1940 hindered the president. Indeed, Roosevelt's initial anti-interventionist stance led him to remain largely silent in March 1938 when Germany invaded Austria. In March 1939, when Hitler's troops rolled into Czechoslovakia, the president again did little more publicly than send an "urgent plea" to the leaders of Germany and Italy asking them not to invade thirty-one other nations, a request that led Hitler and his high-ranking officials to roar with laughter.[16]

Even after Germany invaded Poland on September 1, 1939, Roosevelt promised Americans during one of his "fireside chat" radio addresses that the United States would remain neutral in the face of Nazi aggression.[17] Yet, the president also was pragmatic. Despite his public pledges of neutrality, Roosevelt asked Congress that autumn to repeal the ban on foreign arms sales to help America's British and French allies.[18] He also began assessing America's military capabilities, sending trusted advisor Harry Hopkins on a tour of airplane manufacturing plants.[19]

Roosevelt, therefore, faced both political and psychological battles in his efforts to prepare the nation for the possibility of war. The Soviet Union's invasion of Finland on November 30, 1939, only heightened the president's state of anxiety as he watched the global crisis escalate. Roosevelt knew it was only a question of time before the U.S. came under threat. Neither the Atlantic nor the Pacific oceans provided Americans with protection from aggressor nations when those countries possessed submarines, other naval vessels, and airplanes.[20]

The German Blitzkrieg ultimately helped Americans to understand that threat. Early 1940 proved to be an anxious time for much of the public. Citizens, politicians, and journalists alike debated whether—and when—the nation would be drawn into the conflict, as well as whether America would face a direct attack. By late fall, however, the public's fear of a German invasion of the United States had subsided, and citizens once again slid into an uneasy, yet passive frame of mind.[21] Roosevelt used his December 29, 1940, broadcast as a means of awakening the nation by choosing his words carefully, reiterating key points from his May radio address. "This is not a fireside chat on war," he said. "It is a talk on national security."

After calmly reminding Americans of the dangers of the Axis powers and the threat they posed to the nation, the president attempted to make Americans understand that their country's security and its inability to stay out of the war "hinged on the survival of Great Britain." That nation needed war materials that Americans could provide. With the groundwork carefully laid, Roosevelt got to his key message, calling on citizens to shift to a wartime footing by helping produce the materials necessary for America's national defense, as well as those for the defense of European allies. The United States, he said, must become "the great arsenal of democracy."[22]

THE BATTLE OVER PROPAGANDA

Setting the public on the path to engage in yet another world war required a federal publicity effort. But the use of the word "propaganda" made many Americans uneasy. Propaganda, in many people's minds, was a multi-headed hydra with seemingly unlimited power. As Allan M. Winkler states, much of the public realized that well-crafted propaganda could be so subtle "that people might not even be aware they were being taken in. Under those circumstances democracy itself seemed endangered, for the mythical marketplace of ideas could no longer be truly competitive if ideas could be so easily manipulated."[23]

That concern was warranted. Much of the public remembered the propaganda created during World War I by the United States' first federal propaganda office, led by journalist George Creel. Creel had been tasked with persuading the public to support intervention into that conflict.[24] His blandly named Committee on Public Information (CPI) was anything but innocuous. Although President Woodrow Wilson had established the committee to dispense information about the war to the public, the CPI staff quickly mobilized into a propaganda entity with a reach that extended into all aspects of American life by using every form of mass media available at the time. John Maxwell Hamilton calls the CPI's propaganda effort "stunning in its extent and range." CPI officials, Hamilton adds, had an "overwhelming desire to convince ... to pluck at emotions and use information tendentiously." It was not "the house of truth."[25]

CPI officials had also created educational materials about the war for schools and developed speeches on a variety of topics that could be delivered to community groups. They developed short, four-minute talks on war topics that could be given at theaters before motion pictures were shown. From coast to coast, the public was targeted with emotion-laden messages that quickly turned an anti-interventionist nation into one whose citizens had flocked to recruiting stations. Creel's post-war book, which explained how a group of writers, artists, journalists, and bureaucrats sold the nation on warfare, led to a public outcry concerning the CPI's reach, as well as its pervasiveness.[26] As Winkler states, "Creel accomplished his task all too well." His efforts created fear of enemies abroad and at home during the war and bitterness afterwards.[27]

Post-World War I realities also angered the American public and drove them toward isolationism. President Wilson's failure to deliver on his promise of a peaceful world, one made safe for democracy, prompted many Americans to ask why—and for what outcome—so many Americans had died (52,947 U.S. servicemen had died in combat, another 63,000 had died of non-combat related issues, including influenza, and 202,628 others were wounded).[28] Much of the public became convinced that the fight to protect other nations was not worth the sacrifices that Americans had made, especially since arms merchants and bankers profited handsomely from the war, while allies had failed to pay their war debts.[29]

As 1940 dawned, American citizens and officials' distrust of—and distaste for— propaganda shaped federal policies toward using such tactics again. The president found propaganda distasteful, but he recognized—as did the leaders of European nations—that World War II involved what strategists have termed "total war," that is, a conflict which required nations to focus their whole civilian industrial, scientific, and economic resources behind the war effort to help win the conflict. Motivating and involving those civilians required government-created propaganda. Roosevelt also knew that civilian morale was a key factor behind military success. Propaganda was, in the words of David Welch, "an essential weapon in the national arsenal."[30]

With most of the nations involved in the conflict in possession of well-developed media resources, World War II combatants and civilians alike witnessed a parallel propaganda war—the largest in the history of modern warfare, although American propaganda agencies were never accorded the power nor the scope of activities as was given to the much-derided Committee for Public Information.[31] Despite the establishment of less powerful propaganda agencies, Americans, like European and Japanese citizens, could not escape their government's patriotic messages. That messaging encouraged citizens to support the war and contribute to winning the conflict, while troops were informed about their enemies and their respective nations' goals.[32]

A "STRATEGY OF TRUTH"

President Roosevelt's dislike of World War I propaganda initially led to him to decide in 1940 against establishing one powerful, overarching federal publicity agency that would be tasked with creating and distributing information about the nation's defense buildup.[33] Instead, he created several government agencies which produced propaganda, including the Office for Emergency Management, the Office of Facts and Figures, the War Manpower Commission, and the Office of War Information.[34] The latter agency was created on June 13, 1942, by executive order after the president realized that his other agencies were stymied by overlapping mandates and infighting on message strategies. At times these agencies distributed conflicting information, which hindered rather than helped the public's morale, as well as citizens' general understanding about the need for defense preparations. The Office of War Information included both domestic and overseas propaganda units, the latter of which worked to help counter Axis propaganda while also engaging in long-range nation building by presenting America's democratic system and way of life as superior to any other in the world.[35]

The federal government's World War II-era propaganda agencies did not possess the unity of voice nor the message simplicity that were so crucial to the success of Creel's operation during World War I.[36] And unlike Germany's well-run propaganda machine, none of America's federal propaganda agency directors had been tasked with a clear mandate as to what messages they should create, according to Sydney Weinberg. As Weinberg states, "In the tangle of overlapping jurisdictions no one agency seemed authorized to explain what America was doing at home and abroad to win the war or what goals it hoped to achieve by fighting." The president deserved part of the blame since he remained vague on his war goals beyond seeing fascism defeated.[37]

Despite their operational and messaging difficulties, the directors of the nation's propaganda agencies tried to calm citizens' fears and sway public opinion toward acceptance of war propaganda by stating that the information they disseminated would be factual, based on a "strategy of truth" as a means of helping citizens stay informed about the war. Their offices, they said, would not disseminate propaganda based on fear and manipulation.[38] Archibald MacLeish, a noted poet, critic, playwright, and Librarian of Congress who was appointed by the president to run the Office of Facts and Figures, put a positive spin on the federal government's propaganda efforts at a January 21, 1942, press conference. He promised that this democratic strategy of truth was in opposition to the propaganda produced by the Axis powers, which he labeled a "strategy of terror." "Democracy," he said, "is based on the proposition that the Government can trust the people and that the people are entitled to all the facts and figures necessary to enable them to make up their own minds within the limits of national security."[39] The Office for Emergency Management's innocuous-sounding mandate appeared to support MacLeish's statement. Its employees were tasked not with producing propaganda but with "show[ing] the public [through words and photographs] what it is getting for the money it spends on national defense."[40]

Elmer Davis, the popular, pro-interventionist CBS radio commentator who ran the Office of War Information, also promised that the "strategy of truth" would serve as the ethical motivation behind the information and photographs that his agency disseminated. Davis recognized how controversial the creation of propaganda agencies was to both members of Congress and the public. He therefore positioned his agency as an innocuous information provider when discussing its role. Certainly, that agency, like the Office for Emergency Management before it, produced propaganda, but both agencies' tactics were subtler—focusing less on fear than did the propaganda produced by Creel's Committee on Public Information.[41]

Despite claims from officials that government agencies would be purveyors of fact, America's pre-war and wartime information agencies were indeed propaganda entities whose staff members engaged in persuasive communication. The public needed to be convinced to help their nation's allies, to buy bonds to help fund the war, to donate aluminum and other metals to scrap drives, and to accept the rationing of food and goods. Civilians who worked in defense industry jobs were portrayed as heroes, fighting at home for the cause of democracy.[42]

The strategy of truth, therefore, was an exercise in card stacking of facts and images.[43] Many federal officials saw propaganda as a weapon. They used all forms of mass media, including photographs, illustrations, posters, and films, as tools to shape public opinion and to educate the public to understand who their enemies were.[44] And that propaganda also reminded Americans that their democratic system and personal quality of life were worth preserving. But regardless of how innocuous federal propagandists characterized their efforts to sell the war, both Republican members of Congress and Southern Democrats remained suspicious of the propaganda agencies, questioning both their budgets and their existence. Many Congressmen were especially wary of the Office of War Information, believing that the agency's true mandate was keeping Roosevelt in power and his New Deal policies in vogue.[45] But as historian John Morton Blum has stated, the fact that Roosevelt gave the green light to a resurgence of government propaganda "spoke more to the dangers of defeat than to the opportunities of victory."[46]

PHOTOGRAPHY AS A PROPAGANDA TOOL

While debates ensued in Washington, D.C., regarding whether federal propaganda agencies should even exist, how they should function, and what messaging they should deliver, the artists, writers, filmmakers, and photographers from those agencies were busy producing the often-derided materials for both domestic and international audiences. Photography played a central role in the government's propaganda efforts from the start. The widespread use of photographs in wartime propaganda reflected its centrality to the government's efforts to persuade the public. Those officials understood—or at least assumed—that the public's emotions could be manipulated via visual imagery.

The World War II generation that propagandists were trying to reach had come of age in a visually rich environment. Noted journalist and social critic Walter Lippmann acknowledged the importance of photography as an information source in his 1922 book, *Public Opinion.* Americans "relied on photography to communicate with each other," Lippmann said. Equally importantly, he acknowledged that much of the public viewed photography as a relatively pure form of communication, seemingly free from manipulation. Photographs, he said, "seem utterly real. They come, we imagine, directly to us without human meddling, and they are the most effortless food for the mind imaginable."[47]

Other influential Americans agreed with Lippmann's assessment of how the public perceived photographs. Publisher Henry Luce banked on photography's "ability to astonish" when the first issue of the pictorially focused *Life* magazine

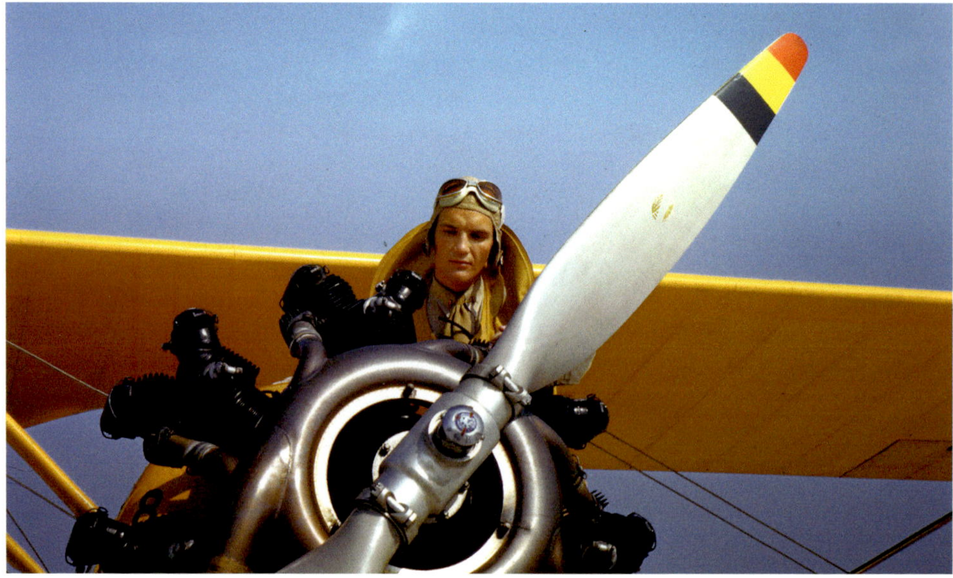

Marine lieutenant with the towing plane for the gliders at Page Field, Parris Island, South Carolina, May 1942. (*Library of Congress*)

hit the newsstands on November 23, 1936. The issue, which featured a cover photo of the Fort Peck (Montana) Dam's spillway, taken by Margaret Bourke-White, sold out its entire press run—all 250,000 copies—within hours. Sales of the magazine soared as the public embraced the new magazine format: one that allowed visuals to drive the narrative, rather than the traditional approach of using photographs to illustrate the text. By 1937, 1.5 million copies of each issue were being printed, and imitators, including *Look* magazine, were established as competitors.[48]

The average American indeed viewed photographs as possessing "literal, matter-of-fact realism," rather than seeing such images as potential tools for manipulation. But, as Roland Marchand states, both wartime propagandists and advertising executives were able to exploit this belief in photography as an honest purveyor and portrayer of truth, even though many commercial photographers and others who used cameras to create art during the 1920s and 1930s engaged in various forms of manipulation. Not every photographer embraced the straight photography aesthetic. Many had developed their own "artistic self-consciousness."[49]

Yet images also proved to be valuable communication tools because they were able to convey information clearly to individuals regardless of what language the target population spoke or that public's level of literacy.[50] The August 1941 issue of *U.S. Camera* contained a similar argument. In an article titled "What About Photography in National Defense?" the unnamed author grandiloquently promoted the value of images as a tool to inform the public or to propagandize, stating: "The photograph can be more eloquent than the report or communique;

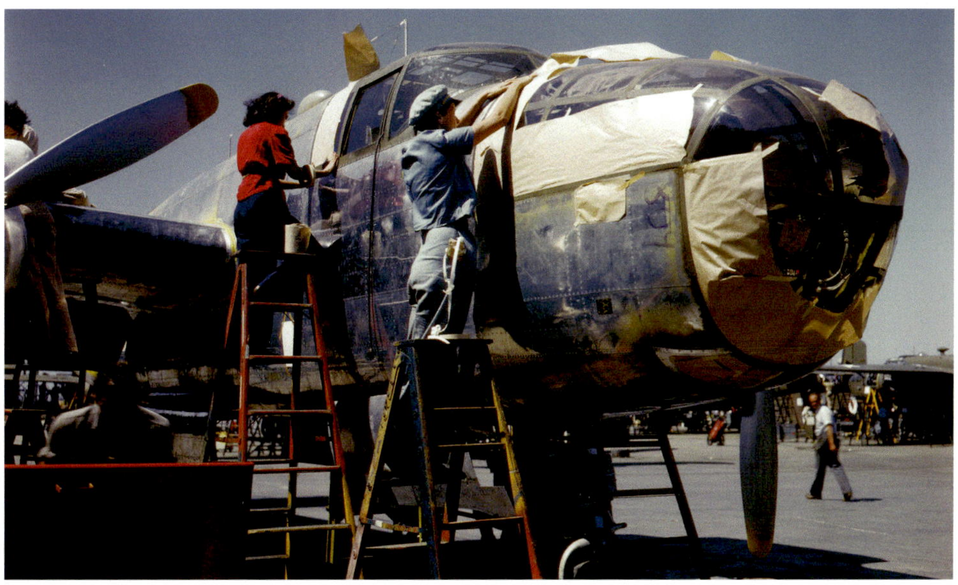

North American B-25 bomber is prepared for painting on the outside assembly line, North American Aviation, Inc. Inglewood, California, October 1942. (*Library of Congress*)

more concise and less suspect than the literature of the correspondent. The camera not only speaks to us as a witness; it sings to us as a bard. It boasts of our might and of our heroism, gloats over the damage we have done our enemy, laments the damage he has done to us." Both British and German propagandists, the article acknowledged, made highly effective use of photographs as a persuasive tool.

The article's writer worried, however, that government officials had not yet realized nor recognized "the full possibilities of photography as a medium of information and propaganda." Only the photographers working for the Farm Security Administration proved the exception, the writer stated, adding that the FSA's photography section "has been setting a notable example since 1935 in arousing public interest in the problems and achievements of the agency."[51] Much of that credit had to be given to the FSA photographers' supervisor, Roy Stryker. Stryker had a very clear understanding of what visual documentation was needed to promote the FSA's accomplishments in helping the rural poor. And Stryker's unit had five years of consistent documentary experience as compared to the photographers who worked for the Office for Emergency Management or for the Office of War Information.

Although those pre-war and wartime agencies lacked the years of consistent direction and singular vision that so marked the FSA's Historical Section, the offices were helmed by veteran journalists, photographers, filmmakers, editors, and advertising executives who knew how to reach the public with persuasive messages. But those employees, including Alfred Palmer, also were dedicated to democratic ideals. Winkler states that while the nation's social faults and failings were acknowledged, the propaganda agencies' directors' careful selection of facts and visual imagery presented a hopeful view of American society that stressed the "spiritual and material" components of American society that made the nation great.[52]

And while President Roosevelt was vague in expounding on his aims and goals if the nation had to go to war, he did give federal publicists some broadly worded rhetorical fodder they could use for propaganda purposes when he encouraged the nation to become the "Arsenal of Democracy." The president created more propaganda possibilities via his "Four Freedoms" argument, which he delivered on January 6, 1941, during his annual State of the Union address. Needing to explain his rationale for assisting the British and other European allies, Roosevelt told Congress that by helping those nations, the U.S. was fighting for the universal freedoms that he claimed all human beings possessed. The president enumerated those as freedom of speech, freedom of worship, freedom from want, and freedom from fear. Alfred Palmer proved adept at depicting those rhetorical constructs.

Having witnessed Japanese aggression first-hand in 1937 in Shanghai, Palmer supported the government's efforts to "rouse people to the dangers" of unchecked foreign aggression. As he began his job to depict American defense preparations in May 1940, Palmer agreed with his government supervisors that the country's citizens were passive. Wanting to awaken Americans to the threats from Europe and Asia to the American way of life, the photographer made "pictures that had guts." He knew that newspaper and magazine editors "wanted pictures with impact." And that is what he set out to shoot, he said, recalling his wartime work.[53] In doing so, Palmer brought his commercial advertising experience to bear, creating archetypal heroes—and heroines—who, in the words of Jeanie Cooper Carson, "could personify and simplify Americans' roles in the complex international struggle."[54]

From May 1940, when he was hired by Robert Horton, until December 1941, when the United States entered the war, Palmer may have been the only photographer under government contract whose job was devoted solely to one task: taking propaganda photos that depicted the nation readying itself for self-defense. With the media divided into pro- and anti-Roosevelt camps, the publicity photos were needed as a persuasive tool. The public, collectively, needed to see that its tax dollars were being well spent. Then, too, as much as Horton preferred public relations and straight factual detail over propaganda, citizens also needed to see through visual means that others like them were contributing to protecting the nation's defenses if federal officials were going to coax hundreds of thousands of individuals to undertake war work.

The Office for Emergency Management's staff grew rapidly in late 1941 and into 1942. The Division of Information soon included sixty-five staff members. Its Division of Photography and Newsreels was just one of fifteen different divisions housed within the Division of Information. William Nelson, whose background was film production and screenplays, was hired by Horton as the photographic assignment editor. He served as Palmer's direct supervisor.[55] The hiring spree reflected Horton's realization that as America prepared itself for war and then entered the conflict, the agency's information production had grown exponentially.

Photographs of the defense buildup became a pressing need. By the spring of 1942, Nelson estimated that the Division of Information was receiving approximately 300 requests per week for photographs.[56] The need for photos grew so acute that the Still Picture Unit, which initially consisted of Palmer, Nelson, and a secretary, was increased in May to twelve photographers, six of whom were part-timers under contract. The new staff members, along with Palmer, would transfer to the newly established Office of War Information the following month. Nelson hired the most talented photographers that he could find, including Howard Hollem, who, like Palmer, had taken photographs for *Fortune* magazine, Howard Liberman (a former FSA photographer), Al Freeman, and European immigrants Fritz Heinle and Andreas Feininger. Palmer served as chief photographer but also was tasked with supervising the agency's darkroom facilities and serving as technical advisor.[57]

Collectively, the unit produced more than 18,000 images. Palmer contributed approximately 8,000 of those photographs. The images appeared in federal agency publications for domestic and foreign readers, in war department publications, in brochures and pamphlets, in mainstream magazines like *Life*, and in a variety of newspapers. The photographers' work also appeared in posters and other visual displays during the war years.

When President Roosevelt abolished the Office for Emergency Management and folded its information division into the newly established Office of War Information on June 13, 1942, Nelson supported his unit's transfer and expansion. He argued that even though photojournalists working for the nation's press might be able to give "quantitatively adequate coverage" to depicting certain home front subjects, including the issue of women's entrance into factory labor, the very nature of a free press meant that editors could not be forced to cover the topics and angles that government propagandists created. Even when journalists did pick up on certain topics, government officials could not guarantee that those press members would cover the issues with the emphasis that officials believed that they should have. The agency, Nelson said, needed photographers like Palmer to produce the news feature photographs that federal officials believed were vital to successfully carry out their wartime campaigns.[58]

DIFFERING AESTHETIC VISIONS

The ever-increasing need for photographs led the Office of War Information's Domestic Branch to contain not one, but two photography units that operated separately: the Still Picture Section of the Domestic Branch News Bureau, in which Alfred Palmer was employed, and Roy Stryker's FSA team, which was attached to the agency's Bureau of Publications and Graphics. The Stryker unit was folded into the agency in October 1942 after Congressional budget cuts to the FSA forced the transfer. Although both units took photographs for domestic consumption, both Palmer's photographs and those taken by the FSA photographers were used by the Office of War Information's Overseas Branch as well. The two divisions remained separate until September 1943 when Stryker resigned to take a position at Standard Oil. Many of his photographers had already departed. Several photographers enlisted in various branches of the U.S. military, while other shooters pursued varying opportunities.[59]

The two photography divisions often produced images with diverging aesthetic visions, in part because the two units were assigned different tasks that served different purposes and were meant to reach very different audiences. The photographers' backgrounds, training, and direction further influenced what they photographed and how they did their work. Palmer, who was in his mid-thirties when he was hired in 1940, had fifteen years of commercial photography experience. His pre-war images were used in pamphlets, window displays, and other forms of advertising.[60] While wartime brought about a change in Palmer's clientele, he continued to shoot images using his already established commercial advertising aesthetic, an aesthetic that William Nelson encouraged other members of his photography staff to use, as well.

Unlike Palmer, some of the FSA photographers, including Dorothea Lange, Ben Shahn, and John Vachon, had artistic training. Others (i.e., Rothstein, Gordon Parks, and, again, Vachon) were young and relatively new to photography. A third group of Office of War Information photographers had previously worked as photojournalists. Then, too, as discussed in Chapter 1, Palmer's extensive global travels gave him an international perspective and opened his eyes to foreign aggression, experiences that many of the other home front photographers lacked.

While both Palmer and the FSA shooters largely concentrated on producing feature images, officials in Washington, D.C., used many of Palmer's images in posters, leaflets, and other print media where single shots could illustrate a story or a campaign. Those images regularly depicted America's pre-war and wartime industrial, cultural, and civic strengths, while other photographs were designed to bolster the public's morale and instill confidence that, with public support, the war could be won.[61] Occasionally, some of Palmer's work was bundled for feature stories in magazines and for newspaper rotogravure sections, with accompanying stories that stressed the same government policy objectives.

In contrast, editors in the Office of War Information's New York office, who produced propaganda for international audiences, also sought visually compelling images from FSA photographers, but played to that unit's strength by seeking documentary packages that could tell a complete story for use with feature stories and in picture booklets.[62] For example, although FSA photographer Arthur Rothstein photographed common wartime visual fodder, including power plants and defense workers, he also continued to shoot in the FSA's established aesthetic in 1942, a style that photographer Cornell Capa later termed the "concerned photographer" approach, as he took pictures of migrant labor camps in Texas and housing for low-income families in New York City.[63]

The aesthetic involved not just social concern but also often involved the photographers taking their pictures as unobtrusively as possible. Many of the most iconic images taken by FSA photographers were inspired by the photographers' intuition, vantage point, and timing, an approach that later would later be termed "the decisive moment" by noted French street photographer Henri Cartier-Bresson.[64] Those documentary projects reflected a continuation of the FSA's longstanding mandate from Stryker to capture American life in detail. But Rothstein, like other FSA photographers, also undertook documentary projects that showed America in a more positive light for propaganda purposes. For example, he captured small town autumn harvest festivals, complete with their picnic lunches and hog calling competitions—visual proof that a democratic political system offered a high standard of living for citizens, as well as one that was free from the type of fear and intimidation encountered in fascist-led nations.

That small town documentation was used extensively in overseas propaganda. Playwright Robert Sherwood, the director of the Office of War Information's Overseas Branch, used the images to counter not just Nazi propaganda, but also long-standing beliefs that Europeans had developed about American society. While the agency's officials blamed Hollywood filmmakers for presenting an image of the United States as a one of gangsters and money, motion pictures were just one factor that led some Europeans, including the Dutch, to have developed a pre-war view that the United States was little more than a nation of "skyscrapers, violence, inventions, and Hollywood stars."[65]

In addition to the photographs that Palmer and other federal photographers produced, federal officials also carefully selected American films that they felt were more reflective of the nation's culture to be shown in European nations. Illustrated magazines were another crucial component of the agency's foreign propaganda campaign. As Marja Roholl states, Sherwood wanted Europeans to understand that "America had its own genuine culture, something to be proud of …" Sherwood's vision of America regularly focused on small town life. To Sherwood, small towns served as the embodiment of American democracy. Images of those communities demonstrated that Americans indeed had their own unique culture, one that centered on the importance of family, the church, the town hall as a center of free speech, and the nation's strong sense of community.[66]

Russell Lee's work for Stryker also reflected the same mix of positive propaganda images and social documentation. Lee photographed mining operations in Montana and bountiful wheat harvests in eastern Washington state, images that federal propaganda officials could use to depict abundance. Lee's wartime portfolio, however, also includes topics that were less tangential to the war effort, including street scenes in Los Angeles that included gas stations, theaters, drive-in restaurants, and dance halls—the types of images that he had taken prior to the outbreak of war as a means of creating a detailed visual record of a community.

By shooting their images in the unit's longstanding social documentary style to which they had become accustomed, the FSA photographers' images often were aesthetically different from the positive and often glamorous images taken by Palmer. The latter photographer took a series of photographs of scrap metal recycling at the Douglas Aircraft Company, located in Palmer's boyhood home of Long Beach, California. Rather than document images of a recycling yard filled with aluminum, copper, or steel, as did FSA photographer Russell Lee in an image below—a photograph that required a caption for the public to understand what they were seeing—Palmer asked an attractive employee, Annette del Sur, to serve as a model. Wearing a crown of scrap metal, del Sur is well dressed, with carefully applied makeup. Palmer depicts del Sur and her long, shapely legs in an aesthetic style that loosely parallels many "pin up" posters coveted by the war's soldiers. Palmer's photograph showed del Sur's willingness to help with the scrap metal drive, which demonstrated American unity during wartime. The photograph clearly employed what FSA boss Roy Stryker denounced as "cheesecake" imagery; however, as Winkler states, the Office of War Information's campaigns were well-run. Because of the positive reception to many of the government's propaganda campaigns, officials continued the "sales promotion ideas and techniques" in those campaigns.[67]

Each of the two photography units had its supporters and detractors within the Office of War Information. The Stryker unit had the support of Gardner Cowles, Jr., the Midwestern publisher who supervised the agency's Domestic News Bureau, as well as Archibald MacLeish, who served as the agency's assistant director. Both administrators viewed the FSA shooters' work as superior to that of Palmer and the other photographers who made up the Domestic Branch News

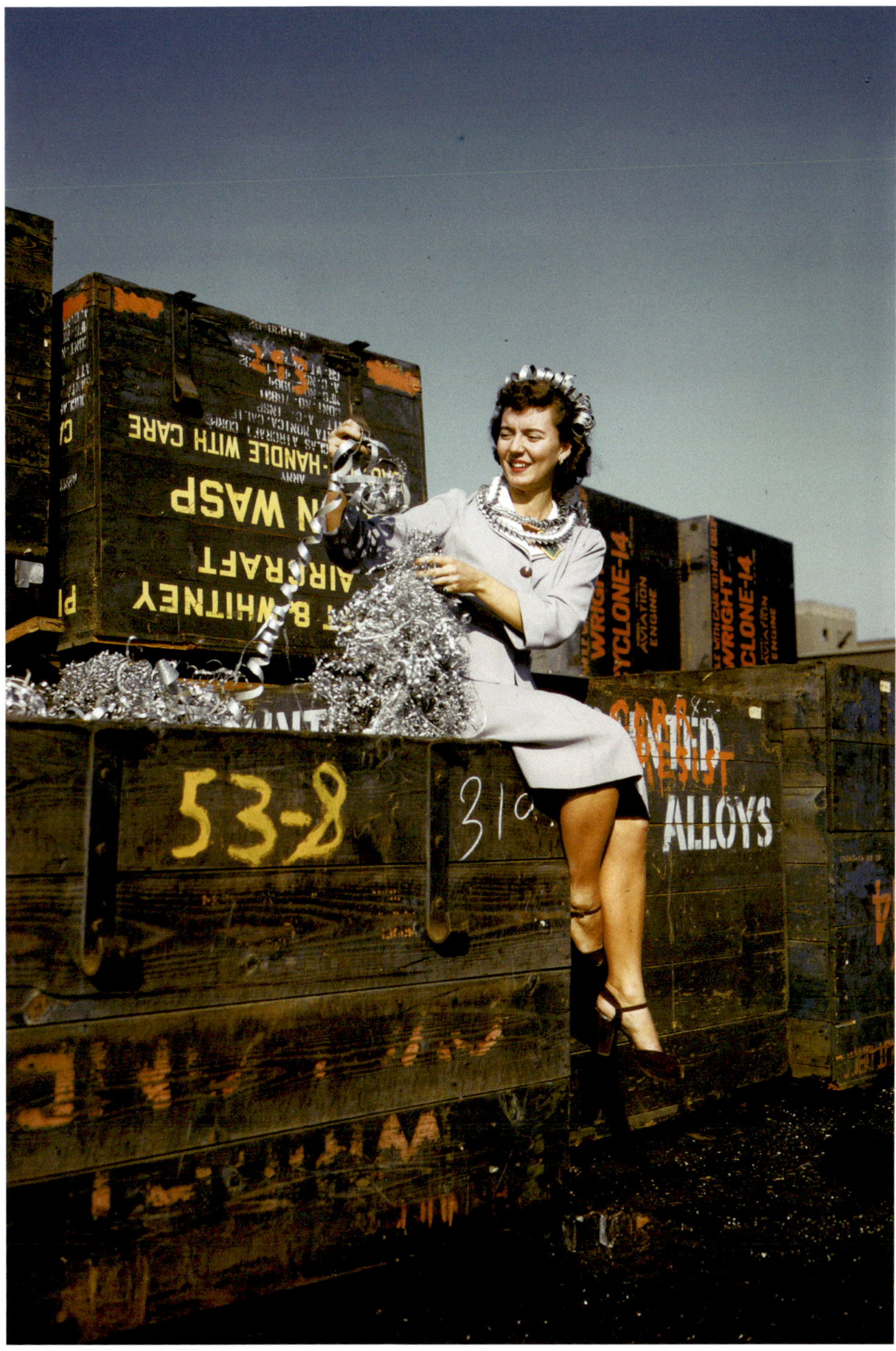

Douglas Aircraft Company employee Annette del Sur publicizing a salvage campaign in the company's yard in Long Beach, California, October 1942. (*Library of Congress*)

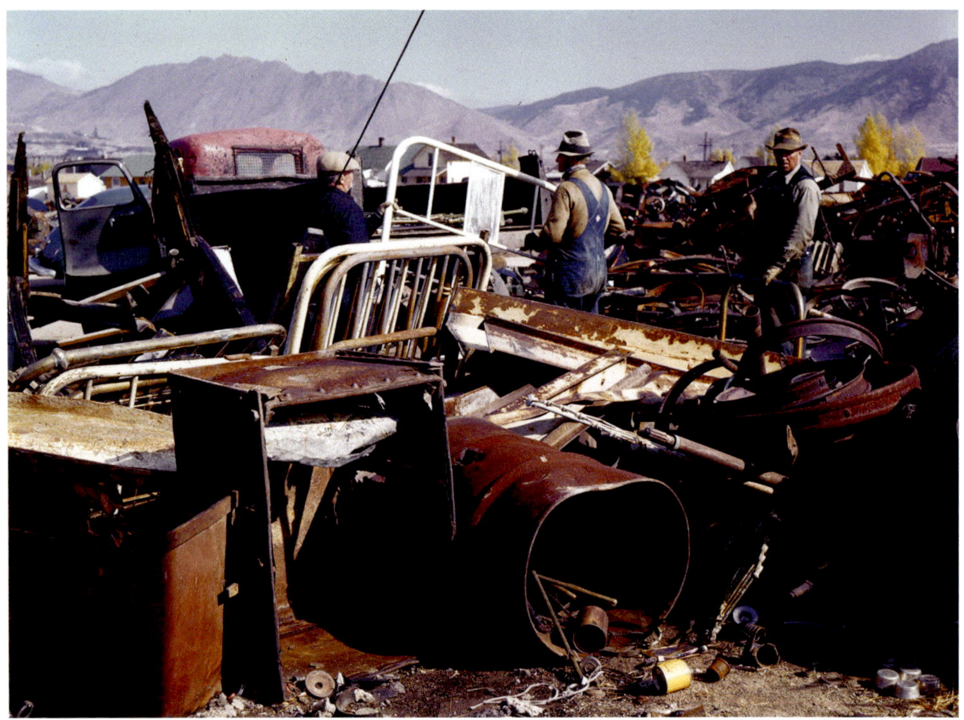

Scrap and salvage depot, Butte, Montana, October 1942. Photograph taken by Russell Lee. (*Library of Congress*)

Bureau unit.[68] Yet, Palmer's idyllic and idealized aesthetic ultimately prevailed. His images were regularly reproduced since they served as visual representations of the agency's policy of presenting the country and its citizens in the most positive light possible. As Winkler states, Robert Horton and other agency officials "stressed the components—both spiritual and material—that to them made America great. And perhaps most important of all, the general image seemed consonant with the way ordinary Americans viewed the war."[69]

Photo historian Nicholas Natanson concurs. In assessing the two photo units, Natanson states: "With Palmer's work setting the standard, News Bureau pictures provided more direct expression (than did the work of the Stryker unit) of themes that went to the very heart of the OWI propaganda program … American industrial might, American adaptability to wartime demands, [and] American unity amid cultural and ethnic diversity." Natanson also raises an important issue concerning the differing aesthetics, stating: "But what is most important here is not the question of who was correct, but the very fact that two ways of photographic 'seeing' existed side by side—with convergences at certain points, and divergences at a great many other points—in the government context." The photo history of the 1930s and 1940s, Natanson argues, has a richness and "complexity," that many scholars have ignored or overlooked.[70]

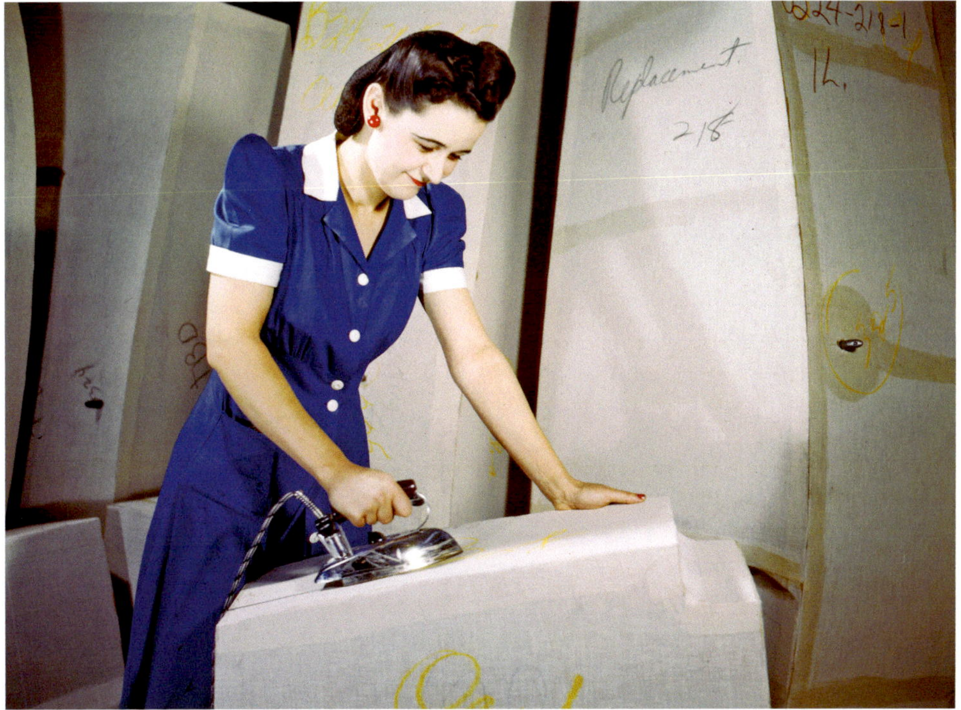

Manufacture of self-sealing gas tanks, Goodyear Tire and Rubber Co., Akron, Ohio, December 1941. (*Library of Congress*)

A CHANGING AESTHETIC VISION

The coming of war necessitated a change in how the FSA photographers represented the nation. Stryker's team continued to document social concerns and agricultural problems; however, the photographers increasingly depicted the nation's strengths, including dam construction and agricultural bounty. An article in the August 1941 issue of *U.S. Camera* acknowledged this pivot toward a more positive photographic portrayal of the nation. But the unbylined article's writer argued that the FSA's documentary approach was a strength since Stryker's team remained focused on educating the public. "The major contribution of FSA photography to national defense has been in helping to acquaint Americans with the country they are about to defend," the article stated.[71]

Stryker undoubtedly concurred with the assessment. He had long been concerned that so many of the nation's citizens knew so little about their own country. It was a theme that he reiterated during the 1930s and again prior to the United States' entrance into the war. In an April 30, 1941, letter to photographer Jack Delano, for example, Stryker bemoaned the public's lack of knowledge about their nation. "The one great tragedy I find is that few of our people know our part of the country. So few of our citizens have any idea of what our country looks like west of the Hudson [River] and certainly do not know what it looks like west of the Mississippi [River]. Distance is the great thing in our land, and how little we appreciate it."[72]

The FSA's humanistic philosophy and the resulting images its photographers took were very different from the often-posed images that federal government propagandists needed for posters, leaflets, and other visual materials. With his commercial photography background, Palmer was well suited to undertaking the propaganda jobs that he was assigned to shoot. Corporations and advertising agencies expected that Palmer would portray their people, products, and services in the most glamorous light possible. Throughout the 1920s and 1930s, photography, rather than paintings or other forms of illustration, had been seen by advertising executives as "the most effective medium" for advertising.[73] For Palmer, then, the U. S. government was the latest client who expected stylish, artistically created images. Unlike some FSA photographers who publicly chafed at the work and viewed the Office of War Information's visual aesthetic as glitzy and one-sided, Palmer enjoyed the styling.[74, 75]

Not every FSA photographer opposed the positive visual portrayals of the nation that America's entrance into the war necessitated. Dorothea Lange was fully supportive of photography's role in propaganda, stating "Everything is propaganda for what you believe in, actually, isn't it?"[76] Russell Lee also was on board. Following the Japanese attack on Pearl Harbor, Lee sent Stryker suggestions for propaganda posters, noting that too many of the ones he was seeing were English in origin, rather than American. He offered to take photographs for war posters and presented Stryker with two pages of ideas for posters, photos, and slogans, then suggested that federal officials should think bigger and use billboards. Lee also asked if officials had plans for a wartime visual propaganda unit. "It would seem to me that a coordinated effort to propagandize the nation, backing up the armed forces, would eventually require such a unit and that that unit would ideally be placed in the economic welfare department."[77]

Stryker and Palmer retained a cordial, if at times strained, relationship concerning the federal government's wartime photography aesthetic. "Roy was a close friend of mine," Palmer recalled in a 1988 interview, "but he used to complain that I was a glamour photographer."[78] Stryker, dismayed by what he perceived to be the lack of well-rounded storytelling, indeed saw Palmer, as well as other Office of War Information photographers and their supervisors, as akin to advertising staff on the federal government's payroll. After resigning in mid-September 1943, Stryker blew off steam by penning a letter to Lange that revealed his belief that the FSA's documentary aesthetic was superior to the commercial photography vision sought by bureaucrats working for the nation's wartime propaganda agencies:

> The whole trend in this town is now against the things which we were doing. I don't think you can really imagine what a dismal atmosphere prevails in our Capitol, though not completely hopeless by any means. There are plenty of good people fighting the

battle and I am sure, in the end, we will swing to better days. Unfortunately, our project is an expensive one and must needs [*sic*] to be sponsored by an agency and administrative people who believe in what we are doing. Unfortunately, the right people in the OWI do not take us too seriously. There are too many second-rate newspapermen who feel that slap-stick cheesecake is good enough to send overseas and to be used on the Domestic Scene.[79]

Stryker's comments to Lange also reveal that the FSA boss could not come to terms with the fact that wartime necessitated a different informational aesthetic, at least for home front audiences, one that diverged from the FSA's sociological documentary approach by providing strong informational images that were created for the purpose of awakening a sense of national patriotism and pride. As Barbara Orbach and Nicholas Natanson state, wartime forced a change "in favor of more encouraging views of bustling activities in American defense centers and a quality of life worth fighting for."[80]

Stryker recognized that Roosevelt's commitment to strengthening American national defense meant that the assignments his photographers shot might shift away from their traditional work of documenting the FSA's assistance to poor farmers and its broader work of documenting the nation during the Great Depression. He was not completely opposed to the new mandate. But given several years of Congressional opposition to the FSA's work, which included budget cuts, Stryker's goal was to keep his team of shooters together and keep his division funded. Stryker was aware of the shifting policy winds in Washington, D.C. In an April 8, 1941, letter to Jack Delano, Stryker stated: "It is very important, as I pointed out to Russell [Lee] and John [Vachon] that we keep our finger in defense activities. The way the whole world is moving now, and particularly the way things happen around this town, we may have to give much more to defense than we are now."[81]

While Stryker, a World War I veteran, agreed with the importance of the work in which the Office of War Information was engaged, he was convinced that detailed, sociologically focused photo documentary work was a superior means of educating and persuading the public during wartime. He thus asked his photographers to document a nation at war with the same attention to visual detail that they had provided during the 1930s. To Stryker, the coming of war and the ensuing domestic response were important socio-cultural stories to document visually for posterity.[82]

Stryker's continued focus on a sociological approach to visual storytelling is revealed in his pre-war and wartime shooting scripts, as well as his letters to photographers. The same April 8 letter to Jack Delano told the photographer that his next assignment required him to go to Hattiesburg, Mississippi, where Delano was to document a U.S. Army training program for cooks. Stryker then gave his usual documentary advice: "My suggestions now ahead of time on this job would be to emphasize the training—bear down heavily on the idea of men learning to cook. You know the old adage that 'the Army travels on its belly.'"[83]

A February 19, 1942, shooting script from Stryker to Russell Lee and Arthur Rothstein was more in line with the Office of War Information's positive, promotional approach to visuals, but it still involved a sociological approach to depicting the nation at a specific point in time. The FSA photography boss asked Rothstein and Lee to take pictures of signs "which indicate a country at war, pictures of men, women and children who appear as if they really believe in the U.S., and small town[s] under war conditions." The same script also directed the photographers to get images more reminiscent of pre-war assignments, including "the long shots for a 'feel' of the country," "housewives in their kitchen," and "pictures of representative small farms."

The key difference between the shooting script from 1942 and earlier, pre-war, depression-era scripts was the emphasis on showing the nation in a positive light as a country at work—from farm to factory—for propaganda purposes.[84] Similarly, in his April 8 letter to Jack Delano, Stryker encouraged the photographer to depict the socio-cultural impact of the nation's defense buildup on its communities. After telling Delano to make his way to Childersburg, Alabama, southeast of Birmingham, to photograph the construction of an ammunition plant, Stryker

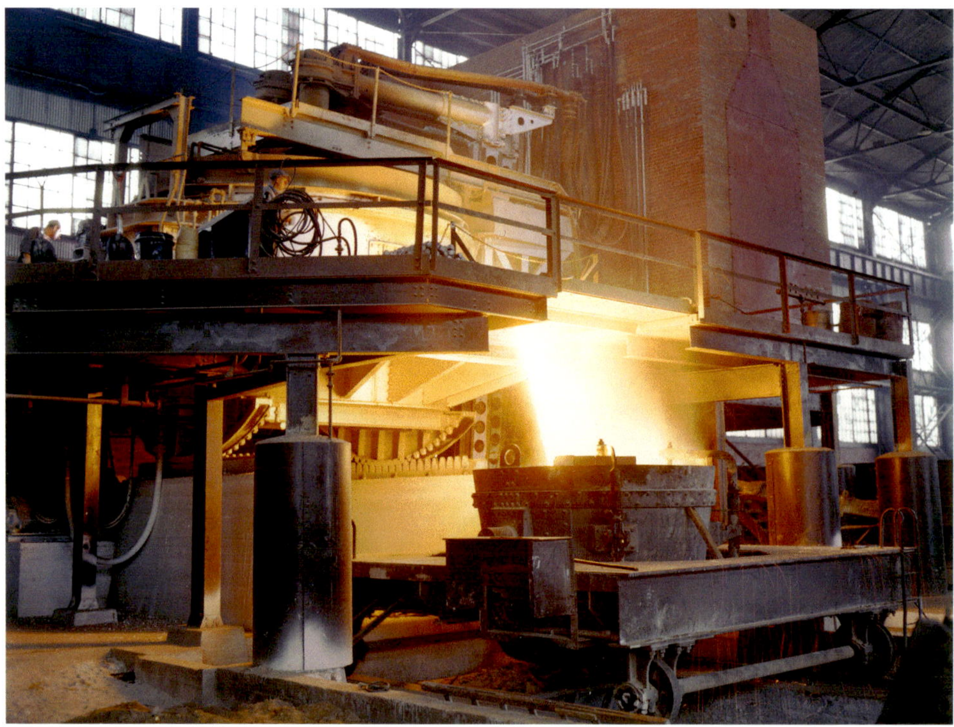

White-hot steel pours like water from a 35-ton electric furnace at the Allegheny Ludlum Steel Corp., Brackenridge, Pennsylvania, February 1942. The finest quality steels and alloys are produced in these furnaces, which allow much greater control of temperature than other conversion furnaces. (*Library of Congress*)

encouraged Delano to take photos of the town before the construction started. "We may be able to develop this into a very interesting story of how one town changes under the impact of defense," he suggested.[85]

Eight months later when the United States formally entered the war, Stryker's staff had plenty of interesting stories to depict, using their well-established social documentary style. Alfred T. Palmer would continue using his stylized, commercial aesthetic, however, his tasks and the federal agencies for which he worked soon broadened. By early 1942, Palmer increasingly photographed promotional and propaganda images that depicted the war's impact on the home front, including Americans' patriotic responses to the war effort, for several different federal wartime agencies. Although their aesthetic styles differed, both Palmer's images and those of the FSA were widely reproduced during the war years in a variety of media for audiences at home and abroad. Photography became central to the American government's war efforts.

3
DEPICTING THE
"ARSENAL OF DEMOCRACY"

By December 29, 1940, the day when President Roosevelt delivered his "Arsenal of Democracy" speech, the war was going badly for America's British ally. The Germans were sinking British ships three times faster than they could be built. And the Luftwaffe had been bombing English infrastructure, including shipyards, since July of that year to force Prime Minister Winston Churchill into a negotiated peace with Germany.

Although Churchill was desperate for ships and other military equipment, American industrial production was only slowly coming back to life in 1940. As the economy spiraled downward during the 1930s, numerous factories and other places of employment had shuttered, leaving nearly one-quarter of all Americans unemployed. Not only did industrial production facilities have to be restarted, but CEOs of companies whose facilities were still in operation often had to be convinced to switch their production from materials for domestic use to producing instruments of warfare.[1]

The construction of new ships was a high priority. A surge of shipbuilding that had occurred during World War I slowed considerably with the onset of the Great Depression. Without robust foreign trade, there was little need for new ships. Congressional passage of two Merchant Marine Acts, one in 1928 and the second in 1936, helped the U.S. resume private ship construction and kept 25,000 men steadily employed during the years of economic downturn.[2] The 1936 Act was, in part, a response to high unemployment during the depression. Yet the Act also was motivated by the realization by politicians and military officials that the U.S. government's reliance on foreign ships to carry necessary military materials to European battlefields during World War I had proven disastrous.[3] A subsequent report from the U.S. Maritime Commission, which found that the nation's merchant vessels were "old, slow, and don't meet military requirements," led to a massive shipbuilding program that was initiated in 1938. Although the federal government's initial plans called for construction of fifty ships per year for ten years, the war in Europe led production to be accelerated to 200 ships per year by 1940.[4]

If the United States was to become the military powerhouse that Roosevelt envisioned, the president required the commitment of those business leaders, especially those with expertise in large-scale manufacturing. The German, Italian, and Japanese war machines simply had to be out built. The conflict became an assembly line war on the home front. Officials at federal propaganda agencies would portray industrial workers as home front heroes who built the armaments that were necessary for the U.S. military and her allies to prevail in the conflict. Palmer's work was a central component in the creation of these heroic archetypes.

American entrepreneurs, including Edsel Ford, Henry Ford's son and president of the company from 1919 until his death in 1943, and industrialist Henry J. Kaiser (whose companies had built the Hoover, Bonneville, and Grand Coulee dams, and the Oakland-San Francisco Bay Bridge), ultimately used bold thinking and American assembly line know-how to accomplish the task. As historian Geoffrey Perrett states, once American businessmen and the public embraced Roosevelt's call to ramp up defense production, "the industrial growth of twenty-five to fifty years had been achieved in less than three."[5]

While all manner of military equipment was manufactured in 1940 and 1941, America's entry into the war accelerated production.[6] That often required that companies stop producing—or reduce the production of—the goods for which they were known. Many major manufacturers had little interest initially in switching to defense production, preferring to restart normal production of goods as the economy began improving. The war in Europe had created a demand for American products; defense production might throw off that economic recovery.[7] For example, the Ford Motor Company did not cease all manufacturing of civilian trucks and cars until February 10, 1942, but under Edsel Ford's direction, the company's executives and thousands of workers used their production knowledge to make not just jeeps and tanks, but a host of other armaments, including B-24 bombers. Production of the latter item required the construction of Willow Run, a massive new plant outside of Detroit.[8] Similarly, Kaiser constructed and launched ships and made fighter planes for the U.S. Navy faster than had ever been done previously.[9] Between January 1942 and September 1945, workers at American shipyards, including Kaiser's, produced 5,304 ships of all classes, including 414 "Victory Ships," a 455-foot-long cargo ship designed for speed.[10]

Palmer set out to capture this optimistic, can-do spirit via still photographs and motion pictures immediately upon being hired by Horton in May 1940. Government officials, including Robert Horton, knew that visual publicity was a necessary tool that could boost the nation's morale, help defeat isolationist sentiment, and, relatedly, also help convince the public to support the president's call to take defensive measures in the face of foreign aggression. But the images also disguised an important reality: manufacturers initially were slow in producing the much-needed military equipment. The armaments that both the U.S. military and its allies needed could not be produced overnight. Factories that once made cars or cash registers had to be retooled to produce airplane engines, barrage balloons, and artillery shells. And vast labor forces had to be hired and trained, a reality which also slowed production.

The scope of the production ultimately exceeded much of the public's imagination. The Fords, for example, hired thousands of new workers, many of whom had never been employed in manufacturing before. Kaiser faced similar issues at his newly established shipyards in Portland, Oregon, and Richmond, California. Parts and tool shortages also slowed production, as did the lack of raw materials. Persistent racial inequalities in pay and treatment of workers occasionally led to strikes, which also slowed production. The story was similar at many other factories across the nation.[11] Such issues, however, never were evident in Palmer's photographs. He believed that strength, not weakness, needed to be depicted as America readied itself for war.[12]

A BROADENING VISUAL MANDATE

Palmer's years with the Merchant Marine provided the photographer with a knowledge of ships and shipping that made him a good fit when he was hired by Horton. Although the photographer would be sent to shipyards to photograph new ship construction, his first job for the U.S. Maritime Commission involved shooting a color, ten-minute short motion picture for theatrical release titled *America Builds Ships*. A month later, Palmer followed Horton to the National Defense Advisory Commission, which was housed in the Office for Emergency Management.

The move from the U.S. Maritime Commission to the new agency immediately led to a broadening of Palmer's assignments. He still went into shipyards; however, Palmer was now traveling the country for weeks at a time, capturing images of defense plant workers, employees at electrical plants, dams, and other infrastructure facilities, and raw recruits engaged in military training at locations including Fort Knox in Kentucky and Parris Island in South Carolina.[13]

Both federal officials and industrialists were aware of the value and importance of public relations by 1940, as well as the potential power of the press in shaping messages. Photography was particularly important to the government's propaganda and public relations efforts since the images provided visual proof to the public of what the government and industrialists were doing to place the country on a defense footing. And those images could be distributed widely and at very little cost.

Palmer's photographs became central to this promotional effort in the year and a half before the nation entered the war, as well as after the country entered the conflict. A memo from Robert Collyer, an operations manager at the Office for Emergency Management's Department of Information, to Horton, dated November 22, 1940, told the latter man that Palmer's photographs were being well received and were widely used: "Business is good, and continues to increase with a big play from the trade papers as well as the photo syndicates."[14]

Horton was undoubtedly glad to hear the news. Although Roosevelt chose to split the federal government's pre-war propaganda and public relations efforts among several agencies, Horton envisioned supervising one federal agency that would collect and disseminate all pre-war and wartime materials to the press,

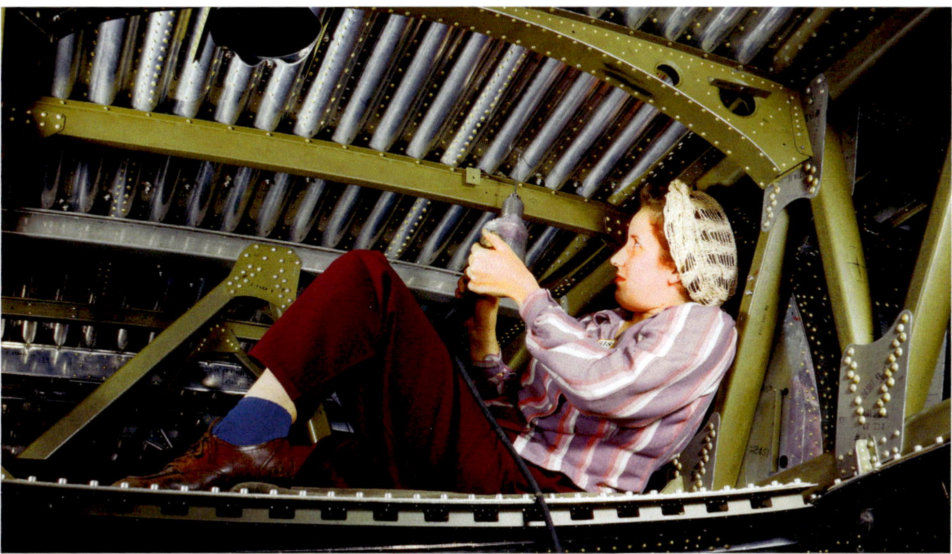

An A-20 bomber being riveted by a woman worker at the Douglas Aircraft Company plant at Long Beach, California, October 1942. (*Library of Congress*)

including photographs and films. Horton's organizational activities did not always match his ambitions, however. Mordecai Lee states that throughout the winter of 1940–1941, the still picture division "continued muddling through" without any clear definition of its role.[15]

That lack of definition did not appear to impact Palmer's job. He was the photography division for many months. Just a secretary and a supervisor rounded out the unit. As such, Palmer spent much of the first eighteen months of his employment on the road, away from Washington, D.C., its political battles, and his agency's offices. Even on the road, Palmer was aware of the general lack of direction for his job, telling historian Jeanie Cooper Carson that he considered his job in these early months to be "a kind of exploratory mission." Because the Division of Information employees were establishing their departments and getting used to their positions, Palmer acknowledged that there was no clear "pattern of operation."[16] Nonetheless, he was able to accomplish his task of depicting Roosevelt's defense buildup because Horton held meetings with military officers, industrialists, and labor leaders who provided suggestions for Palmer's assignments. Those suggestions ultimately sent Palmer to such diverse locations as train yards in Philadelphia, the Ford Motor Company in Dearborn, Michigan, the Douglas Dam in Tennessee, the Goodyear Aircraft Corporation in Akron, Ohio, and the Douglas Aircraft Company in Long Beach, California. The photographer's supervisors did not tell him how to take the photographs, however, which left Palmer free to make his own aesthetic judgments. And that visual judgment led him to portray the nation as strong and unified and its citizens as patriotic.

At the end of his first year of working for the Office for Emergency Management, Palmer took stock of his work. He told officials that he had engaged in two distinctly different visual tasks during the past twelve months. His first task, he stated, was to create "a pictorial chronicle of U.S. industrial production for national defense." Accomplishing this chronicle involved going into defense plants and "emerging … with a complete pictorial continuity describing fully an industrial process, assembly of parts, or method of manufacture."[17] Much of Palmer's time from May 1940 until December 1941 was taken up with making this pictorial record. Because most defense plants were not responsible for making a finished airplane or tank, the photographer often traveled to two—or even three—facilities to provide the Office for Emergency Management's public relations practitioners with the visual documentary record they desired. And given the reality that defense production facilities were scattered across the country, Palmer's work led him to travel from the East Coast to the West Coast several times, ultimately shooting jobs in every region of the country.[18]

The photographer told his supervisors that his second task was "diametrically opposed to the first." His other orders had led him to take photographs for booklets, posters, exhibits, and other publications. This work, he said, required a different aesthetic and different knowledge. "Here a pictorial and graphic (rather than industrial or technical) sense has been called into play, and from the number of repeat assignments which I have received for this type of work, I am able to conclude that my work in this respect has not been unsatisfactory," he stated.[19]

While most of Palmer's images taken at defense plants were clearly posed, the photographer said in a post-war interview that he went to great lengths when setting up his equipment and taking the photographs to never slow down factory production. He set up his lights as his subjects—who were real defense plant workers—continued their work. Most of his subjects, however, were not assembly line workers and, therefore, could stop their labors for a few moments to pose for the necessary photographs. Palmer recalled that once the nation was at war and more photographers were hired to help depict the nation's home front production, another government contract photographer was sent packing from a General Motors facility by the plant manager after that photographer asked the manager to shut off a machine that made bullets so that he could set up his lights, pose the worker who was the subject of his photograph, and get his exposure set correctly. The request may not have been communicated clearly. "Red hot shells" began pouring out of the machine and the worker was fired. Palmer was sent into the factory to redo the shoot.[20]

Palmer clearly enjoyed the commercial photography work that he undertook for the federal government and wanted to continue doing it for as long as possible. He positioned himself as having the requisite knowledge to do industrial photography, telling his supervisors that several industrial arts courses that he had taken during high school, coupled with an interest in mechanical engineering, had helped prepare him for his assignments:

This photographing of industrial production has also necessitated a very thorough understanding of the industrial processes and operations involved. Before one can intelligently photograph a subject, he must understand it, and my previous industrial and mechanical training assisted me considerably in this respect. In this job, I have had to provide caption data for all of my pictures, and because many of the magazines and publications in which my material is used are specialized trade and engineering journals, it has been vital that this caption data be accurate to the nth degree. No guessing or "padding" could have been tolerated here.[21]

Given Palmer's lack of a formal university degree in engineering or manufacturing processes, he may have overstated his knowledge in those areas; however, the photographer clearly relished a life on the road free from immediate supervision.

President Roosevelt eliminated the National Defense Advisory Commission in January 1941, but both Horton and Palmer continued their jobs as part of a separate Division of Information that continued to be housed in the Office for Emergency Management. In June 1942, when that agency and several others were abolished and the Office of War Information was established, Palmer photographed an ever-increasing variety of defense and war-related subjects for several federal agencies, including the War Manpower Commission and the War Production Board.

Although the Office of War Information also produced other forms of visual documentation, including films, photography remained a central component of the agency's propaganda efforts. Gardner Cowles, Jr., who headed the agency's Domestic News Bureau in 1942, understood the importance of photographs and their ability to inform. Cowles, Jr., a Midwestern newspaper publisher, had co-founded and edited *Look* magazine, a pictorial publication that was established as a rival to the popular *Life* magazine.

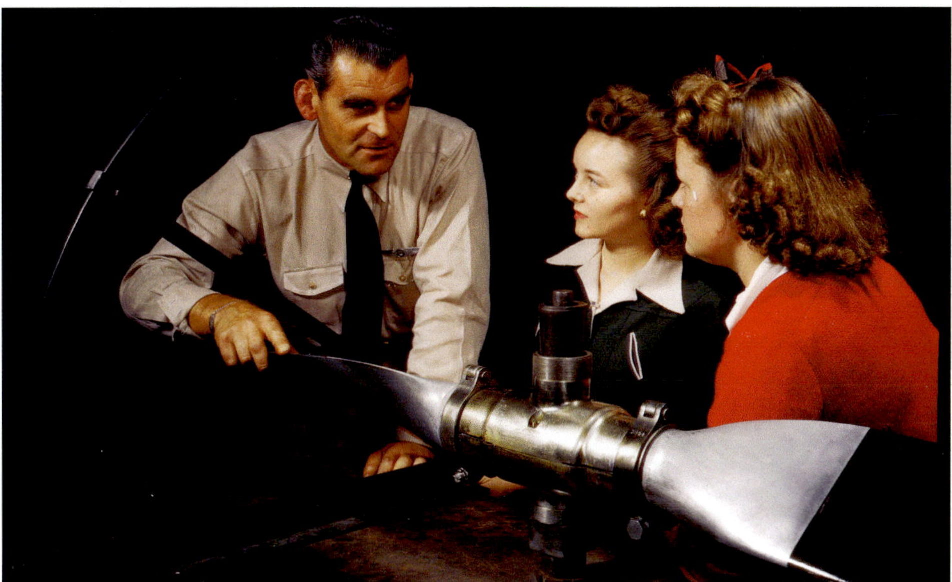

Students at Washington High School training for specific contributions to the war effort, Los Angeles, California, September 1942. Instructor Ralph Angar explains propeller characteristics to students in the aeronautics class. (*Library of Congress*)

While Palmer continued to depict defense plant workers and soldiers engaged in training, he increasingly photographed the war's impact on civilians, depicting the population's unity and readiness, to help illustrate numerous home front information campaigns. Palmer captured images of scrap drives, the conservation of needed materials, price controls, food rationing, the employment of women and minority workers in critical wartime industries, and students learning defense industry skills. Some of the topics that Palmer photographed were developed by Horton or Nelson, while others came via requests from editors at a variety of publications. But the photographer continued to be given the freedom to develop story ideas on his own, as well.[22]

Palmer put a positive sheen on wartime life at home—a view both the photographer and his supervisors concurred was the correct depiction to present during wartime. "At that critical time, America did not need photographs that concentrated on her shortcomings," Palmer told historian Jeanie Cooper Carson. "She needed evidence of her spiritual strength to help her resist the awful threat of the Nazis as they moved relentlessly into a subdued Europe."[23] As a result, Palmer's images of America were both idyllic and inspirational, meant to reflect the strength of the nation, as well depict the best qualities of the American people and their values. For example, a series of images that Palmer took to explain the point system of food rationing depicted both housewives and children as happily accepting the need for rationing—rather than seeing it as an inconvenience—and viewing their participation in the process as a patriotic, home front duty.

Palmer's images largely were meant for domestic use, however, his photographs were used in leaflets dropped by plane over Europe prior to December 1941, to encourage war-ravaged citizens that Americans were coming and bringing their industrial might to the fight. Many of his photographs also were reprinted in government publications aimed at foreign audiences, including *Victory* magazine, which was widely distributed in Europe, and *En Guardia*, which was distributed throughout Latin America. Many of those images showed the American military arsenal under construction. The photographs were meant to give Europeans hope, while showing off America's military might, which Office of War Information officials presented as based on superior technology. But those government propagandists went further, linking the nation's military superiority to Roosevelt's goal of the United States serving as the leader of a new democratic world order. As Roholl states, "Only a strong America would be able to defend democracy at home and abroad. The power and success of America's military forces reflected the industrial might behind it."[24]

Foreign audiences received a largely idyllic view of the United States via U.S. government propaganda: a land of bountiful harvests with flocks of well-fed sheep and cattle, clean, attractive grocery stores filled with food, vast factories, and defense plant workers producing the materials of warfare quickly, efficiently, and in mass quantities. Palmer was consistent in his depiction of the nation, its wartime industrial production and workers, and its military personnel. Both Palmer and his supervisor, William Nelson, believed that "glamour, fashion, and

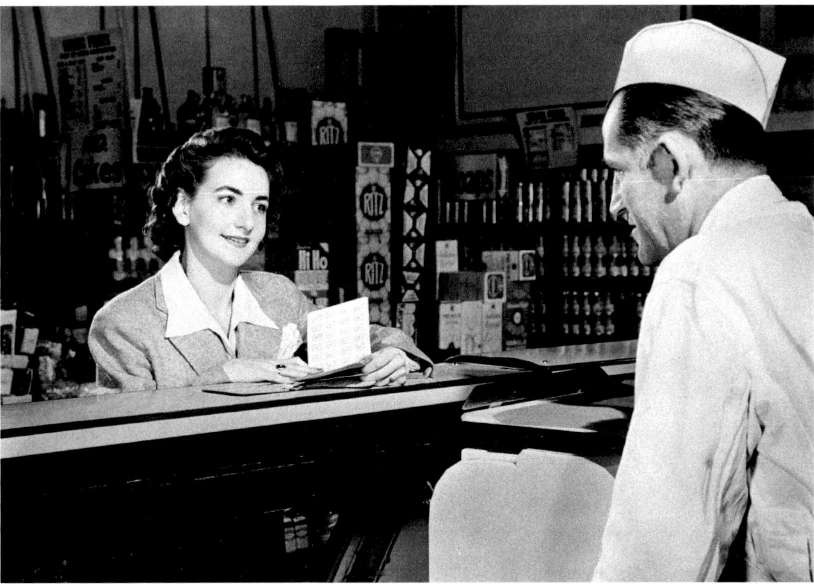

A customer can use the ration books of the whole family. But the first thing she will want to know when she buys pork chops, a pound of butter, or a half pound of cheese is—"How many points will it take?" March 1943. (*Library of Congress*)

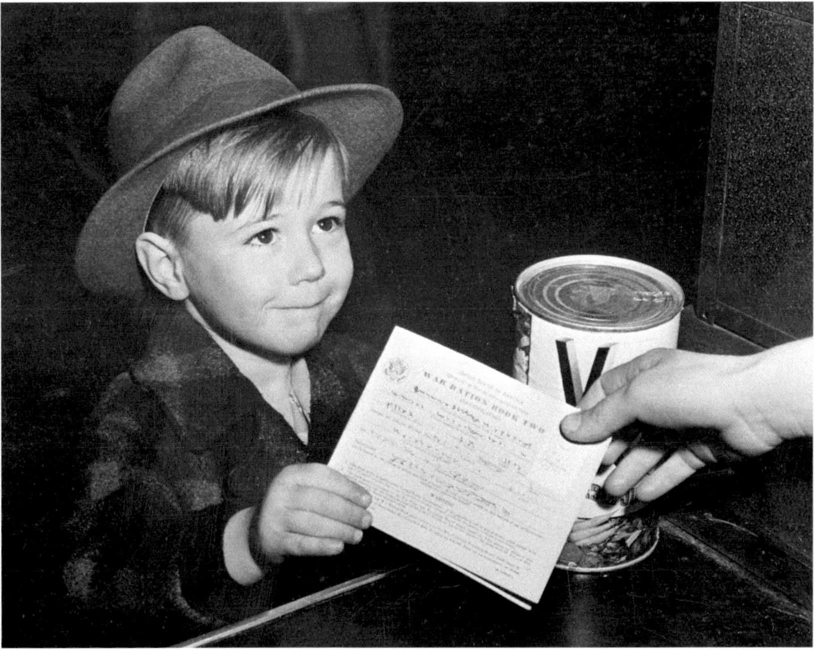

An eager schoolboy gets his first experience in using war ration book two, March 1943. With many parents engaged in war work, children are being taught the facts of point rationing for helping out in family marketing. (*Library of Congress*)

sex appeal" were important and effective factors in drawing readers' attention. These visual traits had become commonly expected aesthetics in magazines and motion pictures in the decades before the war. Then, too, Nelson had come to Washington, D.C., from a career in the Hollywood film industry where glamour and sex appeal reigned.[25]

Based on his previous commercial photography and filmmaking experiences, both of which involved knowledge of lighting and camera angles, Palmer knew how to provide the dramatic images that his immediate supervisors, as well as those at other federal agencies, wanted. Both the workers and the type of work in which they were engaged, especially in defense plants, were accurately depicted, but every aspect of the final image—from lighting to subjects—was carefully considered and styled by Palmer before he snapped the camera's shutter.[26] He recalled his efforts in a post-war interview, stating:

> ... in a defense plant ... you had to select the right models, the right people. We always had to watch out for trash on the floor—all those details. And it was all multiple flash, not flat flash. No, I wanted modeling, character, lighting. Having been in the film business before, I wanted to make these pictures as dramatic as possible, meaning in the sense that they were dramatically lit.[27]

Plant managers, he added, often were skeptical of what Palmer hoped to accomplish when he first arrived. But years of experience had taught Palmer how to reassure clients. "I carried along with me a portfolio, to show them what we were attempting to do," he recalled. "There was such a great need for pictures of defense."[28] Palmer soon won over most company executives. His interior and exterior images of the Ford Motor Company's River Rouge plant in Dearborn, Michigan, tremendously pleased the company's executives. "We've been trying for over a year to get pictures like these," Ford's public relations director told Palmer.[29]

Palmer's photographs also pleased a growing array of supervisors at the Office of War Information. As the war progressed, the agency's Bureau of Campaigns became increasingly dominated by advertising executives, who, according to Winkler, "had their own ideas about arousing the American people." Unlike many of the journalists and writers who preferred producing informational campaigns as part of the strategy of truth, which allowed the public to make up its own mind on issues when given the facts, the advertisers who dominated the Bureau of Campaigns "saw the American people as hesitant customers who had to be persuaded by gut-level appeals."[30]

POSTERS, PRINTS, AND MAGAZINE PHOTOS

Palmer's images were reproduced in a variety of government media forms, including posters, leaflets, flyers, booklets, and pamphlets. Despite concerns about the propaganda tactics used by the Committee for Public Information during

World War I, thousands of posters were produced by the Office for Emergency Management, the Office of War Information, and many other federal agencies from 1940 to 1945. With federal officials perceiving that the posters created during World War I were a success, artists again were recruited to help create a parallel ideological war.[31]

The Office of War Information created more posters than did any other federal agency during the war. And those posters, along with those produced by other federal agencies, became ubiquitous—seen in factories and on city streets across the nation. Between 75,000 and170,000 copies were printed of each design. The images also were reformatted to appear as billboards, bus placards, and materials for office bulletin boards. The posters were meant to influence the public's behavior "through forceful images and simple, direct, and sometimes emotional messages ..." Federal propaganda officials also used posters as a tool to "strengthen the home front bond, build public morale, and develop a sense of community and personal participation in the war effort."[32]

The Office of War Information's Domestic Bureau's poster campaign focused largely on reaching a home front audience. Paintings, illustrations, and photographs were used as visual components for the posters. The agency sought artistic talent through an association called Arts for Victory, which was comprised of twenty-four separate organizations for artists. The group sponsored poster competitions in local communities and produced exhibitions of work that was "designed to focus public attention on the goals of the war."[33]

Palmer's straight photography aesthetic coupled with his use of dramatic lighting led Office of War Information officials to use several of his photographs in war posters. Unlike European war poster artists, American illustrators during the war years embraced a tradition of realism. Palmer's images of war workers and soldiers proved a good fit.[34] Yet, as with so many of the federal government's wartime propaganda campaigns, the posters the agency produced did not reflect the nation's diverse population. Instead, the war posters created by federal agencies largely portrayed white soldiers, sailors, and civilian workers since propagandists were largely trying to influence the nation's white middle-class members.

Federal wartime agencies produced large numbers of posters and billboards because, as Garth S. Jowett and Victoria O'Donnell have noted, perceptions are often shaped through both images and words. How the public perceives the ideas and images is based on "complex psychological, philosophical, and practical habitual thought patterns that we carry over from past experiences." Perception, they add, involves the process of extracting information from both "the world outside us, as well as from within ourselves."[35]

Two of Palmer's black-and-white photographs, one of a welder at a steel factory and the other of a sailor, were used to create a composite image for a poster that proved particularly popular. The two photographs, along with a third image of a soldier taken by FSA photographer Marion Post Wolcott, were used in a campaign that was meant to explain to the public that civilian workers and military members had to be united and working together to win the war. The poster, titled "Men

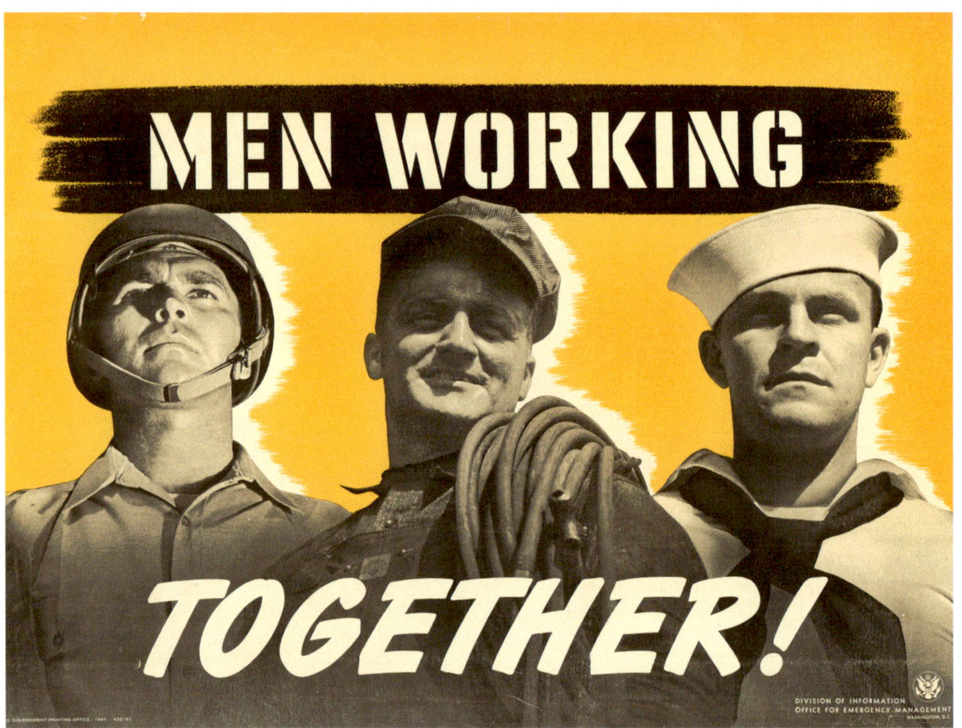

"Men Working Together" poster. Created by the Office for Emergency Management, 1942. (*Library of Congress*)

Working Together," which was created by the Office for Emergency Management in 1942, was displayed in factories around the nation.

The poster's popularity led federal officials to produce a motion picture with the same title, which premiered at Radio City Music Hall before being released to nationwide distribution. The film followed the three men, Sgt. French L. Vineyard, welder George Woolslayer, and aviation-radio chief John Marshall Evans of the U.S. Navy, as Woolslayer showed off the materials being produced for war at the Allegheny-Ludlum steel mill in Pennsylvania where he worked. The film also depicted the three men visiting Woolslayer's home and sightseeing in the welder's community. Because of the creation of the morale-boosting motion picture, the original poster became known as "the poster that came to life." Palmer accompanied the film crew, taking still shots of the men for several days in August 1942, as they toured Woolslayer's factory and community. The images were reproduced in magazines and publications produced by federal propaganda agencies and were made available to newspaper and magazine editors across the country.

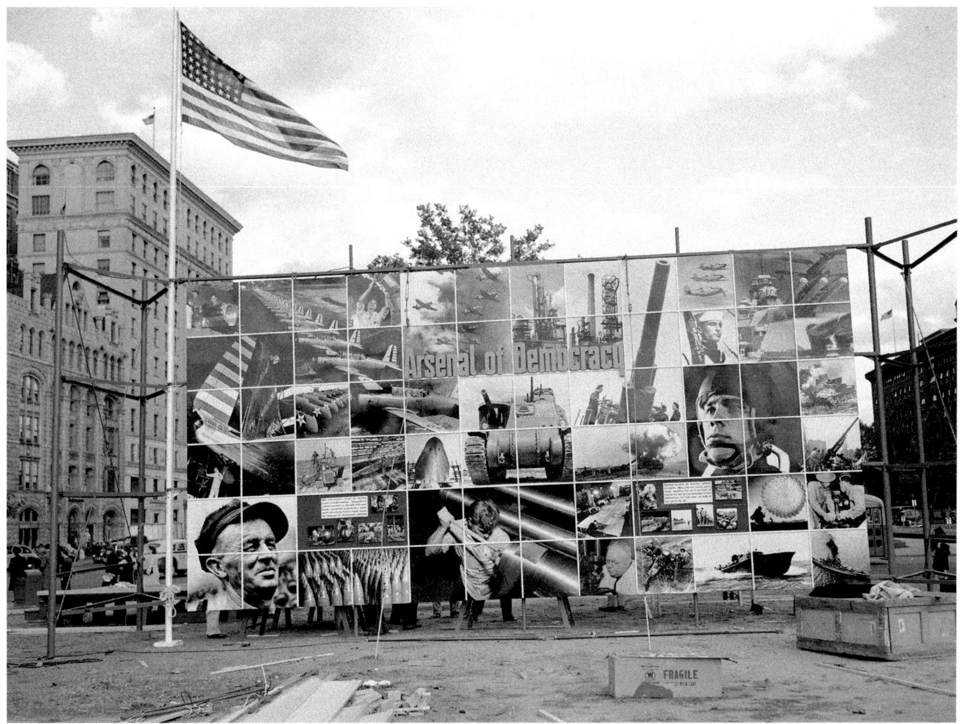

This 15- by 30-foot panel, "The Arsenal of Democracy," and a second, "The Four Freedoms," were displayed in Defense Square in Washington, D.C., for a month beginning November 7, 1941. The panels were designed for the Office for Emergency Management by Jean Carlu, an eminent poster artist. (*Library of Congress*)

Several of Palmer's photographs (along with others taken by the FSA photographers) were also used in a huge, double-sided photo-montage exhibit that the Office for Emergency Management commissioned. One side of the 1942 exhibit, which measured 15 feet in height and 30 feet in length, featured a variety of photographs taken by home front photographers, including Palmer and Russell Lee, which, collectively, depicted Roosevelt's "Arsenal of Democracy." The other side presented the president's Four Freedoms. Palmer used his young daughter, Julia, as a model for the "freedom from want" section of the montage, posing her holding a large glass of milk. French graphic designer Jean Carlu created the two montages, which were unveiled near the White House with Roosevelt present. The outdoor exhibit, which contained no text and was meant to appeal to the public's emotions, was seen by thousands of passersby before being moved by a rail car to New York City. After two months on display, the exhibit toured the country for six months. Palmer stated that the exhibit, in his opinion, was "one of the most effective promotional and information projects yet created to stimulate war production on the home front."[36]

A STRATEGY OF TRUTH, OR NOT?

Did Palmer's photographs that depicted the nation's defense buildup reflect the Office for Emergency Management's (and, later, the Office of War Information's) strategy of truth? The socially conscious editors of the *Survey Graphic* reflected on the issue in the introduction to a selection of Palmer's pictures in the November 1941 issue, but any concerns they might have had were muted in the buildup toward war. "Not all workers are as photogenic as those caught unawares, as they worked on various defense jobs, by [the] OEM's expert camera man, Palmer—you have to give a photographer his preferences. But they are all just as real. On this page and those to follow are people who inspire confidence, pride, admiration," the introduction noted.[37]

Given the aesthetic and persuasive mandates that the government wanted to display, Palmer's photographs often revealed one side of the truth—the one that the photographer's superiors wished to show. But it was a truth. And Palmer supported creating the one-sided approach, rather than undertake the FSA's documentary aesthetic of attempting to provide readers with a complete visual record of the home front. He was opposed to anyone producing FSA-style photographs of hardship or poverty during wartime when clearly the nation's strengths needed to be on display. Palmer's supervisors agreed, refusing to show any photographs that depicted "dignity in struggle and suffering."[38] Take, for example, the photographs that Palmer took of wartime housing for defense workers in Erie, Pennsylvania. The black-and-white images depicted the construction process itself, showing workers framing the buildings and running steam rollers, flattening the land to create roads. Palmer's photographs also depicted the end result: women and men admiring their new homes, which consisted of a combination of defense trailers and apartment buildings. The housing was presented in a glamorous light— clean, new, and lived in by happy families who appreciated their new homes, Importantly, Palmer's photographs demonstrated that these workers truly turned their temporary wartime housing into a community. Palmer captured well-dressed children playing on slides and swings, families relaxing in their living rooms, women having their hair styled in a newly opened salon, and nurses visiting the community to check on the residents' health.

Although Palmer took numerous photographs of the construction and the families who moved into the housing, he focused on one family—thirty-three-year-old B. J. Rogan, a drill press operator at the General Electric Plant in Erie, Pennsylvania, his wife, and their young son—to illustrate how the government was taking care of its wartime workforce. The family initially lived in a government-run trailer park, then, later, moved into a newly constructed apartment at the Franklin Terrace housing project, part of the federal government's defense housing in Erie. The image of Mrs. Rogan (whose first name was not given) and her young son in their new kitchen in July 1941 served as visual proof that the federal government had built comfortable housing for defense workers, tens of thousands of whom had traveled vast distances from their original homes to obtain war work.

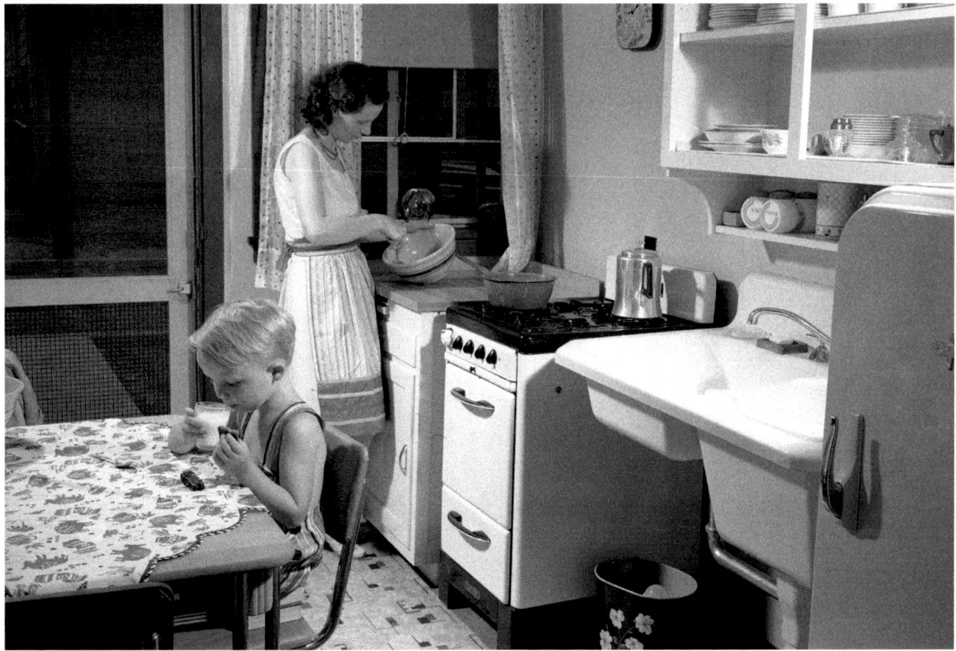

Mrs. B. J. Rogan and her son, Bernie, in the kitchen of the Rogans' new defense home at the Franklin Terrace housing project in Erie, Pennsylvania, July 1941. His father is a drill press operator at the nearby plant of the General Electric Company. (*Library of Congress*)

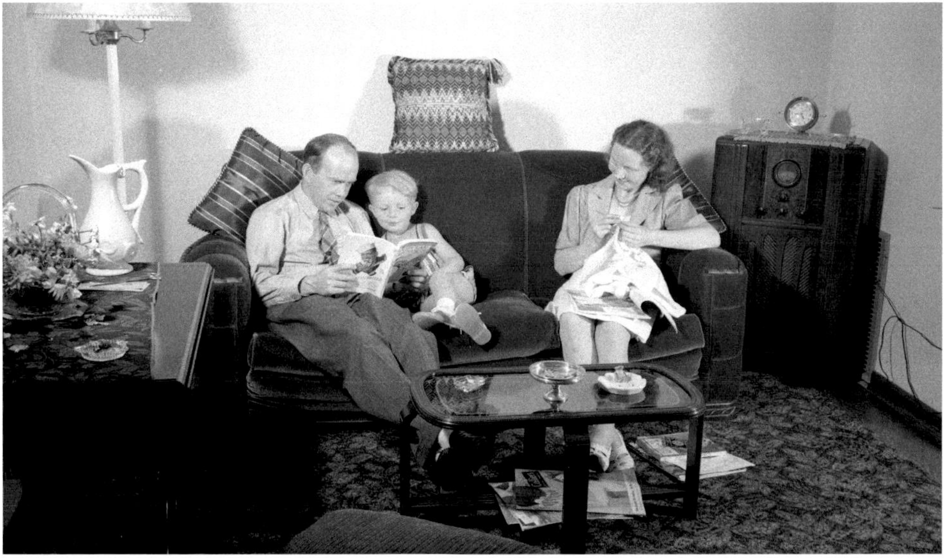

Mr. and Mrs. B. J. Rogan and their small son, Bernie, in the living room of their new defense home in Erie, Pennsylvania, July 1941. Before moving into a newly constructed defense home at the Franklin Terrace housing project, Mr. Rogan lived in a remodeled attic, and then in a trailer. (*Library of Congress*)

The images of the Rogan family's new housing also had psychological value: the couple and their son were portrayed as middle-class—the target demographic group for much of the federal government's wartime propaganda. Palmer demonstrated through his depiction of the Rogan family that they—like millions of other Americans—had a lifestyle that was worth preserving and fighting for. The idyllic image, which displayed traditional gender roles, was meant to help sell war work to middle class, white Americans by showing that individuals could live comfortable lives while engaging in necessary defense production. Another image that Palmer took of the Rogan family again stresses traditional family roles, depicting the father as head of the household reading to his son while his wife lovingly looking on, as the family relaxes in their comfortable, well-appointed living room.

For some defense workers and their families, Palmer's images were a truthful portrayal of reality. After a decade of grinding depression and nagging unemployment, America's defense efforts brought a return to affluence for much of the public, especially for individuals who resided in the Northeast, the Midwest, and the far West. Although gas rationing and a rubber shortage curtailed driving, many Americans once again had money to spend on dinner parties, motion pictures, and vacations, especially to locations where trains could take them. And when the war was over, the money from war bonds that Americans purchased would be converted into new consumer goods, including stoves and refrigerators.[39]

But the images told just part of the defense housing story. The couples whom Palmer photographed in Erie, Pennsylvania, did not include any ethnic minorities. And the images reflected just a fraction of the defense workers and their housing during wartime. Americans of all ethnicities were involved in wartime production. Some workers indeed lived in clean and sanitary conditions, however, the rapid and massive defense buildup led to severe overcrowding near military bases and in cities with defense facilities—images that Palmer was not tasked with taking since the negative nature of such photographs would not boost morale and, worse, might appear in enemy propaganda.[40] In Childersburg, Alabama, for example, the completion of the Alabama Ordnance Works led the town's population to skyrocket from 500 people in 1940 to almost 15,000 in under a year. As J. Leigh Mathis-Downs states, "People came from everywhere. Every house was taking boarders. Apartments, shack villages, dormitories, trailer parks, projects, and boarding houses were going up everywhere to accommodate the workers. Men were living in chicken [shacks] and coal houses."[41] The story was similar in other communities. In Alexandria, Virginia, one man wrote in January 1941 to the FSA's Roy Stryker about the deplorable state of living conditions. "Local people often suffer a double or triple rent raise or get out," he explained. The cost of living in Alexandria rose with wage increases; many locals could not compete for rents with camp workers or army officers.[42]

The FSA photographers who were sent to document the construction or expansion of military bases and factories that produced war materials found similar conditions wherever they went and were appalled at the human cost of defense and war preparations. For example, Jack Delano, writing to Roy Stryker on March 20, 1941, from Fayetteville, North Carolina, revealed the unsanitary conditions and chaos brought on by the mass mobilization. Approximately 8,000 workers had swarmed the community to help expand Fort Bragg. "The camps and settlements around Fayetteville were one hell of a mess," Delano wrote. "Shacks, tents, trucks converted into homes—all along the roadside from the town to the fort and on beyond it. I can imagine what they must have smelled like before the community health department required the owners of the sites to install privies. Some of them are still standing unfinished," he added. The only saving grace, Delano stated, was that the worker population was a transient one. As work was completed to expand the military bases, the men were laid off and moved on to other communities.[43]

The FSA photographer evinced greater concern about the impact of the buildup on African American residents in parts of the South who were forced to move so that defense projects could be constructed. "It's pathetic to see what has been happening to the people in the 'areas,'" Delano stated:

> In Spartanburg [South Carolina], Santee Cooper [South Carolina] and here in Hinesville [Georgia], it's the [same] story. They have lived there so long, are attached to their neighbors and friends, have after many years, perhaps, reached the stage of owning their little piece of land, and now along comes the "guv'ment" and tells them they have to move. Some of the older Negroes especially, who were born and have always lived in the same shack, just can't conceive of having to move—and furthermore can't believe that the government will ever pay them for their land.[44]

Wartime migration upended social stability for many Americans. Approximately 20 percent of the population traveled from their homes looking for work. Some 15 million people worked in other counties than their own, while another 8 million sought employment in other states. The migrants included both individuals seeking jobs in factories manufacturing war materials and servicemen's families who had relocated near training facilities and duty stations to stay together until the male members of their families were sent overseas.

The FSA photographers made a visual record of such wartime living conditions, seeing them as part of the "story" of the defense buildup. But those photographers had another reason for depicting the often-squalid living conditions of the defense industry workers. The FSA had long been mandated with providing better government-funded housing and improved living opportunities—first for agricultural workers during the years of the Great Depression—and, during the 1940s, for itinerant defense workers. Roy Stryker used photography as an educational tool, selecting images to influence both the public and politicians alike to support the FSA's progressive initiative to provide better housing.[45] Alfred Palmer had no such mandate motivating his work. Then, too, images of squalid and overcrowded living conditions near military bases and armaments plants would not contribute to his tasks of making pictures that raised morale at home and encouraging individuals to take positions doing crucial wartime factory labor.

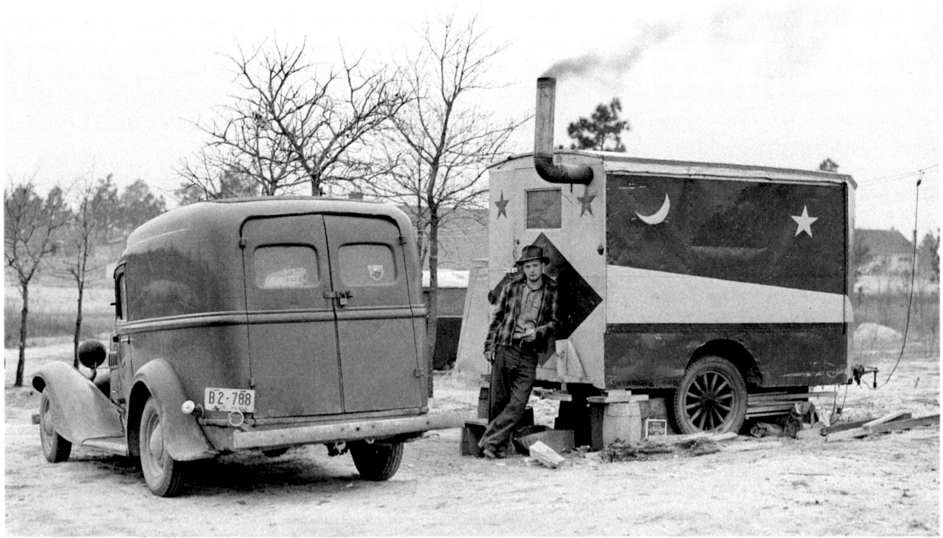

This trailer was occupied by two men working at Fort Bragg, North Carolina, who had come from West Virginia. They bought the trailer from a fortune teller at a circus. Photograph taken by Jack Delano at a camp near Fayetteville, North Carolina, March 1941. (*Library of Congress*)

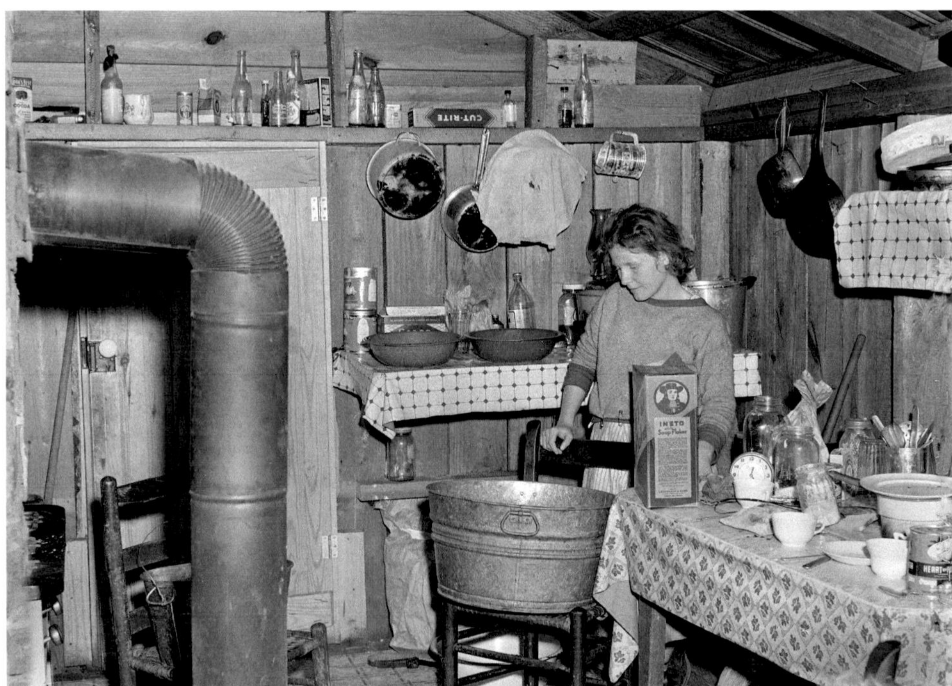

In the second story of a tobacco barn used as living quarters by family of workers from Fort Bragg, North Carolina. Photograph taken by Jack Delano near Fayetteville, North Carolina, March 1941. (*Library of Congress*)

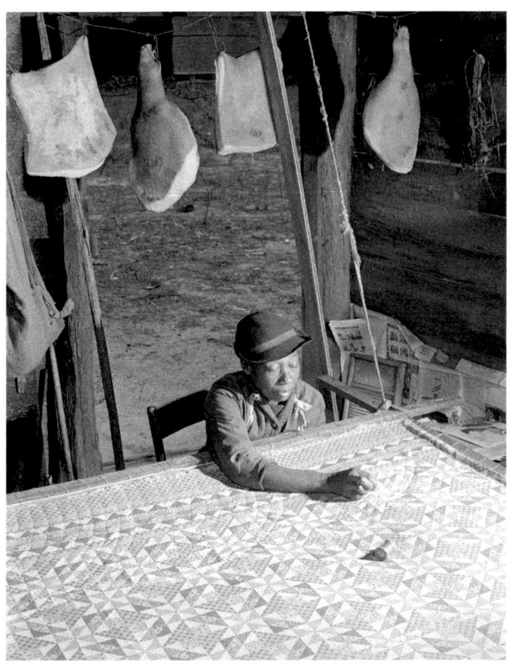

Right: Woman who has not yet found a place to move out of the Hinesville Army camp area working on a quilt in her smokehouse. Photograph taken by Jack Delano near Hinesville, Georgia, April 1941. (*Library of Congress*)

Below: A black woman still living in the Hinesville Army camp area who has not yet found a place to move. Photograph taken by Jack Delano near Hinesville, Georgia, April 1941. (*Library of Congress*)

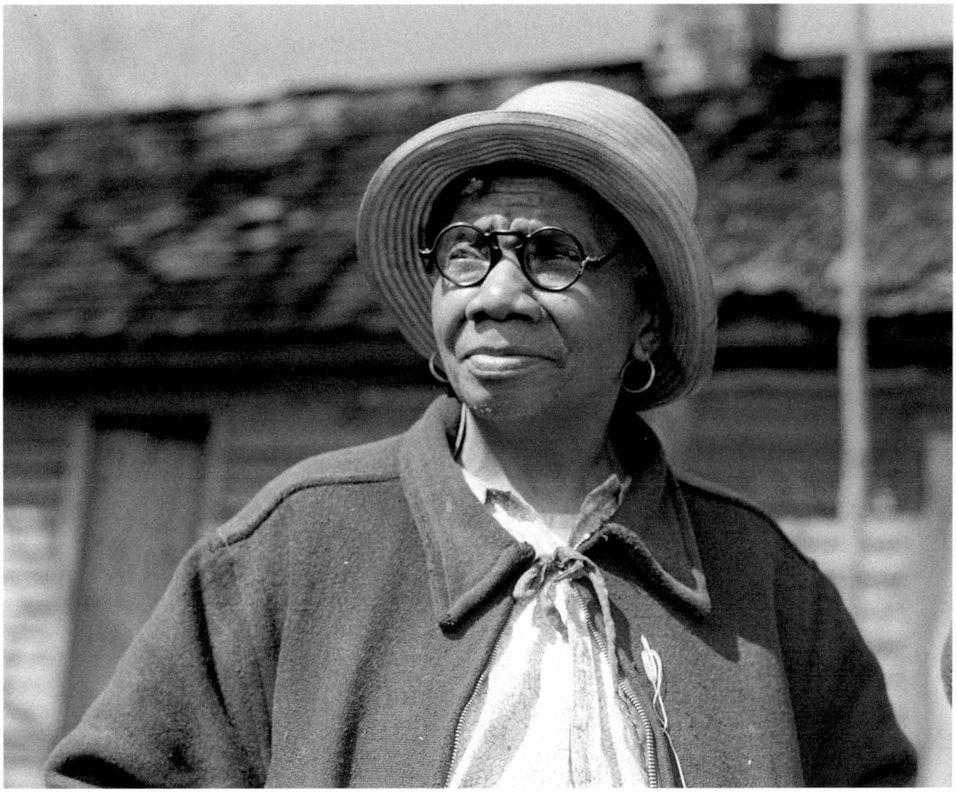

DEPICTING THE "WOMANPOWER" CAMPAIGN

Palmer not only was unique in his technological capabilities as a photographer, he also was socially aware. He was one of the earliest photographers to depict women factory workers as dignified, professional, competent, and patriotic. His visual promotion of such women began before the federal government launched its "Womanpower" campaign in 1942. That propaganda effort, which involved the Office of War Information, the War Manpower Commission, and the War Advertising Council (a private organization that encouraged companies to run advertisements that supported the war effort), was meant to appeal to women's emotions and patriotism to encourage them to take up industrial jobs as rising military enlistments caused the number of men available for civilian labor to dwindle. But the campaign had to hook men as well by convincing them that their wives, daughters, and sweethearts were engaged in temporary positions that would end when the war was over.[46]

The federal propaganda campaign to normalize women's work ignored certain realities. Many women who undertook wartime positions had worked previously. While 19 million women were employed during World War II, statistics show that women who were truly new to paid labor accounted for only 3.5 million individuals. As Lynn Dumenil states: "Women may have worked out of patriotic

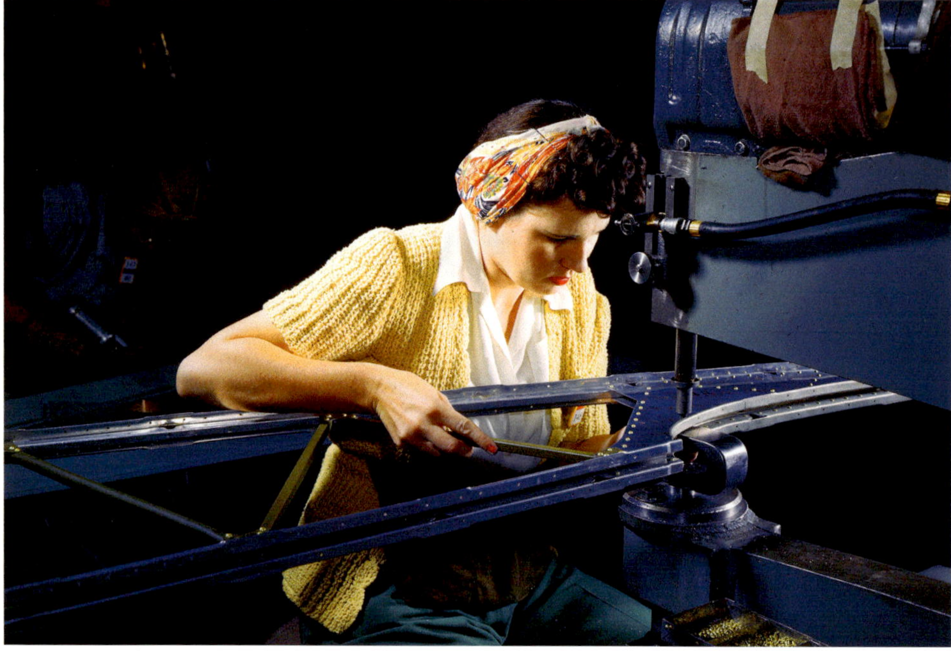

A woman riveting machine operator at the Douglas Aircraft Company plant joins sections of wing ribs to reinforce the inner wing assemblies of B-17F heavy bombers, Long Beach, California, October 1942. (*Library of Congress*)

goals, but they also served their own agendas of financial need and personal satisfaction." Indeed, in 1940, approximately 3 million women who were unemployed actively desired work. Other women, who were already working, switched from lower paying jobs such as waitressing or domestic service to higher paying defense jobs. Although many women were paid less than men for the same positions, those women often were earning more than they ever earned before. And, despite propagandists' claims that war labor was temporary work, millions of women desired to continue working after the war.[47]

Palmer's photographs of women engaged in factory labor had a duality that was unique. His images helped the public accept women workers in heavy industries because those photographs offered a traditional portrayal of such women as still feminine—well dressed (often wearing something attractive that was red or yellow; colors that Kodachrome film displayed well), their hair carefully styled, and their makeup artfully applied—an issue that concerned both men and women during wartime.[48] But the photographer's images also depicted female laborers as serious and competent, an innovative and progressive portrayal that reflected the fact that Palmer acknowledged that war helped bring about cultural change. Through his photographs, Palmer helped legitimize war work for women, but his images clearly are more nuanced than simple glamour shots.

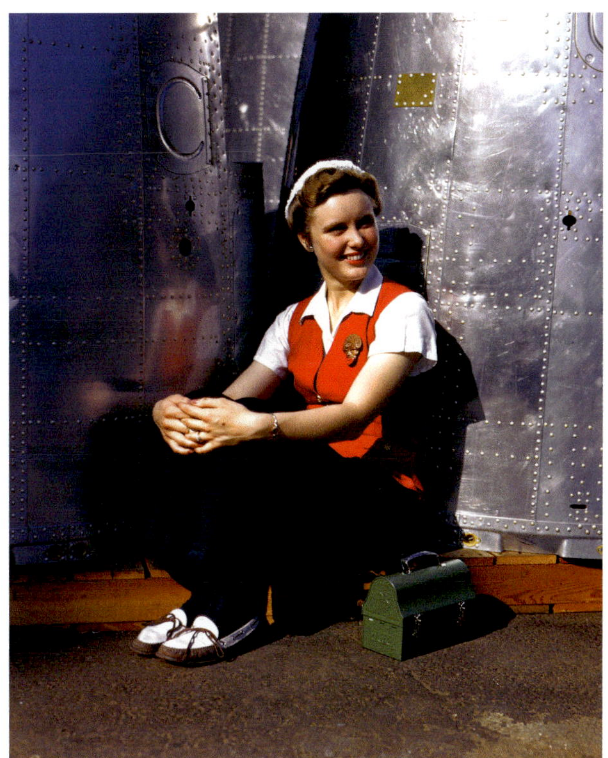

Woman worker at lunch also absorbing California sunshine, Douglas Aircraft Company, Long Beach, California, October 1942. (*Library of Congress*)

Federal propaganda officials used patriotism as the key psychological appeal in the "Womanpower" campaign. Yet, the text that accompanied Palmer's photographs also helped sell war work via a secondary psychological appeal: stressing women's traditional role as helpmates of men. Soldiers, federal propagandists argued, could not succeed on the battlefield if they did not have the tools and equipment that they needed to win. Women, especially middle-class women, were stepping out of their traditional roles at home, but were portrayed as only engaging in much needed factory labor to help their men win the war. The view was, at times, at odds with the reality that many women wanted to work; however, propagandists and advertising executives were hesitant not to upset prevailing gender norms and roles. Therefore, women who engaged in factory work also were portrayed as traditional wives and mothers when they returned home after each shift.[49] Despite the dual portrayals, Maureen Honey notes that women workers became a symbol of the home front's militant spirit as well as models "for proper civilian attitudes."[50]

Although many of Palmer's images of female workers show those women working alone or in small groups, several images portray women as deferential to male authority, listening to male supervisors, or being instructed by men. Such photographs were meant to assure the public that the war had not caused a revolution in gender roles. And the men were frequently depicted as standing above women, looking down at them and their work in paternal fashion.

Even with such carefully constructed imagery, government propaganda officials recognized that their task of attracting women—especially women who had not previously worked—was a difficult one to accomplish. Much of the public, especially those in the middle class, held traditional views of gender roles. Men were seen as the family breadwinners, while women's primary responsibilities involved maintaining their homes and taking care of their children and husbands. This social construction of the "ideal woman" was based on white, middle-class norms and was popularized by the media. Women who "wanted it all"—a husband, children, and a career—often were considered selfish and found themselves chided in popular literature, including magazine articles, for stepping out of their proper sphere.[51]

These broadly held views ignored the reality that American women have always been in the workforce. The industrial revolution that began in the 1820s relied heavily on women workers in cotton and woolen mills. The percentage of women who worked outside of their homes increased following the U.S. Civil War as new work opportunities, including secretarial positions, teaching jobs, and nursing positions, brought women out of the home sphere and into the public sphere. The nation's rapid industrialization also brought many women into the workforce, especially women from lower socio-economic classes.[52] Women's service during World War I and the suffrage movement of the 1920s also helped accelerate the number of women in the workforce. In 1920, 11 million women were working outside of their homes, which accounted for approximately 20 percent of the U.S. labor force. By 1930, that percentage had risen to 22 percent.[53]

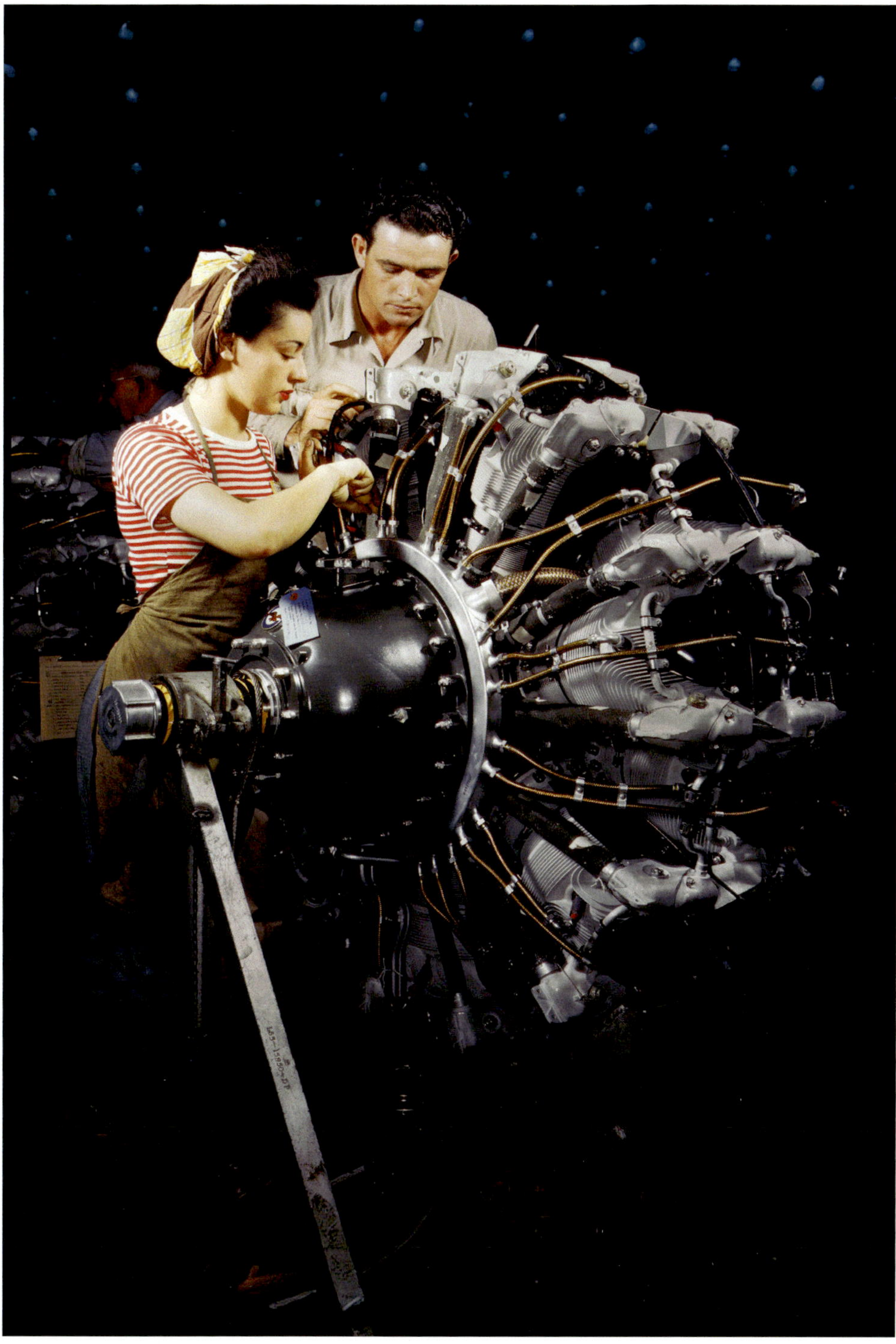

Women are trained as engine mechanics in thorough Douglas training methods, Douglas Aircraft Company, Long Beach, California, October 1942. (*Library of Congress*)

The onset of the Great Depression made the issue of women's work a controversial socio-economic issue, however, given the number of men who were unemployed. In 1936, 82 percent of respondents to a national poll said married women whose husbands could support them should not work because those working women were taking jobs away from men. Magazines during the interwar years reflected a strong degree of ambivalence on the topic, although career women characters increased noticeably in works of fiction, including stories published in magazines.[54]

The coming of war continued this trend. Women workers were increasingly portrayed in newspaper and magazine articles and advertisements positively, even as heroines. That shift in content is not surprising given the large female readership on the home front. Then, too, with 19 million women (both married and unmarried) employed by 1944, editors realized that a reassessment of women's contributions was in order, but editors and writers continued to frame women's entrance into the workforce as a largely temporary measure. They were encouraged to return home when the war was over, ceding their place again to men. Such representations also appeared because federal propaganda officials encouraged editors to promote the depictions as a means of assisting in the war effort.[55]

Alfred Palmer was aware that the images that he took of female workers could upset some citizens, heightening already high wartime anxieties. But the photographer, whose images were often used by the War Manpower Commission, viewed the "Womanpower" campaign as an effective one that would achieve two short term goals: labor recruitment and morale boosting. Then, too, Palmer believed that women who made the sacrifice to work outside of their homes—labeled "two job women" for running their families' homes by day and working by night—served as proof of the nation's spiritual strength.[56] Not all women who were employed during the war years were engaged in industrial production. From 1940 to 1944, women's participation in manufacturing positions increased from 20.2 to 29.9 percent, but so, too, did their entrance into positions more traditionally held by females, including clerical jobs. The latter jobs saw an increase in women laborers from 21.3 to 26.6 percent.[57]

Government propagandists were consistent in their appeals to women's patriotism throughout the years of the conflict. One popular World War II campaign poster pronounced: "The more women at work—the sooner we'll win." Yet Office of War Information officials also used fear appeals to motivate women, telling unemployed women that soldiers might die if women did not do their part by getting war jobs. By making such appeals, propagandists were able to ignore the larger and far more controversial issue of women as breadwinners.

Officials from various wartime propaganda agencies worked within existing social normative constructions of femininity and masculinity when representing male and female war workers. Although Palmer claimed that he sought "typical Americans" to photograph, an examination of his photographs housed at the Library of Congress reveals that Palmer fell back upon his years of commercial photography when selecting the subjects of his images. His archetypical war workers who were helping produce the much-needed armaments often were attractive women and handsome young men, although older workers were depicted as well. Men (and some women) in their fifties, sixties, and even seventies frequently were portrayed as experts who were providing training to younger workers, including women who were serving as temporary replacements for male factory workers who were serving in the military.[58]

Palmer's female subjects might be attaching nose cones to aircraft or working with rivet guns, but those women had carefully applied makeup, their figures were usually trim, their hairstyles reflected the popular trends of the era, and they were clothed in conservative attire.[59] Although the nation's entrance into the war brought about economic and social changes, Palmer and his Office of War Information colleagues attempted to find a balance between portraying women workers as fitting within the traditional gender status quo while also engaging in a small degree of progressive change.

Ultimately, the "Womanpower" campaign that was launched by the Office of War Information and the War Manpower Commission proved successful.[60] Many of the women who were new to the workforce labored in the types of blue-collar industrial jobs that government officials encouraged. For example, in April 1941, just 143 women were employed in the aircraft industry. By October 1943, more than 65,000 women were helping produce the bombers and fighter planes needed to take on the nation's wartime enemies.[61]

DEPICTING WARTIME CONTRIBUTIONS OF MINORITY POPULATIONS

Government propagandists also had to strike a careful balance in their portrayal of minority workers and soldiers, particularly African Americans. Prior to America's entry into the war, military officials in the War Department had no plans to use African American soldiers in combat. Military reports produced during the 1930s played to the worst racial stereotypes, questioning African American men's intelligence and bravery. Pentagon officials determined that the military should remain segregated and that minority men, if needed at all, should engage largely in non-combat roles.[62]

In a nation struggling with separate and often highly unequal facilities, as well as inequalities on all fronts—economic, political, legal, and social—some African Americans were apathetic toward the war. Others showed varying degrees of opposition. As Clayton R. Koppes and Gregory D. Black note, World War II "brought into sharp relief the duality of Black citizens in American society. Roosevelt may have identified Allied war aims with democracy's Four Freedoms but Walter White, executive secretary of the NAACP, pointed out that blacks had to 'fight for the right to fight' for democracy."[63]

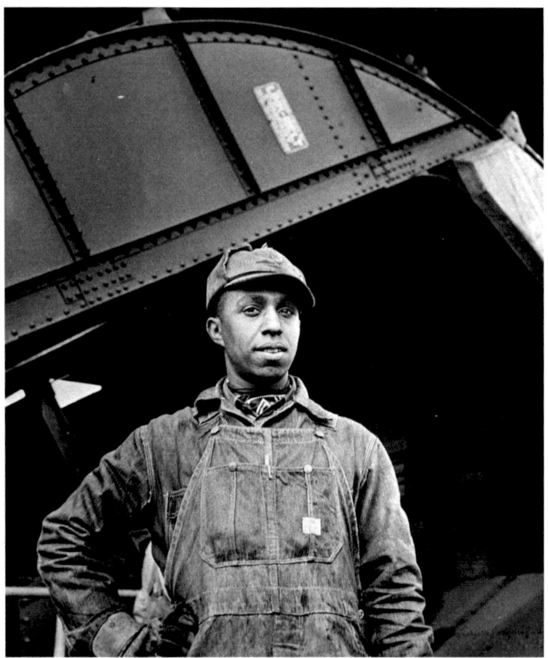

Black workers speed war work for Tennessee Valley Authority. Earl M. Qualls, car dumper operator at Watts Bar, is job steward of the Hod Carriers' local union on TVA Authority, and is active in combatting absenteeism and in furthering war bond Red Cross drives.

The *Pittsburgh Courier*'s "Double V" campaign was one of the most noticeable manifestations of the battle for equality and the fight against discrimination and segregation. Standing for victory at home (for racial equality) and victory abroad (against fascism), the civil rights campaign was born from the reality that little progress had been achieved for African Americans.[64] Polls taken during wartime revealed that 92 percent of the American public supported a policy of continued racial segregation and an anti-lynching bill failed to pass in the U.S. Senate.[65]

Federal propagandists, therefore, knew that they had to be careful in their representations of minorities, particularly African Americans. They ultimately fell back on their original information strategy, representing minorities on the home front and in the military based on a one-sided strategy of truth. As with portrayals of women, wartime housing, food rationing, and other wartime campaigns, officials at the Office for Emergency Management and the Office of War Information downplayed tensions and public concerns in their campaigns, while accentuating the positive. Ethnic minorities were portrayed as hard workers who were helping the nation by producing the materials that the U.S. military needed to win the war.

A publication aimed at African Americans titled *Negroes and the War* highlighted African American accomplishments during the previous fifty years, while also telling readers that a Nazi victory would set back progress. African Americans were portrayed in the pamphlet as fully participating in all aspects of society—going to work, to school, and to church. Prominent African Americans, including boxer Joe Louis, athlete Jesse Owens, and singer Marian Anderson, were featured as examples of minorities who had succeeded in American society. The

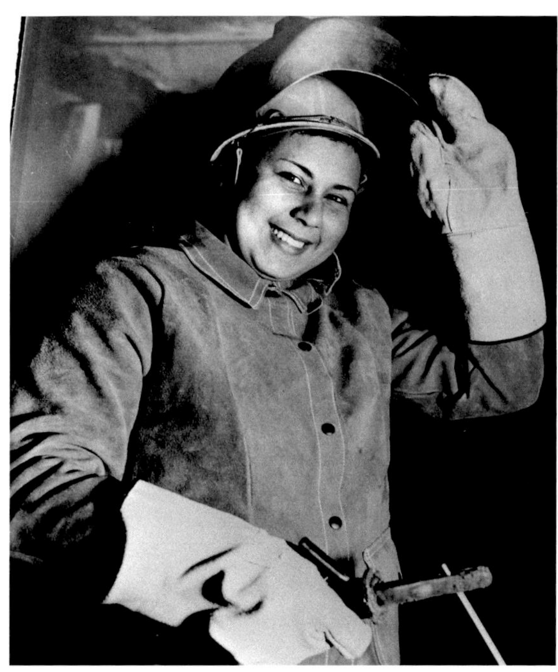

Petrina Moore, a full-blooded Cherokee Indian woman, now a welder at the Todd Hoboken dry dock, New Jersey, 1943. (*Library of Congress*)

pamphlet was meant to assuage any "justifiable doubts" that African Americans had about the Roosevelt administration's commitment to civil rights.[66]

In keeping with federal propaganda agencies' policies of trying to portray minority workers as having made gains in American society, Palmer depicted minority subjects, including Petrina Moore, a Cherokee Indian woman, who worked as a welder at the Todd Shipyards in Brooklyn, New York, with dignity.[67] But the impetus behind the photographer's representations of minority workers and soldiers went beyond what his supervisors desired. Palmer's humanistic values, coupled with extensive pre-war travels that led him to meet individuals from all walks of life, were key factors behind how he portrayed minority citizens. Yet, those positive depictions could be—and were—leveraged by federal officials to visually depict the great strides that minority citizens had taken, a portrayal that was meant to counter Nazi propaganda, which often included Depression-era FSA photographs that depicted the nation as impoverished and deeply racist.[68]

Palmer's photographs of minority workers uniformly reveal their patriotism, competence, and devotion to the war effort, as well as their willingness to defend a nation that, thus far, had refused to give them equal rights. The images conveyed the Office of War Information's stance that all Americans were united against a common enemy. Even though Palmer's images of minority women often did not possess the glamour aesthetic that he used in his depictions of white women workers, his progressive-leaning photographs remained controversial given the era's prevailing racial attitudes.

Indeed, critics quickly pounced on propaganda from the Office of War Information that portrayed racial minorities in a positive light. The *Negroes and the War* pamphlet, for example, was highly criticized by both Northern and Southern members of Congress who believed that the publication was thinly veiled propaganda for Roosevelt's "New Deal" accomplishments. Southern members of Congress complained bitterly that the pamphlet was proof that federal propagandists favored racial equality, and that such propaganda was an attempt to force the concept of equal rights on the public.[69]

Despite Congressional complaints, Office of War Information officials persisted in displaying African Americans' wartime contributions in positive fashion, though much of that propaganda occurred during the latter two years of war when labor shortages became acute. Rather than acknowledge that reality, federal propagandists instead claimed that their efforts were meant to counter viewpoints that African Americans and other minorities were less patriotic than were white Americans. Then, too, federal propaganda also sought to convince minorities that they "had a stake and a share in fighting to preserve the American dream."[70]

Palmer's photographs of minority defense workers and soldiers visually depicted the Office of War Information's stance that all Americans were united against a

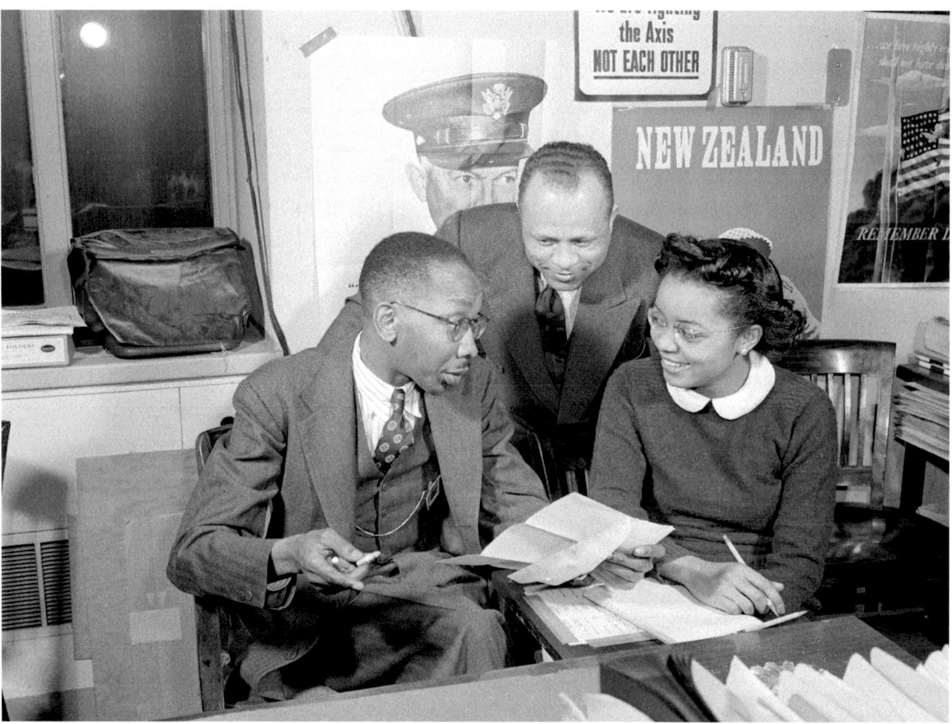

Ted Poston, a black desk editor of the Office of War Information (OWI), discusses a letter from one of the 240 black editors to which he sends war news from Washington, with William Clark and Harriette Easterlin, his assistants, March 1943. (*Library of Congress*)

common enemy. The photographer was fully committed to this philosophy. When in Washington, D.C., he held regular lunch meetings with African American photographer Gordon Parks and Theodore "Ted" Poston, the Office of War Information's News Bureau's Negro Press section chief. The two men helped inform Palmer's understanding of African Americans' war efforts, and, he said, gave him suggestions and advice.[71]

Finding minority subjects proved difficult for the photographer; however, he found some subjects at shipyards, in Midwestern defense plants, at TVA sites in the South, and at military bases. A September 1942 photo shoot at the California Shipbuilding Corporation yards on Terminal Island in Los Angeles, California, proved a particularly fertile source of minority workers engaged in defense production. Palmer captured African American, Filipino, and Chinese shipbuilders working alongside their white counterparts in the construction of the Liberty ship *Booker T. Washington,* named after the famed African American educator, author, and presidential adviser.

Many minorities, particularly African Americans, often were given the dirtiest and least desirable jobs possible at defense factories, a reality that made Palmer search particularly hard to obtain the subjects that could be used to visually depict the Office of War Information's narrative that the nation's minority citizens were as patriotic as their white counterparts in battling against fascist enemies. Minority women were in short supply as subjects for government propaganda photographs since those women often were not hired until labor shortages became so acute that the hiring of white women was no longer a viable option. Separate surveys conducted in 1943 by the United Auto Workers and the National Metal Trades Association revealed that less than one third of factories that employed women to undertake war work hired African American women. And the ones that did often gave those women the most menial of jobs, including janitorial positions. Despite these continued actions of discrimination in the workplace, many minority women increased their income—often giving up lower paying jobs as domestics and farm workers to enter factory labor. Yet, Karen Tucker Anderson notes that stressing improvements in the working lives of African American women workers "understate[s] the extent to which discrimination persisted and ... ignore[s] the fact that the assumptions of a historically balkanized labor force continued to determine the distribution of the benefits of a full employment economy."[72]

The Office of War Information hired African American photographer Robert Smith to take photographs for the Black press, however, many of Palmer's images of African American defense workers and soldiers also were published in those newspapers. That press was at the height of its circulation power (more than 200 newspapers were produced across the nation), influence, and prestige during the war years.[73] Whether any of Palmer's pictures of minority workers appeared in white-owned publications is difficult to say because OWI officials failed to keep records of when and where their images were used.[74]

Palmer's images of minority workers sometimes depicted individuals with exemplary work records, including Herbert Smith, a drill press operator for

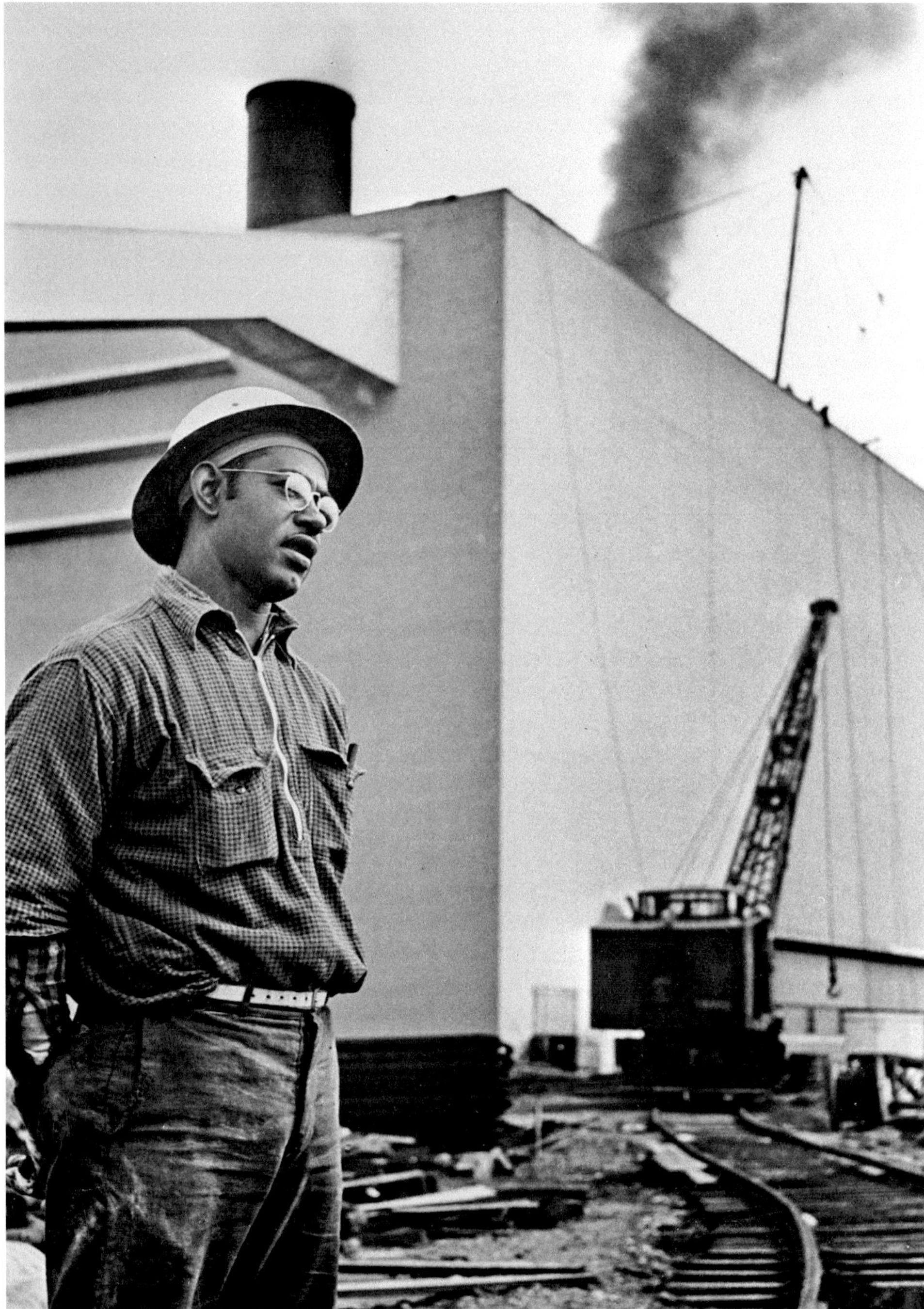

Black workers speed war work for Tennessee Valley Authority, June 1942. Herbert Smith, drill operator, is a member of a local labor-management cooperative committee and is a job steward. He has worked nine years for TVA without a single unauthorized absence. (*Library of Congress*)

the Tennessee Valley Authority, a federal agency which provides power, engages in flood control, and land management in several Southern states. Palmer and other Office of War Information News Bureau photographers took images of African American defense workers and soldiers alike using the most attractive angles possible to portray them as patriotic, hardworking, and serious individuals who were doing their part to protect America and its citizens. As Natanson notes, neither Palmer's photographs of African Americans nor those taken by other government photographers proved to be "biting commentaries of racial injustice." That simply was not the purpose behind the images. Yet, as Natanson adds, Palmer's photographs of minority soldiers and workers did contain what he calls "an important progressive dimension."[75] Ordinary people were portrayed with a respect that was not usually accorded to them. "I did what I could to portray the Black contribution to the huge job we were faced with," Palmer recalled.[76] Obtaining those portrayals led Palmer to drive thousands of miles, enduring heat, dust, rainstorms—and several arrests by local police who thought the photographer was a spy—to depict Roosevelt's "Arsenal of Democracy" for federal propaganda agencies. Armed with his camera, Palmer worked as hard as the war workers and soldiers whom he portrayed.

4

A WARTIME LIFE

"I remember how hard I worked, every day in the week, no matter where I was," Alfred Palmer said, reflecting on his World War II career as a government photographer. "I traveled the country. And I can remember sometimes I would set up and shoot twenty-five pictures in a day." Despite the workload involved in touring industrial facilities, selecting model employees, and setting up his lighting, Palmer reveled in the work, seeing his photography as his contribution to help America win the war.[1]

Palmer spent weeks at a time on the road in his mission to depict the nation's defense buildup. Using both color and black-and-white film to capture the images that his supervisors required, the photographer worked alone, testing his physical and mental stamina. Palmer occasionally sought help from factory employees to clean or paint an area that he sought to photograph. And he often asked for help for someone to carry his lights.[2]

The photographer's days were long ones. Taking pictures by day, Palmer developed his black-and-white film at night when he returned to his hotel room.[3] But he had to send that film and the captions for the pictures to Washington, D.C., where a "two-man, two-woman crew" printed the black-and-white photographs. Those images were then sent on to government censors for examination, clearance, and release to the press.[4] The color film went directly to Kodak facilities for processing.

Palmer had to be confident of what he was shooting as he moved from one factory or military base to another since he did not have a full darkroom in each community from which he could make prints and examine his work. The Kodachrome film he used was "positive" film, meaning there was no negative, but, rather, the film, once processed, came out as a positive image. The tolerance of that kind of film is plus or minus one f-stop, meaning that the film had to be exposed almost perfectly, or it was not usable. With a positive rather than a negative film, there is no ability to fix any errors in the darkroom—there is no postproduction possible, meaning Palmer had to be near perfect.

His anxiety level when shooting color film during the 1940s was much higher than it was for other photographers who were using black-and-white film. In addition to all the other logistical problems that Palmer faced, including lining up his models and dealing with factory executives, the photographer faced the uncertainty of his own perfection while awaiting the results of previous shoots from the Kodak laboratory. Photographers who were early adopters of color film had to be excellent technicians or they had nothing to show for their efforts. Palmer was, in addition to all his other extraordinary skills as organizer, implementer, and conceptualizer, an excellent technician.

Although much of the public never knew Palmer's name, the Office of War Information publicized the photographer and lauded his work ethic in a 1942 statement to the press. The release also revealed the thousands of miles the photographer had traveled in the course of his job:

> The great arsenals, steel mills, aircraft plants, shipyards, the vast TVA projects, military camps such as Fort Benning, GA., Fort Knox, KY., Parris Island, S.C., Mitchell Field, L.I., Langley Field, VA, New River, N.C. … all these and many more have been photographed by Palmer in a comparatively short space of time. At the moment he is on the west coast enriching his coverage of the airplane industry by shooting the North American, Douglas, and Vultee plants.[5]

A writer for *Popular Photography* magazine, a publication read by most professional photographers and perused by a huge amateur photographer readership, also praised the images being distributed by the Office for Emergency Management stating, "OEM photographs are making traditionally dull factory subjects come to life. Already the unit has injected some new ideas into government publicity." Reporter John B. Earle was particularly taken with a set of staged air

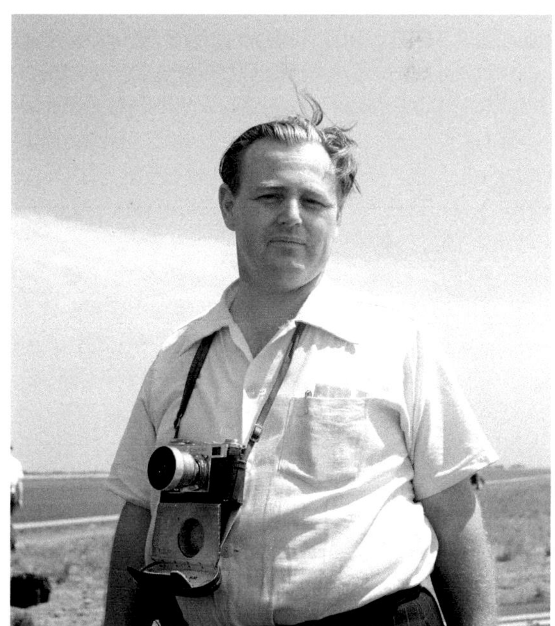

Alfred T. Palmer, U.S. Office of War Information photographer, at the U.S. Marine glider detachment training camp, Parris Island, South Carolina, May 1942. (*Library of Congress*)

raid photos shot by Palmer in New York City. Calling the black-and-white photos publicity and not propaganda, Earle stressed the importance that photography played in wartime. "Their job [i.e., OEM photographers] is to put before the public in the most effective manner, all civilian aspects of our war effort," Earle stated. He explained that a brainstorming session led Palmer to develop the air raid photos. The writer then praised the photographer and other, unnamed Office for Emergency Management staff for working "72 hours without leaving their building to turn out the necessary prints." The resulting images were distributed widely to newspapers across the nation. Many of the photographs, which appeared in *Popular Photography*'s April 1942 issue, reflected Palmer's trademark style: medium shots that featured strong contrast.[6]

The air raid photo shoot was one of several thematic projects shot in black-and-white film for distribution to newspapers and magazines that allowed Palmer to visually depict—albeit in a positive light—the impact of the war on the home front. Other projects included documenting the rapid construction of wartime housing for war workers, publicity the federal government badly needed given the massive overcrowding that occurred in many communities.[7] Another project, aimed at educating Americans, documented the point system for food rationing, while yet a third project, shot in Philadelphia, Pennsylvania, depicted women railroad workers, including conductors and repair crew members, who were serving as temporary replacements for the male employees who had gone to war.

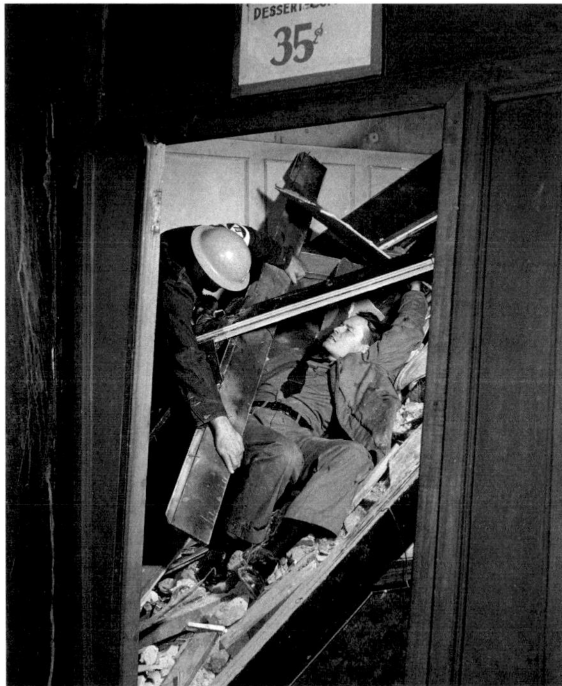

Civilian protection. A rescue worker removes fallen debris which has pinned a victim seeking to escape. He will be given emergency first aid and taken to the nearest casualty clearing station, New York City, October 1941. (*Library of Congress*)

A LIFE ON THE ROAD

Palmer's life of near-endless travel may have seemed glamorous and exciting to many Americans who were emerging from years of economic depression, but the reality was, at times, far different for the photographer himself. Capturing the images that government officials needed for their propaganda work meant that Palmer spent much of his life on the road. Letters penned to his wife, Alexa, reveal that the photographer truly enjoyed the work, and appreciated the challenges involved in shooting in navy yards, at military bases, in factories, and at other locales. But the travel exhausted Palmer, put tremendous wear on his equipment and his automobile, proved challenging for his wife and children (who longed for their husband and father), and made him equally wistful for family life.

A peripatetic life on the road (and at sea) had been the norm for Palmer for almost two decades, as were affectionate written reassurances of his love for his family in every letter home. The photographer cherished his family, but the sea and the open road clearly called to Palmer before, during, and after the war years. Although Palmer's wife was home during the war years with David, Donald, and Julia, the couple's three children, Alexa, who had a background in banking, was an equal partner in the couple's commercial photography business. In addition to raising their children, Alexa handled the bookkeeping, mailed photographs to clients, collected the money owed to the couple, and helped in the darkroom with printmaking when needed. With her husband's encouragement, she also began taking photographs, as well.[8]

Regular letters home allowed the couple to stay in touch and share their daily lives with one another, but they also allowed the photographer—on occasion—to have a safe place to vent his concerns. For example, in a January 1942 letter to Alexa from Louisville, Kentucky, Palmer took his pen in hand to help reduce his mounting frustrations after his immediate supervisor, William Nelson, head of the photography division for the Office for Emergency Management, appeared unable to decide where to send Palmer for his next assignment. "First he had me going South—to New Orleans. Then to California. Then to Detroit. And now to Denver," Palmer wrote to Alexa before adding: "I'm not sore. Just a little bewildered." But the same letter also revealed some real anger when promises made by Nelson were not kept. "He told me that I would be in charge of the darkroom work. And that I would be home at least fifty percent of the time. I am neither," Palmer stated. "I'm always homesick," he admitted later in the letter to Alexa, perhaps to assuage her feelings at his prolonged absence. Palmer's wife bore the brunt of responsibility at home, spending much of her marriage as a single parent while her husband traveled. "I shouldn't be tired," he protested. "I shouldn't be homesick. And above all, I should never wonder what is coming next!"[9]

Palmer's exhaustion was understandable. He was regularly on the road from the time he was hired in 1940 until a promotion in mid-1943 took him away from his itinerant life, making him largely deskbound, supervising other Office of War Information photographers and providing security clearances for their work. But

Palmer also kept his commercial photography business going, albeit on a smaller scale during wartime.[10] He maintained an office and a studio in New York City, where he continued to take photographs for advertising agencies, publications, and shipping lines, including pre-war client Moore-McCormack, whose luxury liners were used during the war years to transport troops. During the 1930s, Palmer had served as a photographer for Moore-McCormack's "Good Neighbor Fleet." The trio of cruise ships made regular trips prior to the outbreak of war to Barbados, Trinidad, and several ports of call in South America before and after the war. The fleet's "Good Neighbor" moniker was drawn from Roosevelt's March 1933 inaugural speech. The president promoted a "Good Neighbor Policy" with South American nations as a means of achieving a variety of ideological, political, and economic goals, including reducing growing German interests in the western hemisphere. The latter goal was a crucial one. Roosevelt attempted to achieve it in part by creating a necessary sense of "community and homogeneity in the Americas."[11]

Whether Nelson's above-mentioned uncertainty as to where to send Palmer for assignments was due to indecision regarding propaganda messaging and goals within the Office for Emergency Management, or was because of the political climate in Washington, D.C., where opposition to propaganda creation remained high, is unknown. Palmer apparently voiced his concerns and complaints only to his wife, Alexa. He admitted in a second letter from Louisville, Kentucky, written on January 25, 1942, that although he was homesick and dismayed at being sent to Detroit, rather than being allowed some time off to return home, he would not complain publicly out of fear that he would be assigned "second-rate jobs to do on civilian defense" while another photographer might be assigned to the more challenging jobs that Palmer relished.[12]

The photographer was aware that his strength lay in commercial work. He was proud of the reputation that he had built in the 1920s and 1930s with shipping line executives and advertising agency art directors and, therefore, had a clear sense of what photography assignments he wished to undertake for federal agencies. But, mindful of the financially precarious years of the 1930s, Palmer often reminded himself that his government job provided steady pay. That was not always the case with jobs he had accepted during the previous two decades as a commercial photographer. Indeed, pre-war letters from Alfred to Alexa were filled with news of what he had earned, his concerns about being paid in installments by shipping companies and other clients, and queries about whether enough cash was flowing in to pay the bills at home.[13]

Despite his steady wartime paycheck, Palmer sought to increase his family's income when possible. He realized that at least some of his images of Asian and Pacific Ocean nations taken during the previous two decades—including photographs of Noumea, New Caledonia, and port communities in northern Australia—might prove valuable to editors. He asked Alexa in a March 22, 1942, letter to comb through his picture files to locate photographs that editors might want to use to illustrate locations in which fighting had occurred. "Who ever thought that our South Seas pictures might someday be worth something," he marveled. Palmer also encouraged his wife to reach out to the Associated Press news agency and to two stock photo agencies, H. A. Roberts and Ewing Galloway, in an attempt to sell prints or negatives when possible. "Anyhow let's get what we can now," he wrote, acknowledging that the timing was right to sell the images. "They [the photographs and negatives] probably won't be worth that [much] a year from now." Recognizing that the war would be a long one, Palmer then provided ideas to Alexa on how to spend any cash from the sale of those photographs: "We can put the money into Defense Bonds—groceries—clothes—and additions to the house. And get all set for the worst to come."[14]

FROM THE OEM TO THE OWI

When the Office for Emergency Management was dissolved by President Roosevelt via an executive order on June 13, 1942, and replaced by the Office of War Information, Palmer continued as chief photographer. Although he was assigned to the agency's Domestic News Bureau, the bureau's name was something of a misnomer. Palmer was not engaged in photojournalism, although some members of the growing photography staff did come from newspaper backgrounds. Instead, Palmer continued to produce the same highly stylized and posed medium shot photographs that had become his hallmark while he was employed by the Office for Emergency Management. Experience had taught the photographer that newspaper and magazine editors did not want stock photos from the Signal Corps or other federal agencies during the nation's period of defense buildup nor during the war years. "They wanted pictures with impact," Palmer stated. "And that's what I went out to shoot." He largely avoided taking wide-angle shots, seeing them as lacking both dramatic and artistic qualities.[15]

Feature photography work suited Palmer. The war had indeed increased opportunities for photojournalists who were needed to take pictures for hard news stories, but photojournalism was not an occupation that Palmer desired—not in 1942, nor in the future. He admitted as much in a January 25, 1942, letter to Alexa, stating that he did not wish jobs that were "more or less on a news slant." Photojournalism was, in Palmer's opinion, a different aesthetic, "a very different sphere than mine." He was content with his government assignments. They allowed his artistic impulses to shine via proper lighting and experiments with color. Then, too, the government photo shoots allowed Palmer to work alone with little direction, just as he had done before the war. "I find myself extremely fortunate to be interested and qualified in the highest paid bracket in the entire photographic field," he told his wife in the same letter. "I've had too much freedom until now to take orders from a *boss*! My spirit does not like direction—or restrictions of any kind—not even for a warm—fairly definite security."[16] Palmer's letter reveals not only his preference to be self-employed when possible, but his mindset as a commercial photographer, as well. He was focused on the creation of the images themselves, fulfilling his client's needs by making the best images possible.

Palmer enjoyed the challenges that shooting in different locations and under different conditions brought, although outdoor shoots on military bases—to which the photographer was increasingly assigned after the United States entered the war—provided weather-related challenges that did not occur when he was shooting inside industrial plants. For example, a May 31, 1942, letter to his wife from Elizabethtown, Kentucky, told Alexa that he had spent "a hot and dusty week chasing tanks over hill-tops and thru [sic] creek bottoms," getting images of soldiers training at Fort Knox with his Graflex camera. "This job has been a hard one," he added. "My cameras are wearing out and sometimes I feel like I am, too."[17] A second letter from Fort Knox, penned four days later, again acknowledged both a longing to be home to get "reacquainted" with his family and to get his equipment and vehicle much needed servicing. "My cameras need a thorough overhauling and the car needs a paint job," he stated.[18]

Palmer's concerns about his equipment and vehicle were real, but his worries about relations with his wife, when he was away for such long periods of time, were a bigger issue. A June 4, 1942, letter from Elizabethtown, Kentucky, expressed Palmer's concern that he had not heard from his wife in six days. "Every day I call in at Captain Henson's office—looking for a letter from you. It's become somewhat embarrassing. Tonight he suggested that I'd better get home quick." He

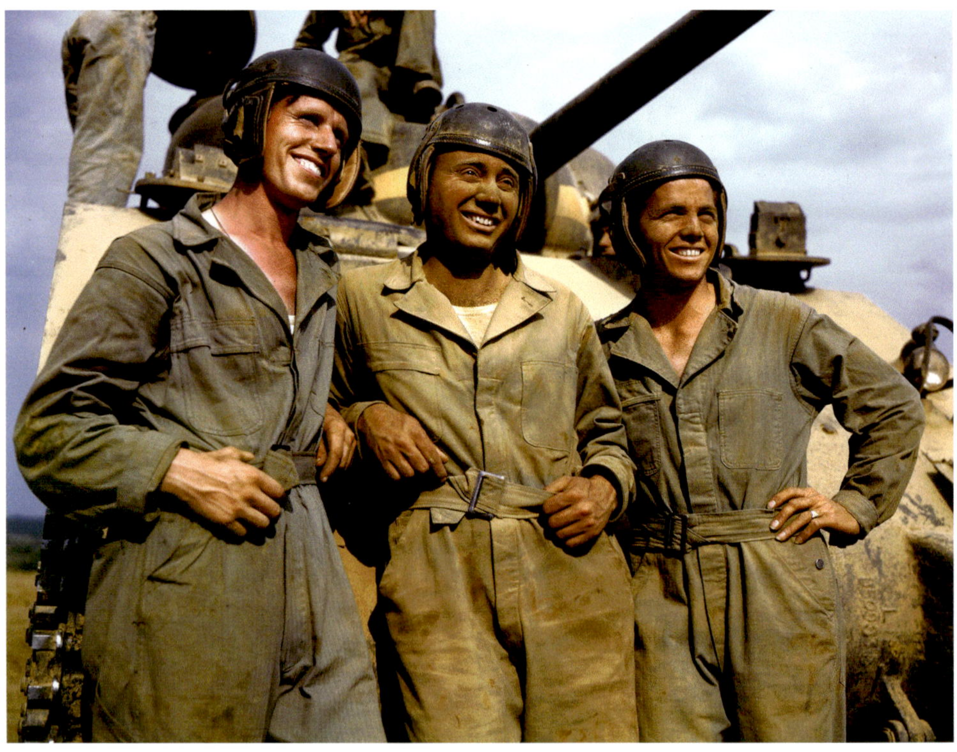

M-4 tank crews of the United States, Ft. Knox, Kentucky, June 1942. (*Library of Congress*)

added: "If you sent me a penny post card each day I'd appreciate it every much. I'd at least know that you thot [*sic*] about me once each day."[19]

A final letter, written as he wrapped up his Fort Knox work, reiterated that the southern climate was taking its toll on the photographer and his equipment. Yet, Palmer also was convinced of the quality of the images that he was sending back to Washington, D.C., which led him to conclude that it was time for him to ask for a larger salary. "It has been very hot and dusty. I certainly have earned my salt this trip—as before. And I think it is just about time that we can ask for a raise since it was promised us." He added that he intended to ask for $4,600 a year, arguing that the amount was not unreasonable. But he admitted that even without a raise, "I'm still highly paid for a govt. photog."[20] Palmer's boss William Nelson put the photographer up for that raise four days after Palmer penned the letter, asking Rachel Brown, a fiscal officer at the Office for Emergency Management, to have Palmer reclassified at a higher level and to make that promotion retroactive to April 1, 1942.[21]

Travel, at times, proved difficult, especially when inclement weather struck. Writing from Rocky Mount, North Carolina, to his wife on March 8, 1942, Palmer explained that he had to take shelter for the night while driving to his next destination. "There's a terrific rain smashing down outside. Much like a tropic squall. I'm glad that I didn't want to go on to Raleigh tonight. I'd be right in the middle of it on a narrow road."[22] That rain followed Palmer throughout the south in the spring of 1942, dogging his efforts. "I've worked hard today. Made pictures of tanks in action," he told Alexa, but then mentioned that getting enough top-quality images was slow going since the weather would not cooperate. "I'm getting some pictures—but not anything like I would get if the sun would only shine."[23]

Wartime rationing also proved to be another occupational hurdle. The thousands of miles that Palmer was required to drive led the photographer to worry about obtaining tires and gasoline, and keeping his personal vehicle maintained. Since Palmer's work was considered essential to the war effort, he was issued "C" gasoline coupons—supplemental coupons that allowed him all the fuel that he needed to drive from one community to another to photograph the nation's pre-war and wartime defense buildup. But Palmer was required to have the gas coupons with him to obtain his fuel. He panicked one time in Detroit when he could not find his booklet. Worrying that he had left the coupons at home, he asked his wife to search through her purse for the missing booklet. "I've gone through everything I own. I'm just hoping that you have them," he stated in a letter.[24]

Of equal concern to Palmer was the fact that none of the federal agencies for which he worked provided him with a car. The job required him to put thousands of miles on his own vehicle, which made maintenance a priority. "I'm having the poor old Pontiac washed and greased," Palmer told his wife in a June 6, 1942, letter. "It certainly deserves the best of treatments. What that little car has been through these last few weeks wouldn't be fit for a jeep."[25]

Just five days after the Japanese attack on Pearl Harbor, the photographer had realized that tires would soon be in short supply. He voiced his concerns in a December 12, 1941, letter to his wife, stating: "The other day I wanted to get word to you to buy some tires quick. I didn't let you know. Now [i.e., with the U.S. entrance into the war] you can't buy tires for any price. But since I'm doing defense work we can certainly get some tires someplace."[26]

Palmer's concerns were well founded. With Southeast Asia producing 90 percent of the world's natural (i.e., non-synthetic) rubber, the Japanese conquest of the region in 1942 forced President Roosevelt to announce gas rationing in May. The policy would go into effect in seventeen eastern states to help conserve tires by discouraging non-essential travel. He expanded the rationing for the duration of the war to all states by the end of the year.[27] In response to the president's actions, Palmer's supervisors sent him to the Salinas Valley in California in November of that year to photograph the harvest of Guayule, an evergreen shrub that produces rubber. Those images—if published—may have reassured the public that Americans would no longer be hamstrung by their previous dependence upon other nations for the much-needed raw material.

Reaching his supervisors while on the road proved another wartime difficulty. Unlike FSA boss Roy Stryker, who sent regular and lengthy letters to photographers as a means of discussing the types of images he needed, Palmer and other Office of War Information photographers relied heavily on telephone conversations as a means of discussing and clarifying assignments and wartime objectives.[28] At one point, the photographer tried three times over the course of two days to reach Nelson to no avail, prior to sending approximately 200 negatives taken at Fort Story in Virginia Beach, Virginia. But Palmer knew he had done good work; his letter home revealed a calm certainty about the images Nelson would receive. "Among them he is going to find plenty of good material," Palmer said. "I've done the best job I could."[29]

Hotel living—another necessary part of his peripatetic life—sometimes proved as irksome as the rain, dust, and heat. Rooming houses often were dirty, hotels frequently had loud occupants in nearby rooms, and his housing assignments in officers' quarters on bases often were located near kitchen facilities. Further hampering his travels, communities near military bases often were so crowded with soldiers and civilian defense workers that it was hard for Palmer to get meals at restaurants or, on a night off, get a ticket for a motion picture at a local cinema.[30]

Life on the road also proved increasingly expensive as prices for almost everything rose due to wartime demand. Palmer noted in a December 12, 1941, letter that "a mediocre room" at the Hotel Auditorium in Cleveland, Ohio, had cost him $2.75, which he viewed as too high. But the photographer was philosophical, acknowledging that it was one of the better rooms he had rented while on the road. "It's warm and quiet here and I won't have to make my home here."[31]

Palmer was in Akron, Ohio, photographing military barrage balloon manufacturing when he learned that the nation was now at war. "I've just heard the President's speech," he said in a letter to Alexa. "I guess we know where we stand now. We're in for a tough siege. And a long one."[32]

A SATISFYING WARTIME CAREER

Despite the arrival of warfare, Palmer counted himself fortunate. His job helped him provide for his family and allowed them to live in Silver Spring, Maryland, a community that the photographer considered safe. He admitted that he had peace of mind that his private life—and the lives of his family members—were secure in his December 12, 1941, letter to his wife. "I'm glad that we're not in Berkeley. Also N.Y.C. Not because of any physical danger involved. But because of our peace of mind. We will be in the middle of things—in Washington—and yet have a pleasant place to live. And be quite sure all the time—of the duration—that we will have an income. We should be very—very thankful for our present lot." He asked his wife to consider bringing his mother from Long Beach, California, to the family's home in Silver Spring, Maryland, since blackout conditions had been imposed in that California coastal community. As an enticement, Palmer said that his mother could pack negatives of his pre-war South Pacific images—pictures that Alexa could then print and sell "anywhere—and everywhere while it's worth something. I'd like to sell it all—lock stock and barrel—for a thousand—or two— or three. No reason why we shouldn't."[33]

Palmer's letters from the road did more than keep his wife informed of his activities. They also provided Alexa with a vicarious view of her husband's life. During a March 1942 stay at the U.S. Hotel Chamberlin in Old Point Comfort, Virginia (a building that was taken over during wartime by the federal government and used to house military members and their families), Alfred told Alexa that he had attended a lecture for military personnel that explained why the nation was at war. "It was good," Palmer said, adding, "But one of the boys fell asleep and started to snore. Was he embarrassed when they woke him up. After that lecture—I attended a movie with several officers entitled 'Sex Hygiene.' Oh—my gosh!"[34]

Although Palmer's images were meant to help inform citizens about the war effort and encourage their participation, his near constant travel meant that the photographer was not always well informed about news of the actual war itself. The irony was not lost on Palmer, who acknowledged as much in a December 1941 letter written from Cleveland, Ohio, to his wife. "You probably know a great deal more about the war than I do," he admitted. "I'm busy inside all day. And can't always find time to read the news." But Palmer reiterated, to assuage Alexa's concerns about being a single parent much of the time, that he knew that his position was a plum one. "But I keep thinking we are so damned fortunate. It sort of makes me feel good—by comparison—to have such a good job—such a good family and home—and about as secure a future as anyone in the world," he gratefully acknowledged.[35]

Palmer clearly thrived when undertaking his wartime work. He looked forward to shooting "right down in the dirt" when he arrived at Fort Benning in Georgia, stating in a letter home that the pictures would show his efforts. "No work I've ever done before has given me as much 'lift' as this present job. Watch me go to

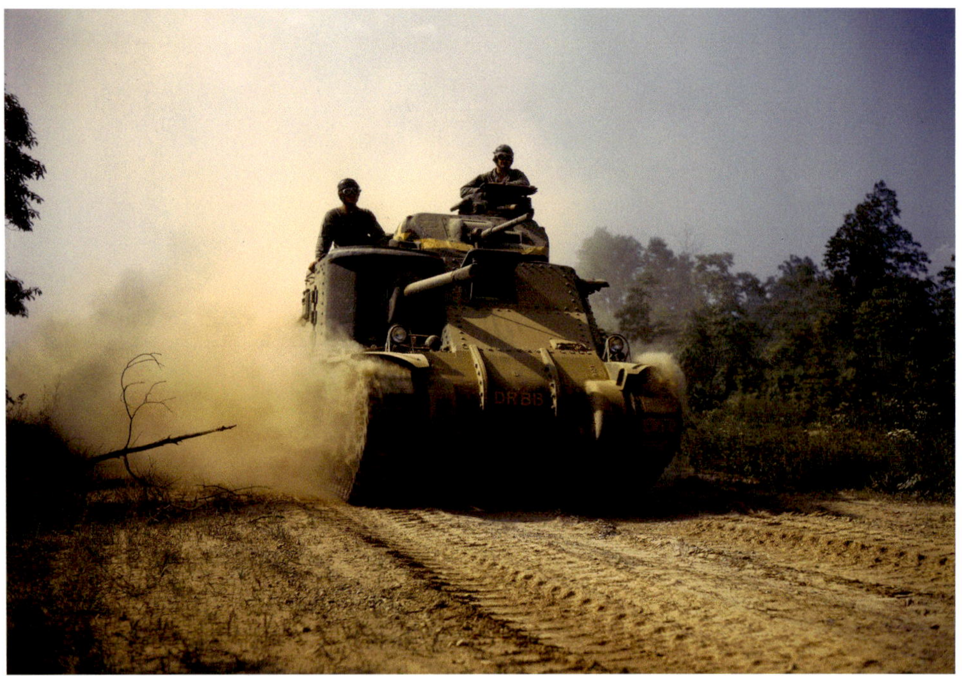

M-3 tanks in action, Ft. Knox, Kentucky, June 1942. (*Library of Congress*)

town," he promised Alexa.[36] That promise would take a few days to realize. Bad weather—a photographer's old nemesis—greeted Palmer's arrival in Georgia. "What a dreary day!" an impatient Alfred told Alexa. "It's raining outside. There's nothing to do inside but read. The town is ten miles away. And has only two shows [i.e., movies]—and I've seen both of them." The rain soon stopped, allowing Palmer to shoot tank maneuvers in a "steamy" atmosphere.[37]

THE PHOTOGRAPHER AS DIPLOMAT

Palmer's perpetual life on the road meant that he was always the new and unknown person in a community. His genuine gregariousness, a necessary personality trait for a self-employed photographer, usually put both his subjects and their superiors at ease. But the range of personalities that Palmer encountered while on the job occasionally required him to engage in as much diplomacy as he could muster. He admitted as much when reflecting on his work to his OEM superiors in 1941, stating: "When visiting these plants it has been necessary not only to be a photographer with a sense of pictorial journalism, but also to be somewhat of a diplomat to get past and around various officials, from Admirals to petty publicity agents who sometimes consider that my work is not of the greatest urgency. I have had very little trouble in convincing such people as to the contrary."[38]

On rare occasions, including during a shoot at the Cincinnati (Ohio) Milling Machine Company, Palmer's professional demeanor and competence as a photographer failed to work as diplomatic overtures. His escort through the Cincinnati factory was the company's own photographer—a man whose work Palmer privately viewed as "quite mediocre." Jealous that an outsider was hired to shoot promotional photographs for the government, the unnamed photographer attempted to keep Palmer from completing his work by taking Palmer out for long lunches that often stretched from noon until almost 3 p.m. After the second such lunch, Palmer recognized the stalling tactic for what it was and realized that he would not finish his work if he did not put a stop to the passive-aggressive treatment. "He knew that I was planning to make four or five dozen shots this day," Palmer told his wife in a letter. "And I had been going good. But thru [*sic*] one device or another he kept me away from the plant until 3 o'clock. And most of the workers quit at four…. He was trying to cut down my production. (Also, the quality of my work)," Palmer added. The two-day job ultimately took three days to complete.[39]

Palmer later learned from the photographer's assistant of his boss's jealousy of Palmer and his well-paid government job. The candid admission led Palmer to muse about whether a post-war career in industrial photography might prove both lucrative and satisfying. His numerous photography assignments in defense plants had given Palmer both the experience and the portfolio material that he would need to succeed. "The field is wide open. And there's good money to be made," he acknowledged in encouraging fashion in a letter to his wife. He added that he knew of one industrial photographer who was bringing home $100,000 a year.

Palmer, who was seriously mulling the work as a post-war career, attempted to persuade Alexa to support his plan by acknowledging her desires to travel and to have her husband home more frequently. "And if I were an industrial photographer, we could choose our customers and our time to work—and our place to live. *And you could go with me*," he emphasized. Palmer added that he planned to begin a scrapbook of industrial images to prove that he was a talented industrial photographer. "My angle now is to plan on the moment this war is ended—and American businessmen are again ready and eager to spend money on advertising and publicity and photographs," he stated. "Uncle Sam—whether he knows it or not—is setting me up in business. He is paying me well to make my future business contacts and to amass complete sets of pictures covering almost every industry. Before I'm through, I plan to know more about more industries than any other photographer in America."[40]

War-wary officials at times impeded Palmer's work. On at least three occasions he ran afoul of police officials, despite his government-issued identification and letters from his supervisors stating who he was, what he was doing, and for what government agency. Police in Youngstown, Ohio, arrested Palmer in November 1941, interrogated him, and tossed him in a cell thinking they had captured a spy. A local newspaper article gave the photographer a sympathetic hearing while simultaneously schooling the police on their mistake, stating: "Palmer probably has taken more 'forbidden' pictures of American defense plants—navy yards, naval vessels, ordnance plants, steel works, powerhouses and others—than any other man in America; for he is official photographer for the Office of Emergency Management and is loaded down with FBI and OEM credentials. But they haven't entirely saved him from trouble."[41]

Palmer's sojourn to Youngstown, as well as to surrounding communities in eastern Ohio and western Pennsylvania, proved successful. He shot images of workers in action at Aetna-Standard Engineering Company's Ellwood City, Pennsylvania, plant; at Westinghouse Electric and Manufacturing Company's Sharon, Pennsylvania, plant; at the Republic Steel Corporation in Youngstown; at Mullins Manufacturing Co., in Warren, Ohio; and at Shenango Pottery Co. in nearby New Castle, Pennsylvania.

The run-in with police at Youngstown was not Palmer's first. Officers in Pittsburgh, Pennsylvania, jumped out of their vehicles and tackled the photographer to the ground, also assuming they had caught a spy, when Palmer was spotted setting up his tripod near steel mills for an evening shoot. Presenting his credentials led the officers to assist Palmer with his work, but police in Kearny, New Jersey, were more wary, arresting then interrogating Palmer for eight hours after he was spotted taking photos of a shipyard from a nearby bridge. The photographer's naval clearance for admission to the facility had not arrived before he reached his destination and Palmer decided to shoot some photos of the shipyard from the bridge to not waste time. Police paid little attention to his federal credentials and only released Palmer once a telegram from his superiors arrived.[42]

Nelson acknowledged the security challenges that photographers like Palmer faced during wartime, telling a reporter for a photo magazine: "We've found it is unsafe these days to wander around the country with a camera, even with a stack of official credentials. A heavy proportion of production now is confidential and police and guards are quick to nab a man spotted taking pictures of industrial exteriors. Once they are identified and admitted, our men are unmolested in making interiors, but many have been picked up at one time or another outside plants."[43]

Bureaucratic red tape in Washington, D.C., also led to occasional frustrations. Palmer's lack of set hours on the road proved problematic for government accountants to understand. After being declined reimbursement for his expenses, Palmer had to involve Nelson to get paid. Palmer's boss, in a June 10, 1942, letter to the agency's fiscal managers, clarified the photographer's "arrival and departure on travel," by explaining the unconventional nature and hours of his work:

> Palmer's customary schedule while shooting is to work all day, as long as light permits, and to spend the evening on negative development. He has to relax sometime and generally picks Sunday to do it. Moreover, his assignments have recently been in Army camps where there is no Public Relations Officer on duty on Sunday. Consequently, he has worked for a portion of the day and relaxed the rest. I think that it [is] perfectly justifiable for him to claim per diem for the Sundays spent

in this fashion because it helps to equalize the very large amount of overtime spent working nights on developing negatives during the week.[44]

Nelson also made clear that his chief photographer's tasks went far beyond his job description as it was written. The photo chief reassured the agency's accountants that the federal government was getting a good value from Palmer's many and varied services, stating:

> I should like to mention that in addition to his own photographic assignments, he is supervising four staff and seven contract photographers; that he plans independently and gets many stories, operating almost entirely on his own initiative and judgement [*sic*] when in the field; that he makes final recommendations about laboratory equipment, supplies, technique, and procedure, and is responsible for final say on the complete technical end of the photographic equipment and processes employed by the Photographic Section.[45]

At times, Palmer was treated as something of a celebrity. His image and a brief cutline adorned the front page of the September 25, 1942, *Skywriter* newsletter produced by North American Aviation. The blurb announced that Palmer was at the company's Inglewood, California, plant the previous week shooting photos of war production.[46]

The following year, editors at newspapers in Michigan's Upper Peninsula voiced their pleasure at Palmer's arrival for a photo shoot for *National Geographic*, claiming his photographs would help publicize the state's often-ignored far northern region. During his visit, Palmer took pictures of war industries, including logging and mining operations, as well as scenery throughout the rural area.[47] An article in the October 8, 1943, issue of the *Escanaba Daily Press* reminded readers of *National Geographic*'s treatment of their region fifteen years previously, stating the Upper Peninsula was "treated in a sketchy and slightly condescending manner." But *Daily Press* reporter Clint Dunathan reminisced that the region's residents "took it all in good part, for they were used to being looked upon as a slightly unpopular stepchild." Palmer's visit, Dunathan said, would finally give the region its due: "For Mr. Palmer came to the Upper Peninsula prepared to stay a few days and shoot a few pictures. He has long overstayed his original time schedule and is still going enthusiastically ahead."[48]

A BRIEF FORAY TO *NATIONAL GEOGRAPHIC*

Palmer's shift from government work to a position as a *National Geographic* staff in mid-1943 came after promotion to a supervisor position at the Office of War Information left him unsatisfied. No longer out in the field taking photographs, Palmer was deskbound in Washington, D.C., in an office in the Social Security building, checking the images that were coming in from his team of OWI photographers, as well as those from military shooters, to select the best ones for distribution to media. "I never regretted it," he said of his transition to supervisor of the News Bureau's photography staff, "but I did miss the action." Selecting other photographer's images to send onto the Pentagon for clearance led Palmer to rethink his government job. "I was doing so little, sitting behind a desk, and the war was going on," he recalled.[49]

Congressional budget cuts were a factor in Palmer's reassignment. The Office of War Information's Domestic Branch had its operating budget slashed from $9 million to $4 million, which forced the agency to engage in restructuring. Many members of Congress never were supportive of government propaganda, while others feared that communists had infiltrated the agency. The latter fear was born of Office of War Information pamphlets that praised minority soldiers and minority defense plant workers, suggesting an equality that many American citizens and politicians were not yet ready to accept.[50]

Faced with an unsatisfying job, Palmer left the OWI in June 1943. Roy Stryker would depart a few months later, in October. Many of his photographers had been drafted or had volunteered for military service. Stryker noted in his resignation letter that the reorganization of operations at the Office of War Information "have made such drastic changes that there is no longer a need for my particular type of talents." He voiced the same dissatisfaction as did Palmer in his resignation, adding: "The reduction of the number of photographers, the decrease in the editorial staff, and the curtailment of distribution functions have changed the position from that of an editorial director to that of an administrative operator."[51]

Wanting a more active career as a photographer, Palmer soon was hired by *National Geographic* based on his pre-war relationship with the magazine's editors. While still a member of the Merchant Marine, Palmer began sending— and selling—images from China, Japan, and the Philippines to the magazine. Some of these photos were published, including a series of pictures taken in Shanghai, China, while others, including this 1935 photograph of a kitten walking across a giant lily pad in the Philippines, were not.

Palmer's foray as a staff photographer at *National Geographic* ultimately proved brief and unsatisfying. The photographer had gone to the magazine with the expectation of starting a documentary film division. And the production work on those films would, of necessity, allow Palmer to sate his wanderlust by again traveling to international locations. "I thought it was more important that I should do that than sit behind a desk, doing nothing, with the OWI," he recalled. The magazine's editors had a different plan, seeing Palmer as a staff photographer, not as a documentary filmmaker. Ultimately, Palmer's plan for an ancillary film division was a vision that was ahead of its time. With the war still on and international travel a difficult prospect, the magazine's editors decided that the timing was not right to engage in film production—a view they would rethink in the postwar period.

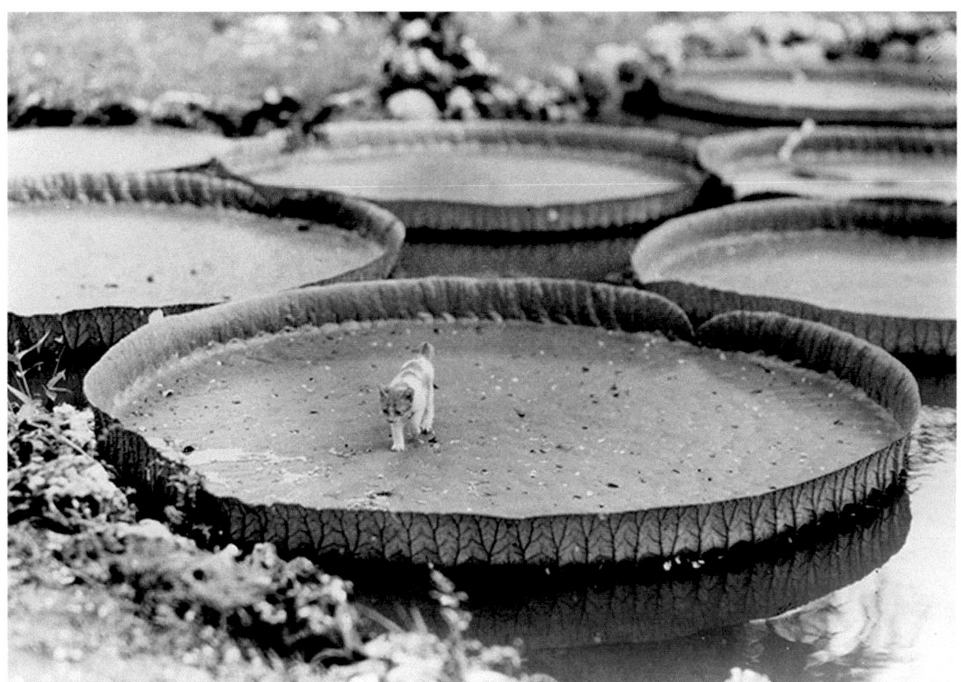

A kitten walking across a floating Victoria water lily pad in the Philippines, 1935. (*A. T. Palmer Collection, privately held*)

PROMOTING THE MERCHANT MARINE'S WARTIME CONTRIBUTIONS

Palmer resigned his position as a staff photographer for *National Geographic* following his assignment in Michigan and spent the rest of 1944 pursuing commercial photography projects before returning to government work once again—this time to the people and the office that first hired him: the U.S. Maritime Commission. Robert Horton had also returned as director of information for the commission, while serving simultaneously in the same position for a "sister" agency, the War Shipping Administration.[52] It was a fortunate turn of events for Palmer, who pitched a final wartime project: a motion picture that promoted and detailed the Merchant Marine's contribution to the war effort.

Without the Merchant Marine, the war might not have been won. The group's sailors were responsible for conveying much of the necessary materials that the nation's military branches needed to fight the war. As Bruce Henrickson states, between December 7, 1941, and V-J day, "nearly 270 million long tons of cargo, three-quarters of it dry cargo[,] was carried from the U.S. to support the war effort."[53] Merchant Marine crew members had paid a heavy price during World War II as they ferried war materials to U.S. servicemen in combat zones: 733 ships were sunk, approximately 6,830 men were killed, 11,000 were wounded, and 604 were taken prisoner—10 percent of whom died in POW camps.[54] Their sacrifices were largely ignored during the war years, however, and Palmer, as a former Merchant Marine quartermaster, found that lack of publicity unacceptable.[55]

Upon his return to the Maritime Commission, Palmer had hoped that the U.S. Navy, Coast Guard, and Marine Corps would supply the necessary film footage that could be edited into such a film, but when that failed to happen, Palmer pitched the film idea to Horton. Horton quickly agreed, and the two men went to Admiral Land to approve the project. The admiral, who was the force behind America's rapid ship building program prior to America's involvement in the war, was the right person for Palmer and Horton to approach. Land served as both chairman of the U.S. Maritime Commission and as the administrator of the War Shipping Administration.[56] Described by the *New York Times* as a "peppery man with an active dislike of red tape and stuffed shirts," Land quickly approved the film following a meeting with Palmer and Horton.[57]

Horton and Palmer did not have any difficulty selling Land on the project. The admiral had previously written to Admiral William D. Leahy, the chief of staff to the commander-in-chief of the U.S. Army and Navy, on August 18, 1944, requesting "adequate" press coverage of the Merchant Marine's wartime activities in combat zones. Leahy had punted on the issue, however, telling Land that various war theater commanders "had different ideas" on publicity. Leahy stated the project's details should be worked out between Land's public relations personnel and public relations officers attached to the War Department and the U.S. Navy.[58]

A letter to Palmer from Land—dated January 16, 1945—made the Merchant Marine project official. Land directed the photographer to promptly "proceed to San Francisco," where the photographer would report to the regional director of the War Shipping Administration for assignment to a vessel. Palmer was given the title of technical director and was to be accompanied by Sergeant Robert W. Russell. Palmer's final directions from the admiral revealed that all the film footage shot was "classified as confidential and not subject to inspection or review until it is delivered into the hands of Security Officer, War Shipping Administration, Washington, D.C., through appropriate War Shipping Administration Channels." Land added two important caveats at the end of his letter. The first gave Palmer free reign on the film's subject matter and focus. "You are authorized to make whatever film shots of merchant marine, naval and military activities, installations and equipment as you think necessary to carry out this project," Land's order stated. The second point demonstrated the admiral's support for the film. "Any difficulties which you may encounter in carrying out this project are to be reported to me immediately by cable," Land added.[59]

One difficulty quickly became apparent: no funds had been provided to make the film. Palmer brought his own cameras, but he and Horton also managed to acquire "70,000 feet of outdated, or expiring 16mm Kodachrome" and seven "expendable cameras … a bunch of junk," in Palmer's opinion, from the U.S. Naval Air Station Anacostia, in Washington, D.C. Once Palmer, Horton, and Russell arrived in

San Francisco, they began searching for a ship to board by studying the bulletin board at the War Shipping Administration's office at 220 Bush Street. The ship's destinations were not listed due to national security concerns; however, Palmer's intuition led him to choose the *Hannibal Victory*. The ship had recently been completed at Henry J. Kaiser's Richmond, California, shipyard and was ready for her maiden voyage. Once Palmer learned that the ship had a cargo of locomotives, "we knew damn well it was headed for the Philippines."[60]

The photographer's desire to publicize his former Merchant Marine shipmates at war took him on his one and only sojourn into a combat zone during the conflict, an assignment which understandably worried his wife. Although the Battle of Leyte Gulf (October 23–26, 1944) largely crippled Japanese naval power and allowed American forces to begin their liberation of the Philippines, General Douglas MacArthur would not pronounce the Philippine islands as formally liberated until July 5, 1945. Even then, pockets of resistance remained.[61]

Palmer attempted to allay Alexa's concerns in a January 30, 1945, letter from Oakland, California. "We are still here—and plan to be here for several days more. So rest your fears. By the time we get out to the Philippines the fighting will be over. And the Philippines is the end of the run—for us," he said, before offering more reassurance that the ship on which he would be traveling is "a brand-new Victory ship—on her maiden voyage." Palmer said he would be quartered in the hospital area "with plenty of space and a private bath. We couldn't ask for more—just like a cabin on a passenger ship."[62]

Security concerns meant that Palmer could not tell his family about the specifics of the project, nor reveal his destination once he boarded the ship, both moot points since the photographer had already revealed the project and his intended destination to his wife via the letter he wrote from Oakland. But he used the military censorship that followed to gently tease his wife in a letter dated March 10, 1945. "We are almost there," Palmer wrote. "Where is there? Well, I can't tell you. But it is not Cairo, or Chungking, or London."[63] A follow-up letter written "In Port" on March 22 also was subject to the same vagaries of wartime censorship. The photographer, therefore, could provide few specifics of his project to his family, telling them: "We are getting what we came after—and things are becoming more and more interesting."[64]

The letters, while lacking specifics, were meant to provide a sense of reassurance to Palmer's family that he was alive and well. A March 23, 1945, letter, for example, stated: "We are just about halfway thru [*sic*] with our work," which provided the photographer's family a glimmer of a timeline. The nature of the project coupled with the need for secrecy led Palmer to pen one of his shortest wartime letters to his family. Before closing, he stated: "I've reached that point when I don't seem to have much to say that will not be censored." Hoping to return stateside by early May, Palmer attempted to lift his family's spirits with his homecoming plans, stating "I'm looking forward to doing a lot of things around the house with the help of my two big boys. And maybe we can get a real boat to take you girls sailing in."[65]

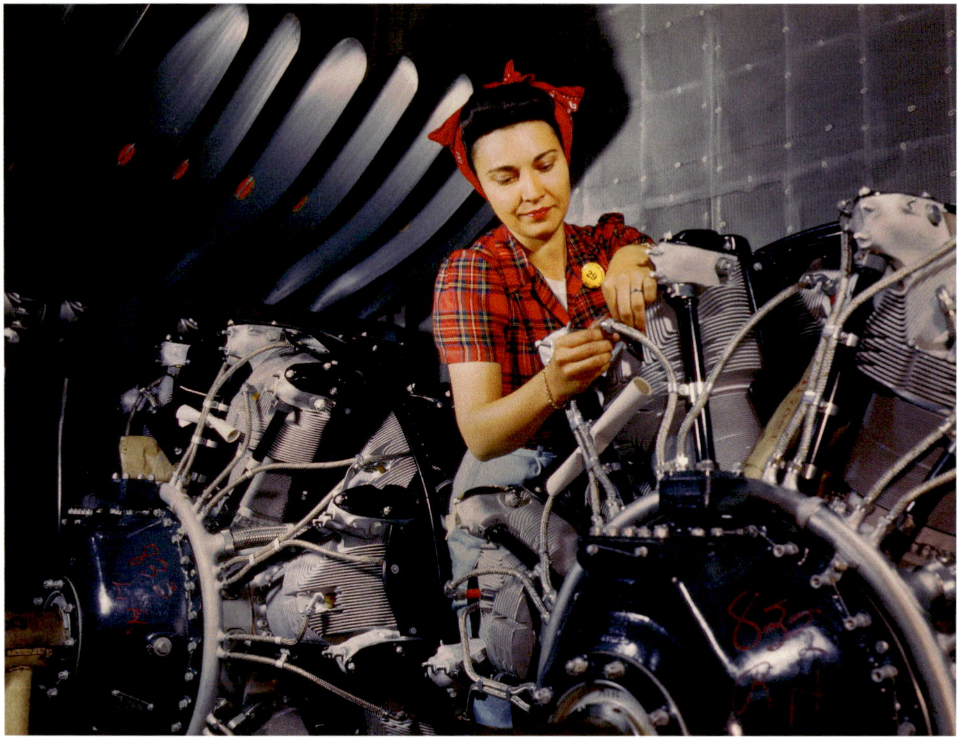

A woman working on an airplane motor at North American Aviation, Inc., plant in California, October 1942. (*Library of Congress*)

Palmer's letters home could not reveal a brutal truth—the photographer filmed the evacuation of British and American POWs who had been held at the notorious Santo Tomas internment camp in Manila, a former university and the largest of several concentration camps run by the Japanese military in the Philippines.[66] "There were 4,000 people, many of whom had been severely beaten by the guards shortly before the surrender," Palmer recalled later. "It was a damn brutal time."[67]

The project would be Palmer's last wartime work for the federal government. With the conflict over, Palmer soon moved his family back to California and resumed his commercial photography career, again focusing on maritime photography for several shipping lines, including APL (American President Lines) and the Matson Navigation Company, while also undertaking work for advertising agencies. But his wartime forays into filmmaking helped hone Palmer's visual storytelling skills and he would pursue both still photography and documentary filmmaking work for clients in the United States and in Asian nations for the final four decades of his career.

5

A PHOTOGRAPHIC ASSESSMENT

Many of Palmer's black-and-white images were marked by a strong tonal range, while his Kodachrome popped with color. The photographs demonstrate that Palmer was a master of flash photography who often used the Chiaroscuro technique—that is, strong contrasts between light and dark—to highlight his subjects in dramatic fashion. Although it is unclear where Palmer learned the technique, that aesthetic, along with tight framing, was used in the 1930s by photographer Edward Steichen to stress beauty in fashion photography shoots for *Vogue* and *Vanity Fair*, both highly popular and influential magazines.[1] Palmer undoubtedly saw—and studied—the images in these popular magazines, but his prewar work for advertising agencies and corporations, including still photography and motion pictures, also contributed to the photographer's knowledge of lighting. His commercial work for the federal government, like Steichen's work for fashion magazines and for the U.S. Navy during the war, is proof that art and commercial impulses do not have to be in opposition to each other.

The photographer's pre-war experiences as a member of the Merchant Marine and as a commercial photographer led Palmer to be as comfortable in factories as he was in shipyards and at military bases. He was used to working independently and clearly enjoyed the travel. Although the photographer never referred to himself as an artist, he was drawn to beauty. Many of the photographs that Palmer took in Japan, China, and the Philippines, as well as in South Pacific island nations, reveal a romantic interest in sunsets, fishing boats, geishas, and temples. A short biographical sketch that Palmer provided for *Fortune* magazine's 1940 "Salon of Photography" exhibit at the Rochester, New York, Museum of Arts and Sciences noted that he "like[d] beauty, and anything structural—including structural quality in a landscape." Those interests often came to the fore in his wartime photography.[2]

Palmer intuitively understood that cameras could capture people and objects in ways in which the human eye could not. "You must remember that the camera lens is very critical and catches every detail. Whereas the human eye does no such thing," Palmer told his wife in a January 27, 1945, letter.[3] The coaching tip to his wife, who was working on developing her own photography skills at the time, reveals that Palmer could see photographically. And much like Steichen, Palmer imbued his assignments for the federal government with his own aesthetic sense of glamour, while also providing his government supervisors what they desired: photographs that spoke to the public on an emotional level. Most of the subjects of Palmer's photographs are not named—and purposely so—as they served as often-heroic archetypes who represented the soul and spirit of the nation, average Americans who toiled hard to protect their country during a time when the need for national defense was exceptionally high. The photographs also proved that for all his curiosity about the world around him and his love of travel, particularly to Asia, Alfred T. Palmer was first and foremost a patriotic American.

His wartime photographs also reveal several other aesthetic techniques and stylistic motifs that were popular in the 1920s and 1930s in advertising, including a classical approach that stressed capturing timeless beauty, and a modernist approach that employed "sharp angles, geometric forms, and streamlined silhouettes suggestive of the dynamic movement of the new society." Art directors at advertising agencies often sought to "create an aura of style" around the products they were promoting and often used "higher art" to create allure, especially if the product did not have it.[4] For example, in December 1927, the Ford Motor Company hired noted painter and photographer Charles Sheeler to take pictures as part of an advertising campaign for the Model A car. Sheeler, who was particularly drawn to architecture and often portrayed the angles and geometric shapes of buildings, spent six weeks in December 1927 and January 1928 at the Ford Motor Company's River Rouge plant in Dearborn, Michigan. Sheeler's modernist impulses led him to produce thirty-two photographs that celebrated industrialism by depicting "gleaming, massive machinery, rather than the human process of labor." The photographs, Jessica Murphy notes, "celebrate the company's—and, by association, America's—

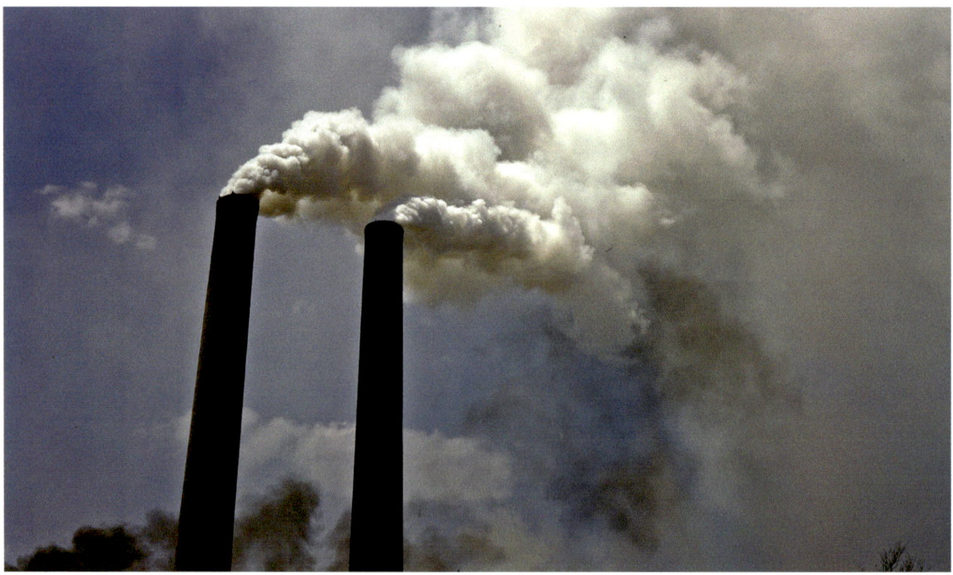

Smokestacks (no location), 1942. (*Library of Congress*)

ideals of power and productivity…"[5] Palmer embraced similar themes of power and productivity in his photographs for the Office for Emergency Management and the Office of War Information. Like Sheeler, Palmer was drawn to the angles and geometric shapes in the manufacturing of the military goods, but he also captured electric lines, smokestacks, and dam construction in his quest to visually depict the nation's industrial strength.

THE LANGUAGE OF COLOR

Palmer's Kodachrome images are particularly striking, both to modern viewers as well as to individuals who saw them during the war years. Kodachrome had been on the market since 1935 for motion picture cameras and debuted in 1936 for still photography use. The public was acquainted with color imagery prior to Kodachrome's development, however. Technological advancements had made the use of color possible in advertisements, posters, magazines, and comics since the late 1800s, but the process was expensive, and the quality of the reproductions often varied. Another important technological change, the development of the halftone process in 1880, allowed for the inexpensive reproduction of photographs. Magazines increasingly became a forum for color advertisements in the decades prior to World War II as improvements in printing presses allowed high quality reproduction of color illustrations. Advertising executives and art directors soon realized that color helped sell products; it appealed to the senses and made consumer goods of all types look more alluring.[6]

The development of Kodachrome film, therefore, proved a boon for Palmer and other wartime photographers, as well as for federal officials who directed the promotional efforts at various federal agencies. They no longer had to sell a war in black and white. Certainly, members of the public were used to the consistent tonal reproduction of black-and-white images across various forms of mass media, but color provided a new language that federal officials unabashedly used to help persuade the public of their need to take part in the war effort. And as Palmer's photographs reveal, the photographer understood how to use color in ways that appealed to the public's emotions and motivated them toward the wartime actions that government officials sought, including taking blue collar factory jobs that previously had seemed uninviting and uninteresting. He made those jobs appear exciting and patriotic, understanding that color reaches emotional places in viewers that black-and-white imagery does not.

Palmer also knew—or instinctively understood—that viewers react to the two different modes of photography—black-and-white and color—in distinctly different ways. He knew that photography is a form of communication and that it conveys ideas no less than does written language. Black-and-white photographs appealed to viewers' intellect, while color imagery appealed to their emotions. Furthermore, Palmer, as a photographer, wanted to communicate clearly and to the point with his photographs. With a good eye for his subjects and careful framing, he eliminated anything that detracted from the viewer or reader understanding the meaning behind his images.

The photographer realized that when he shot in color, the first thing people reacted to was the color itself. Then viewers took in the subjects of the photographs. Therefore, a photograph with a lot of red received an immediate and excited reaction by the viewer, while blue receives a reaction of serenity, a calming emotion. Green, the color of much of nature, gets another calm emotional response from viewers. Of course, most photographs have all the colors. The question is, which is dominant in the image? All of this is to say, in the viewer's eyes, there is a lot more going on in a color photograph than just the subject.

By comparison, black-and-white photography has no color to which the viewer or reader can react. The emotional kick comes from the content, the subject. Of course, black-and-white imagery has its own language: contrast, tonality, grain, etc. But the viewer does not have to deal with the emotions evoked by colors. In Palmer's color photographs, the photographer is very aware of color as language, a language that can be used—that is, made dominant—to excite. He used strong colors: reds, yellows, and blues. For example, when Palmer photographed an airplane engine's cowling, he lit it directly to bring out the color. When he photographed workers, especially women, he had them wear a red bandana or sweater. None of this is accidental; he knew what colors worked to achieve the correct emotional reaction by the public who would view his work.

Palmer also recognized that there are elements of a photograph that a viewer reacts to other than the color. Yet he was worlds ahead of his contemporaries

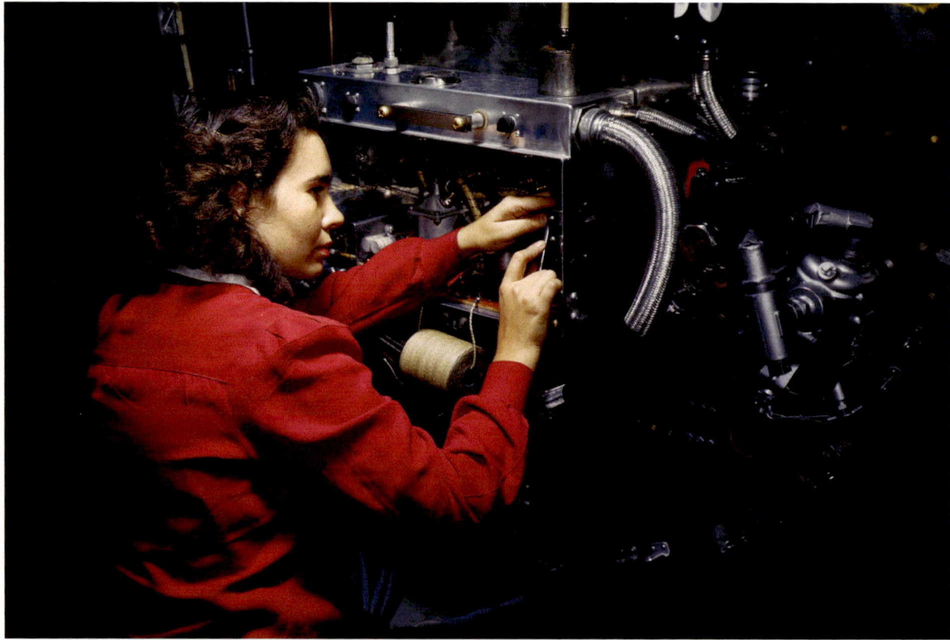

Switch boxes on the firewalls of B-25 bombers are assembled by women workers at North American Aviation, Inc.'s Inglewood, California, plant, October 1942. (*Library of Congress*)

in using color. When comparing Palmer's black-and-white photos housed in the Library of Congress to his color photos of similar subjects, such as workers at airplane factories, his "voice" was strongest in color. Palmer knew that black-and-white photography helped convey facts strongly, especially after the major inroads that the FSA photographers had made in making people believe what they were seeing, while color photography is about physical stimulation of the eyes and the stimulation and motivation of the viewers of his images.

While it is unclear whose idea it was for Palmer to shoot in Kodachrome as well as in black-and-white, the resulting images, used in posters and other forms of propaganda media, helped stimulate and energize the public emotionally. Palmer's photos certainly were propaganda, but they served more than an informational purpose; the images also entertained because he knew the "language of color" and understood when and where to apply his talents to making color images instead of black-and-white. Whether the photographer had ever studied art history or visited some of the world's museums that held paintings done by Renaissance artists or Dutch masters is unknown, but many of his color images look as though he considered and applied in his own work the lighting and the color design "language" inherent in those paintings, creating his own American industrial masterpieces.

A CRAFTSMAN AND TALENTED TECHNICIAN

From a technical standpoint, Palmer's craftsmanship as a photographer is particularly evident in the color images that he shot during the 1940s. While black-and-white photography can be one or two f-stops off—a leeway called "latitude"—and an acceptable print can still be made, the same cannot be said for color film; its latitude is plus or minus a half f-stop. In other words, if Palmer or any other photographer using color film was more than one half f-stop off, the images were unusable. Because the Kodachrome film that Palmer used had to be sent to a Kodak facility for development, there was pressure on Palmer to get his images right blindly—a pressure that contemporary photographers could not even imagine—since he had no ability to see his finished work for days and had already moved on to the next job.

Palmer and his work were highly praised during the war years by government officials. "I have just finished looking at your Allegheny enlargements and comparing them shot for shot with the ones previously made by Farm Security," William Nelson stated in an August 13, 1941, letter to the photographer. "The contrast is amazing and I intend to use this set as a convincing demonstration of the fact that your work is far superior to any government lab in Washington, and as a matter of fact, far superior to any work I have ever seen anywhere."[7] Another official, Ned Evans from the War Production Drive Headquarters Division of Information, was equally enamored of Palmer's work, saying so in a December 14, 1942, letter to Otto Gilmore, chief of Photographic Services at the Office of War Information. Evans lauded Palmer's work and called him "an excellent photographer ... [who] has that rare sense of what makes a good picture. I want to go on record that his work for us yesterday was magnificent."[8]

Palmer preferred using his large format Graflex and Speed Graphic cameras for much of his wartime photography work, although he did use a 35-mm Contax rangefinder camera on some jobs. Some prominent photographers of the era, including *Life* magazine's Carl Mydans and FSA photographers Russell Lee and Arthur Rothstein, grew to favor 35-mm cameras for their portability and for the ease of loading the camera with a film roll, rather than using cameras that either had to be regularly reloaded with a single sheet negative or were the twin lens reflex types like the Rolleiflex, that could only produce twelve images per roll. The Graflex and Speed Graphic cameras were heavier and slower to work with, and the film holder held just two sheets, one on each side of the holder. Despite the slower, more cumbersome process, the Graflex, with its 5-inch by 7-inch film, and the Speed Graphic, which produced a 4-inch by 5-inch negative, provided higher resolution images than did their 35-mm counterparts. The larger the negative, the less the image would be enlarged and thus the better the reproduction quality would be. That, in turn, produced better quality photographs for reproduction in newspapers, magazines, posters, and billboards. As a result, the Speed Graphic, also referred to popularly as a "press camera," remained the choice of most photojournalists and commercial photographers from its invention in 1928 through the mid-1950s.

Most of the images Palmer shot during the war years in factories, on military bases, and in other locales were posed and styled. He set up his lights as his subjects worked, having them stop just briefly to pose. Sometimes the photographer

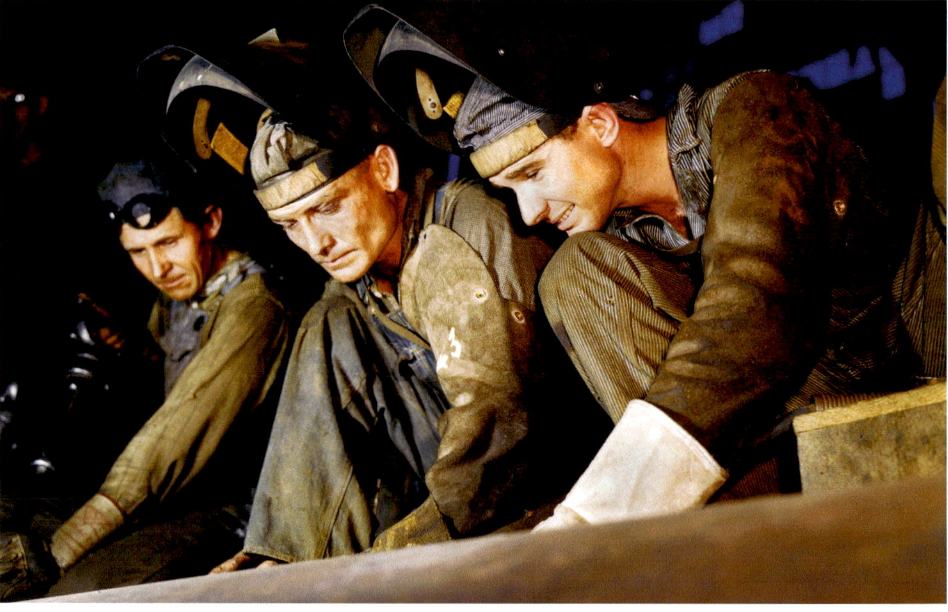

Welders making boilers for a ship, Combustion Engineering Co., Chattanooga, Tennessee, June 1942. (*Library of Congress*)

requested that areas be cleaned, or a coat of paint be applied to a piece of machinery to make a more attractive image. Palmer noted that company officials always were happy to help him get the best images possible. "Right away I always got cooperation to cover up some negative quality in a photograph," he acknowledged.[9]

Palmer's photographs reveal that he used key visual techniques that photographers learn to make their photographs stronger. He noticed the light (quality as well as quantity), got close (or closer) to his subjects, watched out for any distractions in the background, and considered changing his angle-of-view so that their photographs look more dynamic. Indeed, his images demonstrate his mastery of lighting. His images had punch to them, not just because of the subject, but also because of the lighting on the subject. His photographs almost always displayed dramatic qualities. He rarely did not get close enough to his subjects and there was nothing in his frame that was accidental or cluttered—that is, nothing to distract from the main subject he was shooting. When Palmer shot images of people (workers producing military materials, soldiers engaged in training, etc.), he often got as close as he could to his subjects, but because he knew that his images would be used for purposes of persuasion, he usually pulled back to a medium shot, rather than a close-up. Commercial photographers often must make this compromise to satisfy their client's demand to sell a product.

In his mission to make powerful and motivating images, Palmer also often photographed from a low angle, as many photographers learn to do. Why was this a common and preferred practice? First, often, in the factories and on the military bases in which he worked, his subjects were large: tanks, airplanes, cannons, ships, engines, etc. When he first encountered them, standing on the floor of the plant or at a drydock, he had to look up. But this reality does not completely explain his decision to photograph from a low angle. Certainly, the photographer could have gotten a forklift or a scaffold to get him up to eye level, but he knowingly chose to not to do that when shooting such subjects.

To show the enormity of the equipment, he kept his place at ground level and tilted his Speed Graphic upward. By doing so, the images Palmer produced did not just display the facts (i.e., a new bomber was constructed, a new ship was ready for launch). Instead, he was adding an emotional component to his images, displaying the power or majesty of what he was photographing. He captured imposing machines of war, and they were built to be imposing. Whether Palmer might have considered what the enemy might think when seeing a Palmer photograph of a B-24 bomber or a new naval ship is unknown. Palmer's intent was to show power and strength. The angles he chose achieved that. In addition, by taking a low angle, a photographer often can avoid clutter in the background. One sees this in Palmer's photos. He uses the empty sky as a background or the vast and empty space of a factory ceiling.

Shooting a subject from a low angle also gives a sense of nobility to the subject. After all, looking up is subconsciously a reverential point of view, looking up is where we look when we think of a supreme being. Palmer knew, both intellectually and intuitively, that looking up, aiming his camera skyward, would add a touch of the sacred to his photos. When a photographer like Palmer aimed his camera up

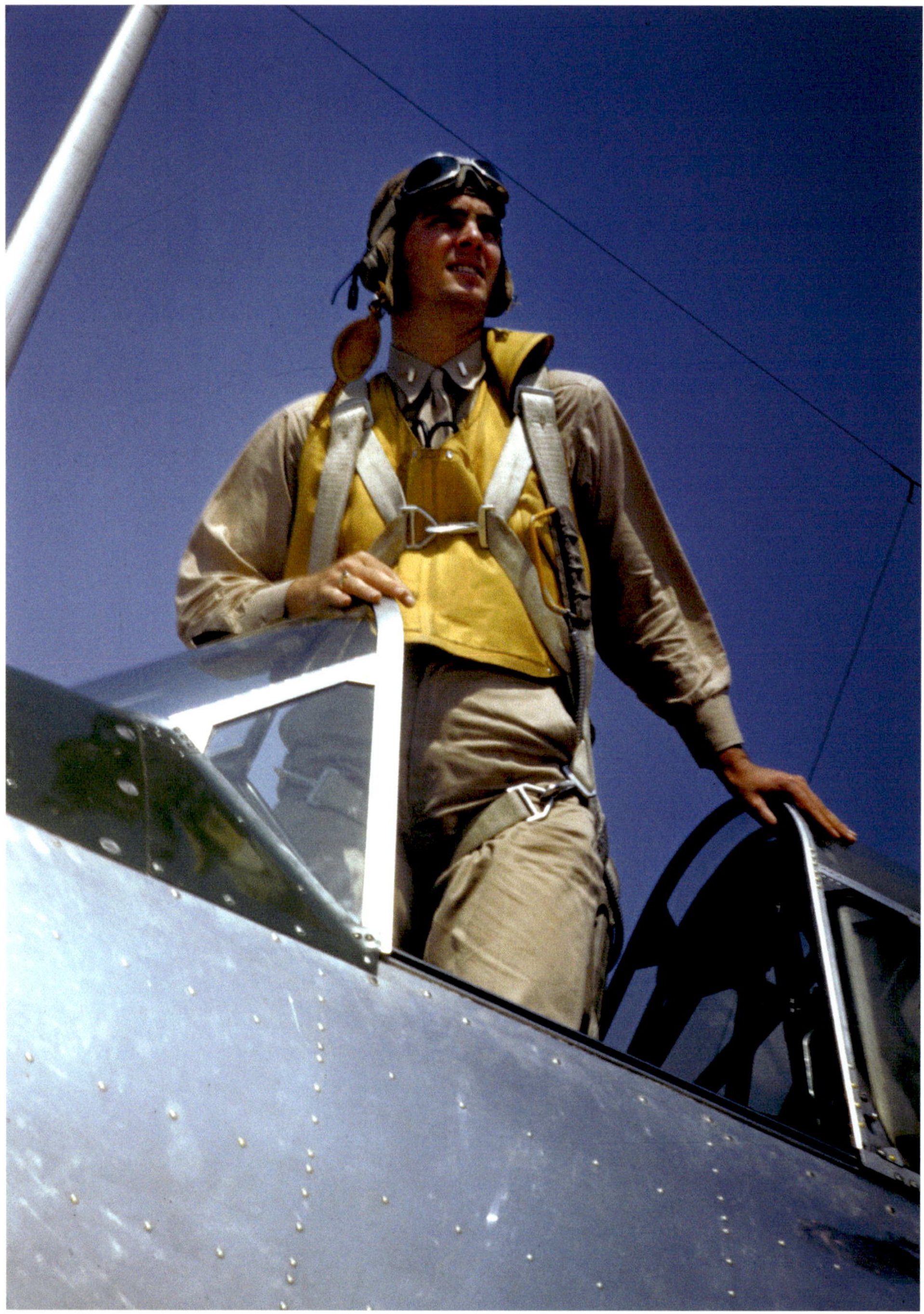

Marine Corps lieutenant studying glider piloting at Page Field, Parris Island, South Carolina, May 1942. (*Library of Congress*)

at an image, the resulting photograph forces viewers to feel smaller, lesser, than the object that was shot. This compositional technique does not always work, however. For some subjects, even, it would be inappropriate. But when it was appropriate, Palmer pounced on it. It is clear, from his numerous uses of low-angle photographs, that Palmer's shooting angles were thoughtful and intentional.

A SKILLFUL VISUAL IMAGINATION

Palmer's images in the Library of Congress reveal that like most photographers he used a technique called bracketing, meaning that he shot one image that was overexposed, one that was underexposed, and one shot "in the middle." The rich colors, strong contrasts, and skillful lighting apparent in Palmer's color images provide proof of his strong technical capabilities, great visual imagination, and artistic sensibility, but his skillfulness as a photographer is further demonstrated by a key reality of 1940s photography, namely, that he had no ability to proof his photographs as did photographers in later decades. Palmer had no monitor to check his work, nor were Polaroids in existence then as a form of proofing.

Palmer's photographs, including this image of a female worker at the Consolidated-Vultee plant in Nashville, Tennessee, demonstrate a different aesthetic approach to documenting the war effort from that of the FSA photographers.

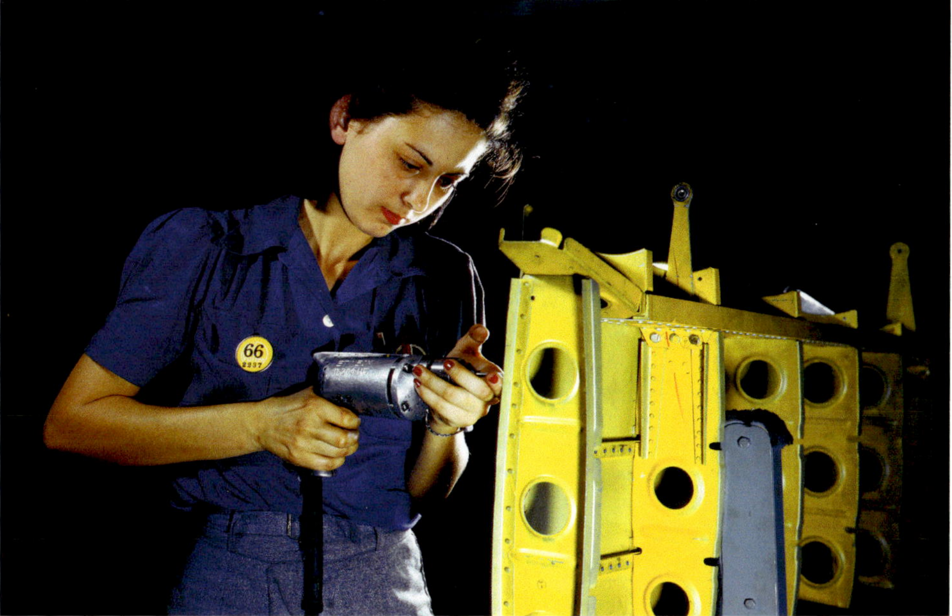

Drilling horizontal stabilizers: operating a hand drill, this female worker at Vultee-Nashville is shown working on the horizontal stabilizer for a Vultee Vengeance dive bomber, Tennessee, February 1943. (*Library of Congress*)

The photograph reveals that Palmer did not display the presumed empathy that was the hallmark of FSA photographers, but instead relied on his craft skills to produce images that were slick and colorful, and that demonstrated his ability to light subjects for dramatic effect. Prior to the war, Palmer had employed these same skills to make ships look powerful and glamorous, which, in turn, made ship travel appear desirable. This image also reflects Palmer's trademark style of powerful color, Chiaroscuro lighting, attractive models, and the use of props to tell the story. His modernistic style of photography is still in use today in industrial and advertising photography.

But his inability to proof his photographs required Palmer to visualize how the final photograph would appear—and he made it so. He did not capture his subjects in the millisecond of time—the so-called "Decisive Moment" of Henri Cartier-Bresson—in the photojournalistic way that so occupied such FSA photographers as Dorothea Lange, Arthur Rothstein, or Russell Lee. He had a job to do, and he was the master of the image. And because Palmer could not develop his own color photographs, he could not—and, therefore, did not—rely on darkroom techniques to manipulate the lighting or contrast in his images as did his first mentor, Ansel Adams, who relied upon darkroom work to enhance the what one photo scholar has called the "artistic interpretation" of his photographs.[10] The quality of the artistry inherent in Palmer's photographs, therefore, was the result of his high technical skills and great visual imagination in pursuit of the very serious objectives of federal wartime propaganda agencies.

Palmer employed the Chiaroscuro technique by using a main light, a secondary light, and often a background light, while rendering the background dark to "set off" the main subject. The photographer perfected the technique of rendering

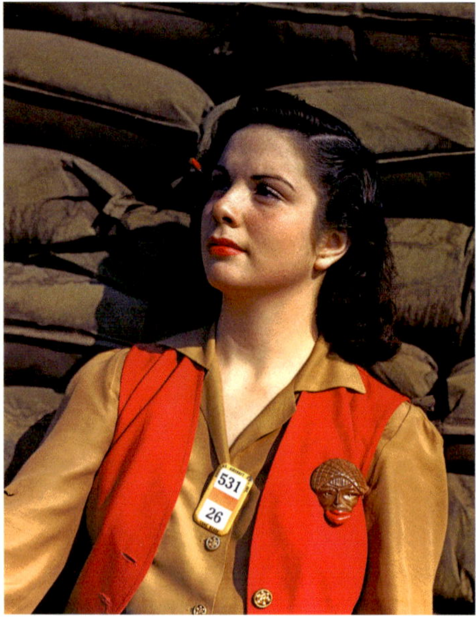

A noontime rest for a full-fledged assembly worker at the Long Beach, California, plant of Douglas Aircraft Company, October 1942. (*Library of Congress*)

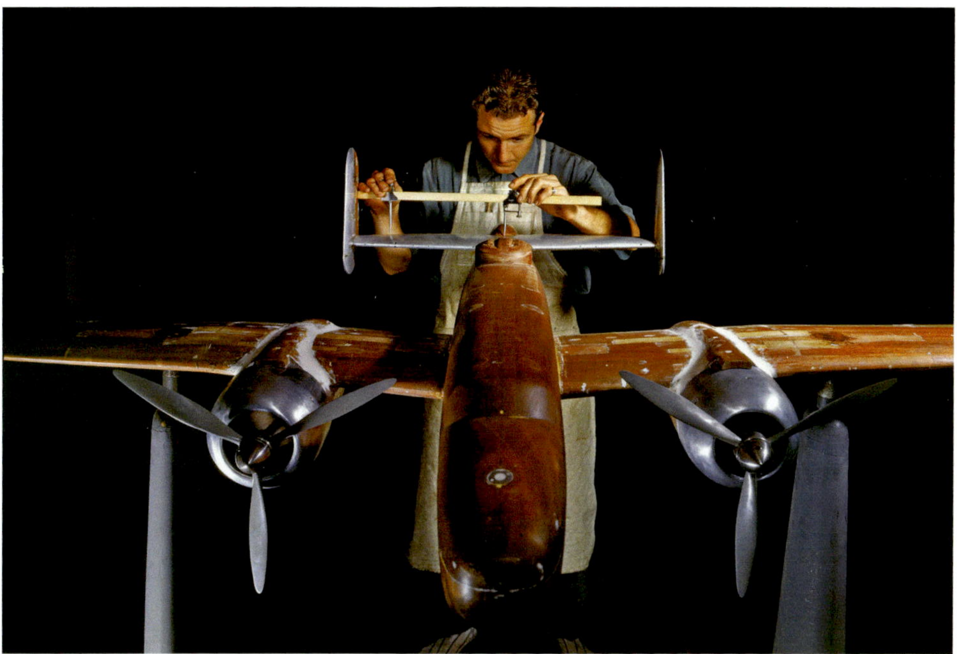

An experimental scale model of the B-25 plane is prepared for wind tunnel tests in the plant of the North American Aviation, Inc., Inglewood, California, October 1942. The model maker holds an exact miniature reproduction of the type of bomb the plane will carry. (*Library of Congress*)

backgrounds dark so that his subject was isolated and dramatic. He did this by underexposing the background by several f-stops and then using his artificial lights—strobes in the case of this image, taken at North American Aviation's plant—to light the main subject. In this photograph, Palmer was using only two lights: the main light is to camera right, probably a widespread floodlight. The second light is to camera left, placed very low and aiming up. His lighting technique was unconventional in the early 1940s. He was working without art direction and was doing what most advertising/commercial photographers and art directors would be wary of doing for fear of shocking their clients and resulting in rejection. Being alone on the job was, it appears, a major asset for Palmer, allowing him to innovate and create a rare aesthetic look for the era.

The image of the model maker, like many other photographs taken of defense plant workers, is obviously staged. If these were photographs done by a journalist, these factory images would be breaking the stringent rules of the National Press Photographer's Association (NPPA). Although informational in intent, Palmer's images are not journalism. His photographs are commercial images achieved with the highest skills, to sell the idea that factory work was desirable work, that it was an interesting thing to do, and, additionally, that the government was hyper-engaged in the production of armaments to win the war.

The quality of Palmer's lighting and the clarity of his images, shot on the highest resolution Kodachrome film and done in large format size, gave a crispness, a powerful-looking energy, to his imagery. The photographs themselves look slick, cool, and modern. Palmer's photographs ended the stark and serious aesthetic of the previous decade that rendered the Great Depression in bleak black-and-white.

The photographer took his established lighting technique outdoors, underexposing the background and then powering up his lights so they become the main light, rather than the sun. He did this for dramatic effect. This image of the carpenter at the TVA's Douglas Dam is obviously posed, as are almost all of Palmer's wartime industrial images. The posed nature of the photographs again diverges from the aesthetic established by the FSA's Roy Stryker and his photographers. The FSA aesthetic was largely a photojournalistic aesthetic: no posing, no direction, capture life as it happens, use only available light—unless there is not enough light.

Palmer's approach was not to render the truth without alteration, but, rather, it was to make whatever he was shooting look as powerful as possible, using any means available. He was after a poetic truth. Palmer was utilizing the latest technologies of color film and electronic lighting. And, as previously stated, he chose attractive-looking workers who served as models who would best sell war work to the American public. He also used color as part of his statement. Color was a new visual area to explore in 1942—more easily produced in wartime via

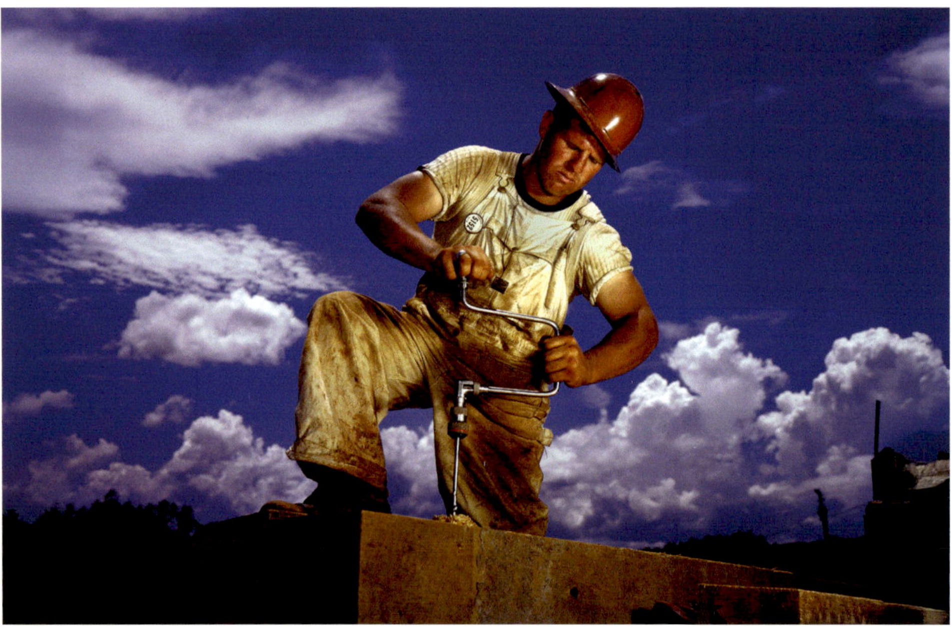

Carpenter at work on Douglas Dam, Tennessee (TVA), June 1942. This dam will be 161 feet high and 1,682 feet long, with a 31,600-acre reservoir area extending 43 miles upstream. (*Library of Congress*)

Kodachrome than any previous or subsequent color processes. It was and shall always be thought of by photographers as the premier color film. Given the new paths in photography, Palmer was ending the dominant aesthetic of the past decade and establishing a brand-new one, pioneering color and lighting usages that prevailed for the next forty years.

Users of color film had two options from which to choose: color negative film from which prints could be made and color transparency film. There is no negative from the latter, yet it was the preferred choice by many photographers for reproduction because color transparency film has no intermediate step necessary. In other words, photographers did not have to make a print. The image could be directly transferred from the transparency to the printing press process; thus, its reproduction was sharper than it would be from capture to negative to print to press. Kodacolor, the first color negative film introduced by Kodak, was manufactured from 1942 to 1963 (with later variations made all the way up to 1985). Palmer used color transparency work exclusively for his World War II imagery.

The image of the two women workers at Vultee's Nashville facility is a classic Palmer photograph in style and technique. He is using his standard two light setup, with a main light to the right and a less powerful fill light, possibly diffused, to the left/front. Here he adds a smaller "kicker" light to the left and parallel to the tubing, skimming the tubes, which is the standard way of revealing texture.

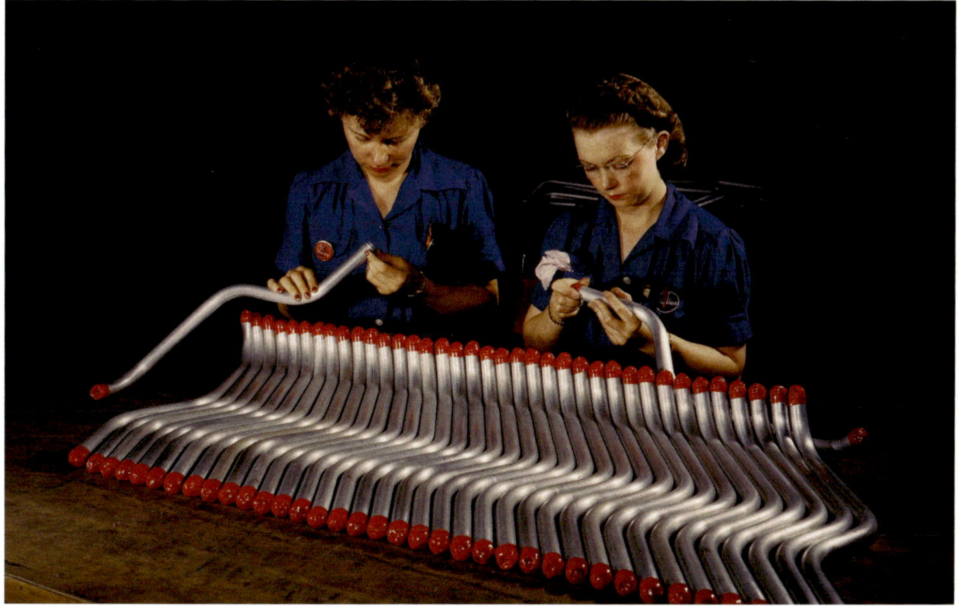

Capping and inspecting tubing: two women are shown capping and inspecting tubing which goes into the manufacture of the Vengeance dive bomber made at Vultee's Nashville division, Tennessee, February 1943. (*Library of Congress*)

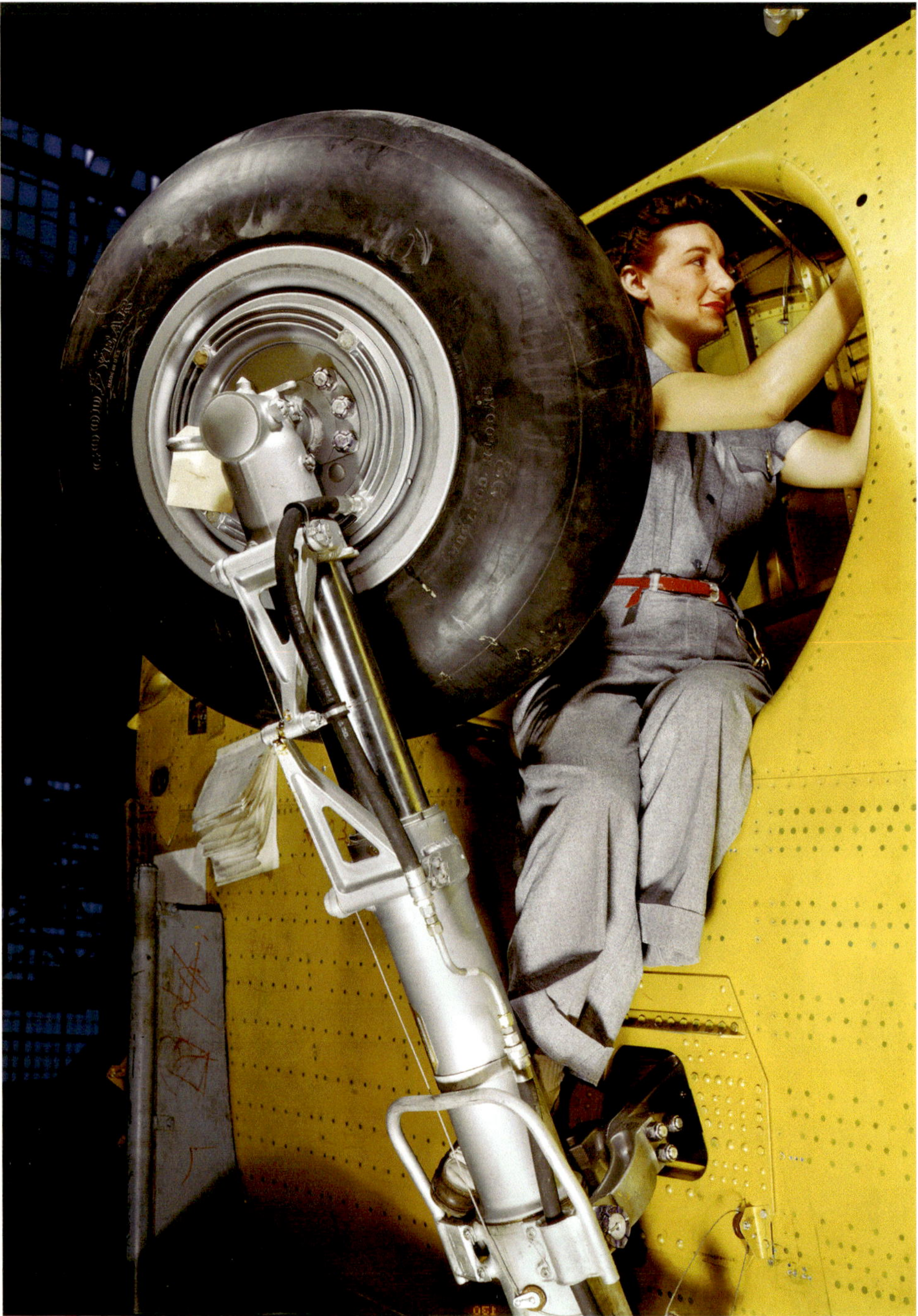

This female worker at the Vultee-Nashville is shown making final adjustments in the wheel well of an inner wing before the installation of the landing gear, Nashville, Tennessee, February 1943. This is one of the numerous assembly operations in connection with the mass production of Vultee Vengeance dive bombers. (*Library of Congress*)

The women are posed, as is the case in almost all of Palmer's wartime photographs. It would have been impossible to pose the women in a factory if they were engaged in assembly line work because the posing would have stopped the workflow. Palmer would have had to engage in the photojournalism style of "run and gun"—meaning using a much smaller camera (thus less reproduction clarity/quality) and a hand-held flash (which would have rendered more "truth" but less attractiveness to the final photograph)—to have achieved assembly line photographs. It is obvious that Palmer not only posed his subjects but gave them time—and possibly advance instruction—on how to appear: clean, perfect hair (nothing frazzled-looking), nice make-up, a well-done manicure, and, even, at times, polished shoes. This is an acceptable way to style a photo when the intent is to promote the product. Palmer was working in a brand-new aesthetic of promotion and persuasion. He wanted his photographs to be gorgeous, and he made sure the people in them were as well.

The image of the female worker adjusting a wheel well is a rare vertical photograph by Palmer, who recognized that the subject itself was vertical. By 1943, Palmer had his technique perfected and, except for outdoor location photographs, he rarely strayed from it. He seriously underexposed backgrounds for dramatic effect, used two lights whenever possible, employed attractive subject matter (the people), and created strong graphics by using whatever element he could to make a strong subliminal reaction to the image; in this case, the circle of the aircraft tire.

Palmer's image of the assembly room floor at North American Aviation in Kansas City, Kansas, with B-24 bombers being assembled, is a straight-up, no artificial light photograph. However, it was not made without a high level of photographic craftsmanship.

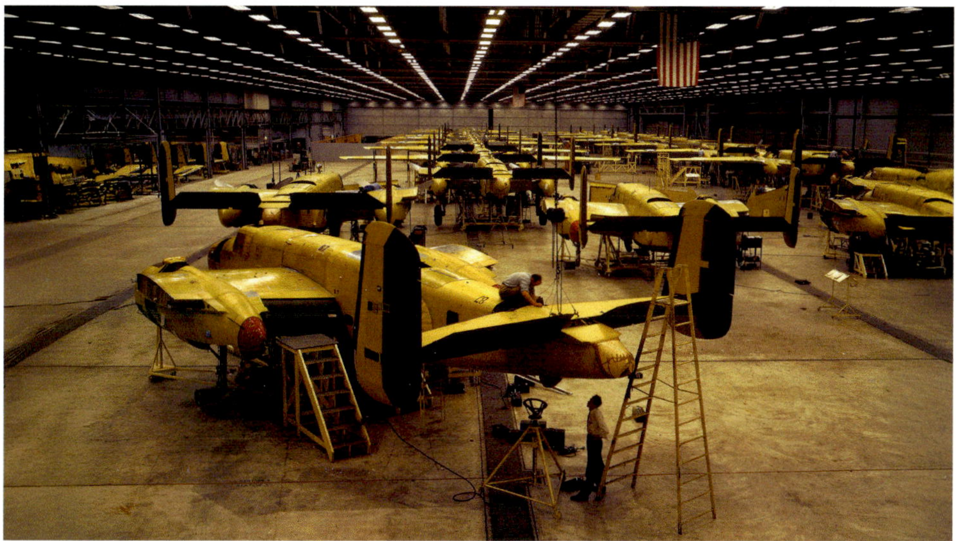

Assembling B-25 bombers at North American Aviation, Kansas City, Kansas, October 1942. (*Library of Congress*)

The image was made on large format Kodachrome sheet film, with a Speed Graphic camera. Kodachrome film was available in three type films: Type Daylight, ASA 10 (the number measures the film's sensitivity to light) and Type B Kodachrome (also ASA 10) for Tungsten lighting, as in this factory photograph, and Type A Kodachrome for use when shooting with flood lights.

The color of light is measured as Kelvin temperature. A photographer has to match one light source to a matching film. In the factory aircraft plant, Palmer had to use Kodachrome Type B designed to be used for that type of light source. For his photographs of people in the various factories, Palmer lit his subjects with photo flood clip lights and used Kodachrome Type A film, a film designed for that kind of light source. The photograph is notable because of true color. Palmer knew how to make his images realistic-looking and brought high craft skill to his choice of the materials that he used. Without the aid of a Polaroid proof or an image on the camera's digital monitor, he was working blind. He had to get it right. There was no going back. (Note: Digital photography has made this issue of true color rendition infinitely easier. Digital cameras have a custom white balance feature that makes off-color rare.)

Palmer was shooting from a high place, possibly a platform, which would be readily available in aircraft construction. This was one of the easier photographs Palmer made, because he did not have to light it himself. However, it did require a high degree of photographic knowledge, gained by Palmer's many years of experience.

Palmer's photograph of a B-17 airplane at sunset is one of the photographer's rare images that is not after detail or even information. This photograph instead seeks mood and emotion. Palmer uses the technique of underexposure to achieve silhouettes of the B-17 Flying Fortress and its full crew of ten aviators (pilot, co-pilot, navigator, bombardier, engineer, radio operator, and four gunners).

Silhouette is achieved by aiming the light meter directly at the lighting source and not adjusting the exposure, then setting the f-stop and/or shutter to the data given. This gives an underexposure, and on most subjects where detail is important, this would be considered a flaw. Palmer knew this. Like all experienced professional photographers, he bracketed to ensure that he made a perfect image. On one of those exposures, the sun would be more sharply rendered, but if that was the case, the crew and airplane would be even darker, possibly unnoticeable.

This photograph is not so much meant to be descriptive, but instead is meant to be symbolic. The B-17 was the backbone of the U.S. Army Air Corps. Developed in 1935, there were 12,731 built. Although heavily armored (thus the nickname Flying Fortress), they were slower (181 mph) than the enemy fighters they encountered (250 mph); 4,735 were lost during combat missions.[11] Although this photo was made only five months into World War II, there were already heavy losses in the European theater of operations. That information may have been on Palmer's mind when he made this somber image.

Strong graphics. Strong light. Low angle. Content. These are the elements of almost every great photograph. In this photograph of the soldier standing next to the 16-inch coast artillery gun, we see the power of Palmer's skill and mastery of craft. We also see that Palmer was, indeed, the forerunner of modern commercial photography.

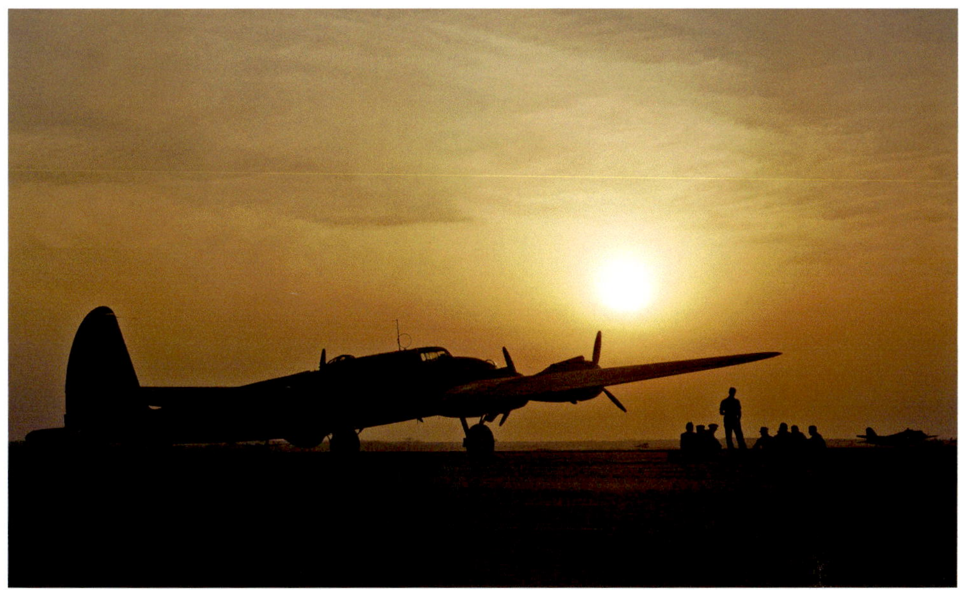

Sunset silhouette of flying fortress, Langley Field, Virginia, July 1942. (*Library of Congress*)

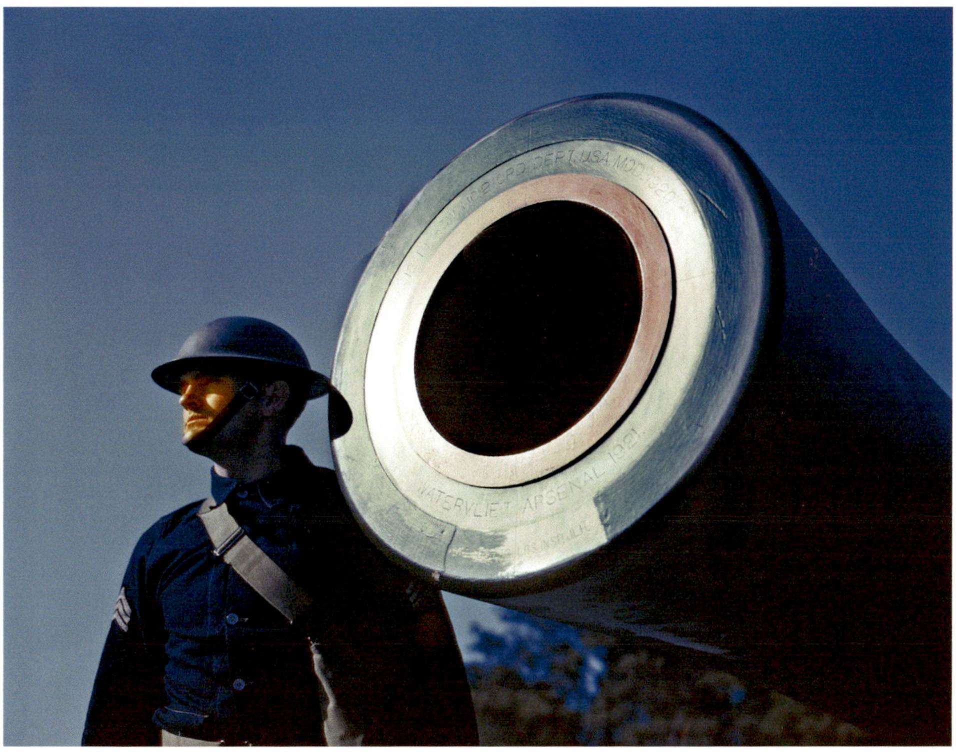

A 16-inch coast artillery gun stamped "Watervliet Arsenal 1921," Ft. Story, Virginia, March 1942. (*Library of Congress*)

Technically this is a very simple image. No artificial light was used, nor were there any reflectors used. Standard practice in such low light was, in that era, to bounce light back into the side that is going pure black (in this case, the side of the soldier's face), so there would be some shadow detail. Palmer chose to forgo this practice, and he did so because he knew that the extreme contrast between light and black would be very dramatic and thus compelling. He knew that any strong artificial light would kill the mood. And, he had little time to work; the sun was almost gone. He also recognized that the muzzle of the canon was a pure graphic element. This is obvious to any observer, but Palmer did more than notice it; he made the barrel the star of the image. He used a composition law, the rule of thirds, so the main elements fell into the third parts of the frame instead of the center.

Palmer photographed this image in either the first rays of sun in the morning or the last rays of light in the evening. This image was undoubtedly a morning shot because the light is cooler in the morning and warmer in the late afternoon. Palmer positioned the barrel of the weapon so the light would be to camera-left and just skimming the muzzle, while making sure that the right shadow went into deep shadow for the dramatic contrast.

The photograph was undoubtedly shot on Kodachrome 4-inch by 5-inch film because of its clarity and deep color saturation. Palmer most likely used his Speed Graphic camera because it was large format but quite mobile—certainly more mobile than the Graflex. He may or may not have used a tripod depending on what platform he was shooting from. Part of the challenge on the day of this shot was to get close enough to be able to do it. There was no rigging under the barrel. He had to have a forklift or construct a platform.

Palmer included the sergeant so that he would be looking at the light, so his face and helmet were lighted. The human figure also gave scale to the gun, showing its enormity. He chose a low angle to show the power of the weapon and, additionally, as all photographers know, shooting up on a human subject subliminally implies nobility. He used this angle repeatedly and for the same reason. While there are no artificial lights at work in this image, a polarizing filter may have been employed to get rid of any unwanted reflections and to saturate the color of the deep blue sky. This is a standard filter used in landscape photography to promote drama by saturating color.

Palmer's image of the M3 tank is a master photograph. The image shows that Palmer did more than work in the narrower space of factories. The power of this photo is that it looks simple, but to produce such an image required a complex and determined effort. At first glance, the image looks as though the tank was shot in natural light. But closer analysis shows it was lighted with auxiliary lighting. There is a spotlight on the tank, but the background is very underexposed, presenting no details in the trees in typical Palmer fashion. He underexposed the background, then punched up the power of his lights for a good exposure on the vehicle. This is a very modern and advanced technique, used by photographers to this day. It is dramatic and compelling and rivets the eyes to the subject, rendering the background to a mere backdrop.

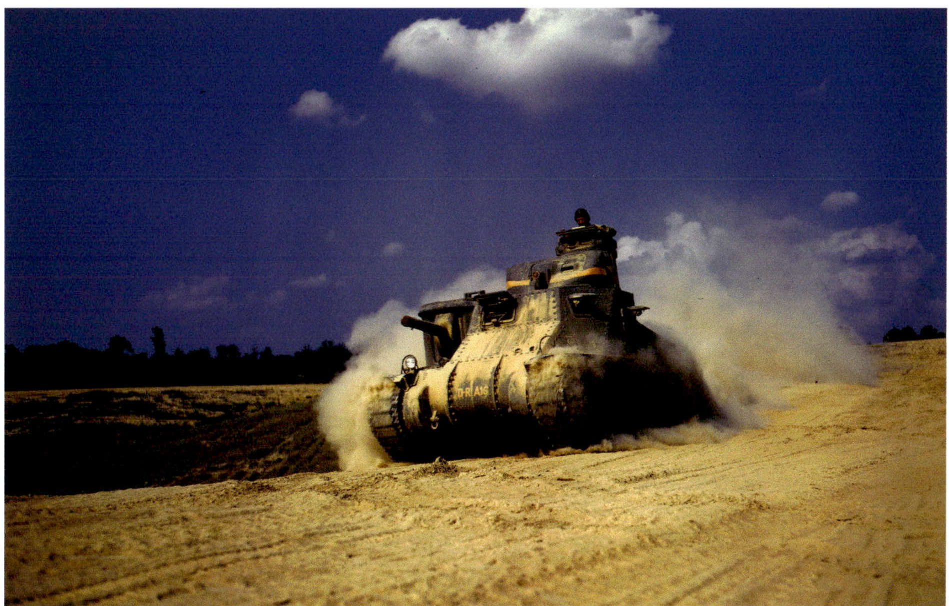

An M-3 tank in action, Ft. Knox, Kentucky, June 1942. (*Library of Congress*)

There is a danger in making this kind of image. Where did Palmer put his lights, and how did he avoid the tank running over them? We cannot know for sure about the latter question, but to answer the former one, the main light is on the left, on a very high light stand, at least 20 feet high. It is aimed down (see shadows on the right side of the tank). It was done—as much of Palmer's work was done—with electronic flash, enabling him to have the stopping power needed. Electronic flash (i.e., strobe) fires at a very high power and can stop motion in its millisecond of a blast, whereas continuous lights are very weak in comparison and cannot stop very fast action. It is unlikely the lights were connected by a cord; it is likely the strobe lights were remotely triggered from the camera, or an assistant fired them from the source.

The camera had to be a 4-inch by 5-inch bellows camera, probably the Speed Graphic. The film had to be Kodak Kodachrome Film Type 5265, the premier color film. Since this type of camera allows only one shot at a time and because of the kinetic nature of the photo, Palmer undoubtedly had the tank repeat the action several times, as any photographer would. Most photographers in pursuit of perfection will ask to take "just one more image" repeatedly. With an enormous vehicle like a tank, this is no small request.

The exposure had to be done at a fast shutter speed. In bright sunlight, to get to an action-stopping speed of 1/250th second, the regular exposure would have been at f-16 (it appears to be) f-5.6 at 1/250th. But this is not a natural light photo. It appears to be shot around f-16 at 1/250th (to stop action), three shutter speeds faster than the above stated natural light exposure.

So, how did he do it?

Palmer powered up his light a massive three extra units of light to achieve f-16. This means he had to have a major, powerful electronic flash of at least 2,000-watt seconds, rare in those early days of electronic lighting. He might have used two or even three right next to each other to gain the proper amount of power to achieve the look he desired. If this all sounds very technical, it is because it is. Palmer brought an unusually high level of technical expertise to these wartime photographs. (Note: there is a possibility he may have used flash bulbs and more than one unit to achieve the high power and slaved the units so he could trigger them from a master flash which would be in his hands.)

To an experienced photographer of today, eighty years later, this would still be a tricky and complex photo to pull off. It would require a couple of assistants or at least a freelance helper. It would require multiple exposure and re-sets. It would be difficult on the equipment and personnel because of the major dust storm each pass of the tank would produce. This kind of shoot can ensure a long night of cleaning lenses and cameras of the dust from stirred-up action.

All of this was done without any way to "proof" the shoot, to check his exposure. He needed to bracket his exposures. Sometimes Palmer was going under a black focusing cloth to double-check focus. The dust was everywhere. This was not just a case of snapping a photo. This was hard work. That is what a truly great photographer does, and it requires patience. The photograph looks exceedingly simple because a master photographer makes it look that way. This photograph is a masterpiece of ingenuity and skill. It also contains that intangible quality that great photographs seem to have: luck. For example, that cloud over the tank is a gift.

This was a long day on location, a physically taxing photo shoot that demonstrates great determination by photographer and crew, including those inside the tank. The styling of the photo looks contemporary to this day.

To take this photograph of five men mounting an engine into the wing of a B-25 bomber, Palmer used two lights, one to the far left, lighting the man working the chain hoist, and one to the right, lighting the men on top and bottom doing the installation. Without the benefit of a digital monitor (or, even, Polaroid test film used in the 1960s through the 1980s, before the onset of digital photography), Palmer has overexposed the man on the left. Normally he could walk around a scene, take light meter readings of each part of his scene, adjust the distance of the lights until all the lighting was even so he could have good exposure throughout. Here, he had no chance to do that, as the action of the scene was unpredictable, and he had to capture the scene fast. He had no time for tweaking. One might say, well, "next time." Palmer's schedule was fierce, producing dozens of photographs per day. There was no "next time" for this scene, because he was off to the next scheduled shoot. Besides, he had no idea there was a problem. He would not see his processed film for days—or weeks. Like all photographers, when seeing errors in their shooting, once they see the final product, there is pain. They cannot redo the image. But they must live with the error and try to learn from it for the next time.

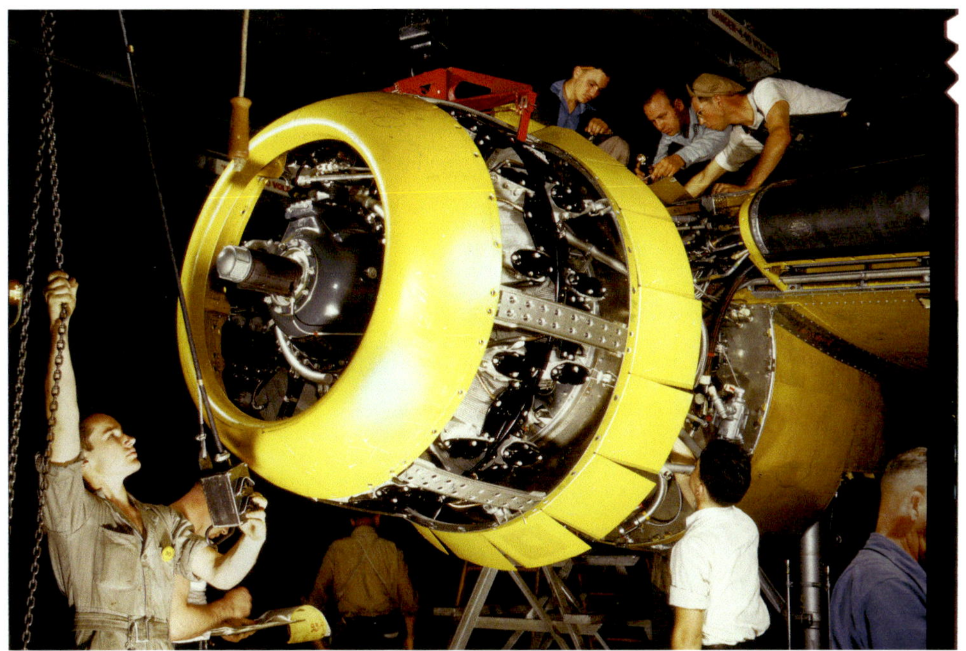

Mounting a motor on a Fairfax B-25 bomber, at the North American Aviation, Inc., plant in Inglewood, California, October 1942. (*Library of Congress*)

Some World War II home front jobs required masculine muscle. Such images also played to federal propagandists' needs of depicting the strength of the nation. Palmer took few photographs of women that show women covered in dust, dirt or sweat. The bulk of the dirty work was conducted by men. This outdoor photograph of a worker unspooling copper wire required no artificial lighting, as did all of Palmer's factory images. It must have been a relief for him to just take a light meter reading, pop the film holder into his Speed Graphic and just snap the photo. Which is not to say Palmer's great skills are not evident in this image. He used a low angle and the half circles of the spool are desirable to have in a composition since circles are a fundamental aesthetic shape and are eye-catching. Outdoors on a sunny day is a perfect time for the use of Kodachrome (as *National Geographic* photographers have come to learn).

As with the FSA, the Office of War Information photographers recognized that America was multiracial and that all Americans were having a shared experience during the war years. Not only did Palmer's photographs invite women into the industrial work force, but the images also enticed minority women by demonstrating that they were needed as part of the federal government's "Womanpower" campaign. Technically, Palmer used one light in his photograph of an African American riveter in Nashville, Tennessee. The 1943 image was shot on Kodachrome film. Palmer employed his now-standard technique of underexposing the background so the subject would stand out boldly.

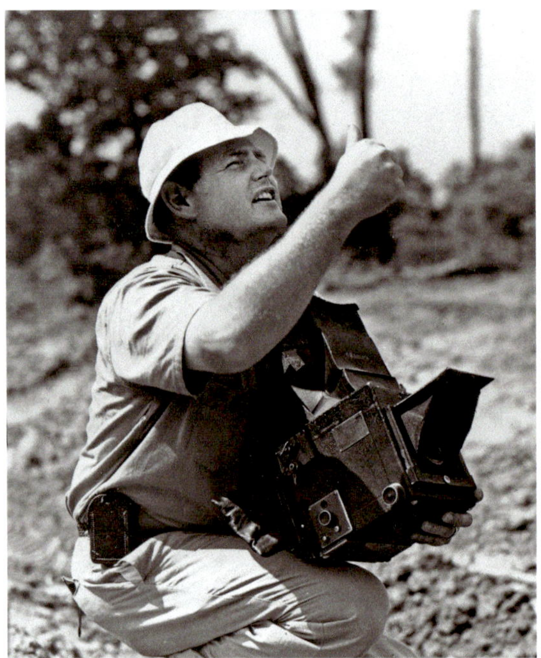

Left: Alfred Palmer shooting tank photos, 1942, location unknown. (*A. T. Palmer Collection, privately held*)

Below: This husky member of a construction crew building a new 33,000-volt electric power line into Fort Knox is performing an important war service, June 1942. Thousands of soldiers are in training there, and the new line from a hydroelectric plant at Louisville is needed to supplement the existing power supply. (*Library of Congress*)

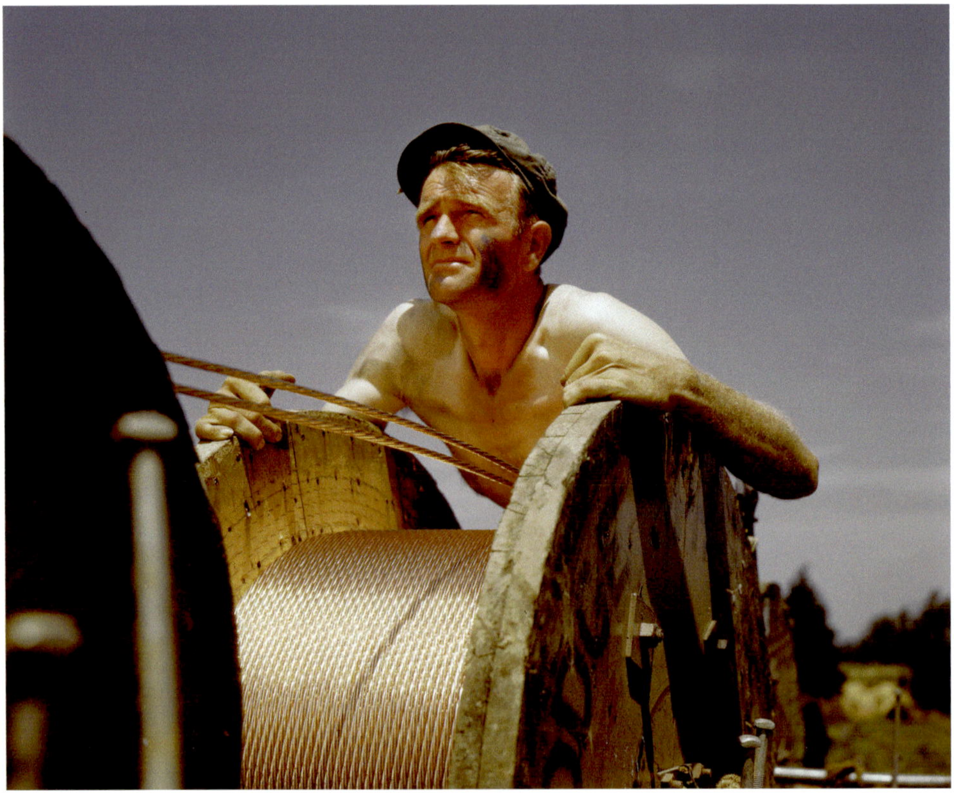

Not all of Palmer's photographs of labor in the World War II era depicted weapons of war being produced. To make planes, ships, tanks, and munitions, the fundamental raw materials had to be produced: nickel, phosphorous, steel, glass, etc. Executive Order #8802 prohibited discrimination in war industries. The legislation led companies to employ "tens of thousands of African Americans, including 400,000 African American women (who) quit work as domestic servants [and other types of employment, including farm work and waitressing] to enjoy the higher benefits of industrial employment," as well as 200,000 Mexican nationals who worked as "Braceros" (i.e., farm workers).[12] Thousands of Mexican and African American workers also went north to work in the steel mills of Chicago, Indiana, and Pennsylvania, as well as to other factory cities throughout the Midwest and West, and along the Atlantic Seaboard.

Palmer lit every subject with attention to detail. His lighting techniques, especially his use of the Chiaroscuro aesthetic to emphasize shadows and light to dramatic effect, would be used by other photographers during the war, as well as in the decades following World War II. Similarly, Palmer's strong use of color, based on his understanding of the language of color, would be embraced by many photographers in the post-war era. While it is impossible to say if Palmer had a direct influence on other photographers and their work, especially those who used dramatic lighting or shot in color, the ubiquity of Palmer's images during wartime meant that they were widely seen and, thus, were undoubtedly influential.

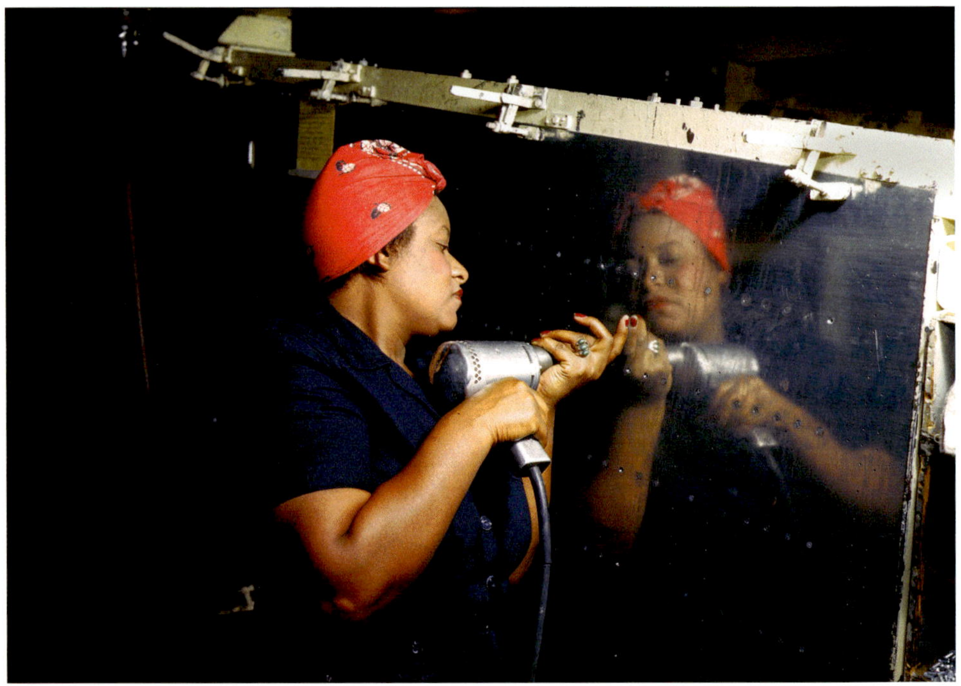

Operating a hand drill at Vultee-Nashville, this woman is working on a Vengeance dive bomber, February 1943. (*Library of Congress*)

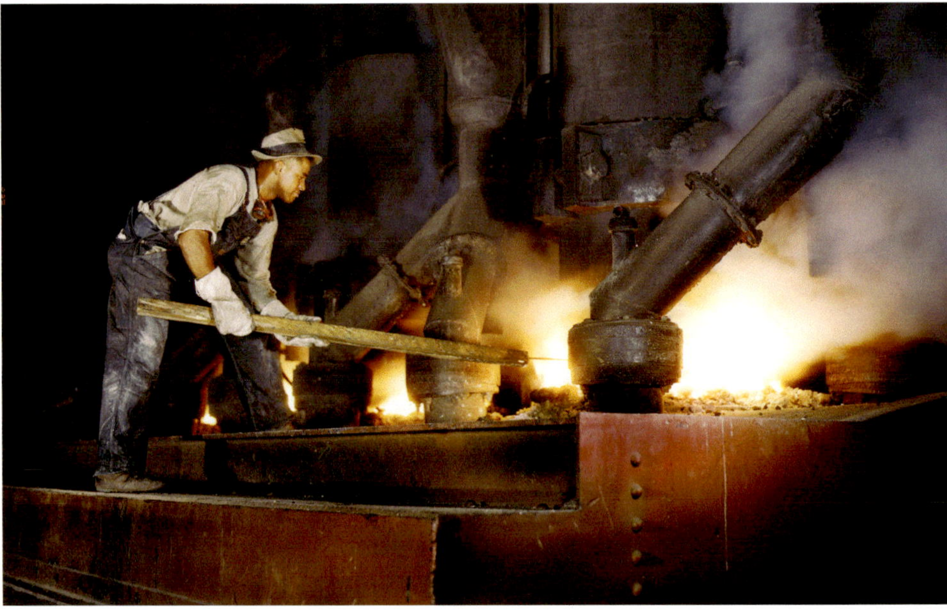

Electric phosphate smelting furnace used to make elemental phosphorus in a TVA chemical plant in the vicinity of Muscle Shoals, Alabama, June 1942. (*Library of Congress*)

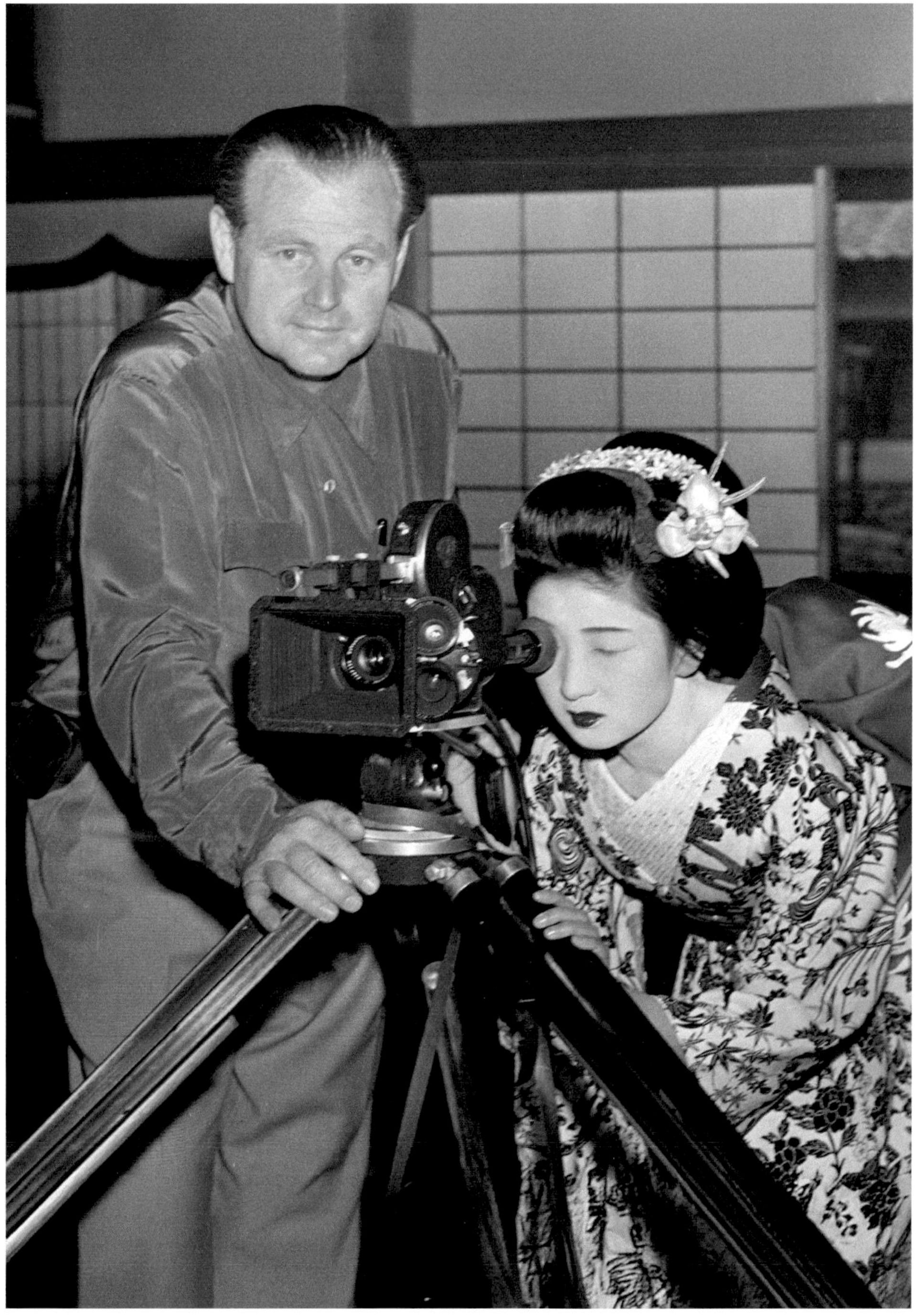

Alfred T. Palmer with geisha, undated. (*A. T. Palmer Collection, privately held*)

EPILOGUE

A RETURN TO THE SEA

In January 1945, Alfred T. Palmer began planning his post-war career. Not surprisingly, those plans included returning to the sea as a filmmaker and photographer. Shortly before he boarded the *Hannibal Victory* to make a film about the Merchant Marine's activities during wartime, Palmer scheduled several meetings with executives from one of his former employers, American President Lines (APL), to discuss future projects. The photographer's enthusiasm for his post-war career is revealed in a letter he sent to his wife. Noting that he and his wartime supervisor, Robert Horton, were meeting with one executive and having lunch with others, Palmer enthused: "… we are all going places. This trip is going to put us right on top—in the Maritime picture business with A.P.L." He noted that the war would soon be over in Europe, which, he said, would make the Japanese "be running so fast they won't even look back—let alone trying to do anything offensive."[1]

By May 24, with the war in Europe over and Japan's surrender a little over three months away, Palmer's post-war plans to get back into commercial maritime photography work seemed a certainty. A letter dated May 24, 1945, from Oakland, California, to Alexa in Manhasset, New York, reiterated an expected return to maritime photography. "We're in solid with the A.P.L.—So solid that big moguls have taken me by the arm and called me 'Al.'" He also admitted his pleasure that executives from the Moore-McCormack Lines had written to Alexa seeking to retain his services, as well.[2]

The war's end in 1945 led Palmer to reestablish his commercial photography and motion picture production business. He set up shop at 11 Broadway in New York, near Battery Park. Within a few years, a desire to return to California saw Palmer relocate to Bush Street in San Francisco. The photographer indeed resumed his work for several shipping lines in the post-war period, including for Moore-McCormick and APL, which allowed him to rekindle another passion: international travel.[3]

The late 1940s and early 1950s saw Palmer return to some of his favorite countries, including Japan, China, the Philippines, Hong Kong, and Ceylon (Sri Lanka), and India, often accompanied by family members. Although Palmer continued to do some still photography work for cruise ship lines, both documenting aspects of shipboard life and engaging in promotional photography for advertising, he increasingly hired and trained others to do the work so that he could devote himself to his other passion—making travel films and educational documentaries for a variety of clients, including the Asia Foundation, Kaiser Engineering, the Bank of America, the Japan Tourist Association, the United States Information Agency, and the Committee for a Free Asia. His filmmaking career would continue into the mid-1970s.[4]

He was particularly interested in producing films that promoted international understanding, an interest and theme that harkened back to his earliest days of international travel and curiosity about the world. Although Palmer would make travel films about silk and Pearls for the Japan Tourist Association and other travel films such as *Destination Hawaii* for the Matson Navigation Company, all of which were meant to inspire post-war travel, Palmer's most successful film, made in 1950, was titled *Cargoes for Peace*. Distributed in thirty-six languages around the world by the United States Information Agency, the film documented how the United States was helping other nations "get back on their feet after the war."[5]

Other Palmer documentaries also were widely seen. An earlier film, made immediately after the war in 1946 for the National Federation of American Shipping called *America Sails the Seas* was viewed by almost a million people the year it was made, and more bookings of the film were planned for 1947.[6]

Palmer's pivot into filmmaking, while personally satisfying, had an adverse effect on his legacy as a still photographer. Many of his contemporaries continued their still photography careers and thus built lasting bodies of work that are studied and remembered to this very day. Palmer's resumption of cruise ship photography and documentary filmmaking created its own legacy (much of which is now housed at San Francisco's Maritime National Historic Park and at the archives at the Mystic Seaport Museum in Connecticut), but his name is not remembered in the same way that the FSA photographers or Alfred Stieglitz is today. Yet Palmer's World War II photographs, especially those that were shot in color, were seen by millions of Americans and Europeans. His understanding of how to use color and his innovative lighting techniques undoubtedly influenced subsequent generations of photographers.

Shortly before his death in 1993, Palmer attempted to get an exhibit of his World War II images shown at the Smithsonian Museum in Washington, D.C. Although his archives reveal numerous letters of support for the exhibition and regular correspondence with Smithsonian curators, the show never occurred. Average citizens were deprived of seeing a body of work that Palmer called "a very important and satisfying period of my life."[7] It is hoped that this book can help reintroduce Alfred T. Palmer and his World War II home front photographic labors to the public. They capture a moment in time, depicting a generation that came together as a nation. A rich legacy of maritime imagery and international photography of bygone people and places also awaits future exploration and discovery by scholars and the public alike.

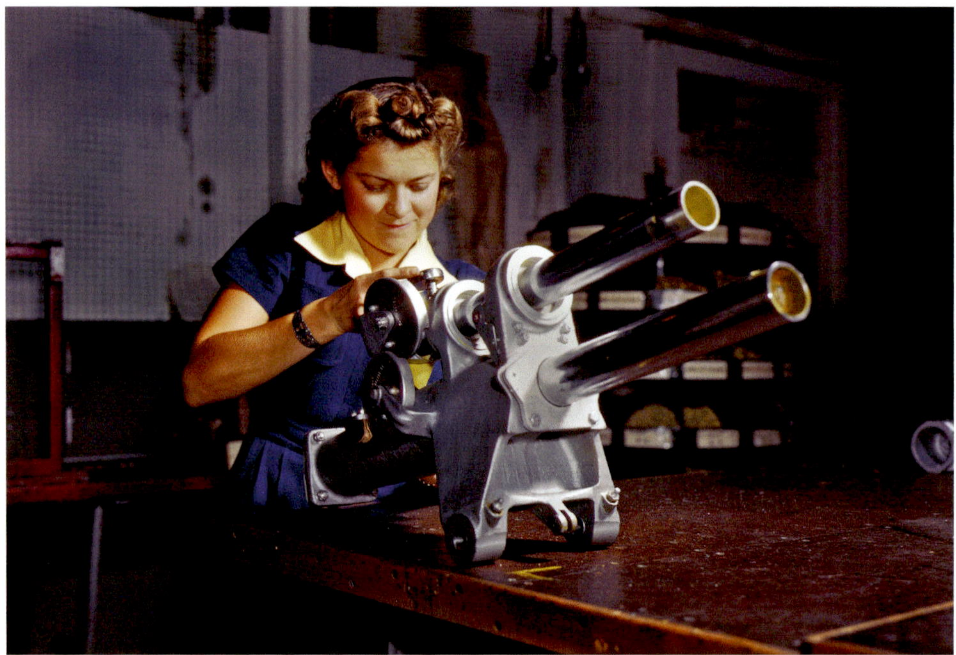

A young female employee of North American Aviation, Inc., working over the landing gear mechanism of a P-51 fighter plane, Inglewood, California, October 1942. The mechanism resembles a small cannon. (*Library of Congress*)

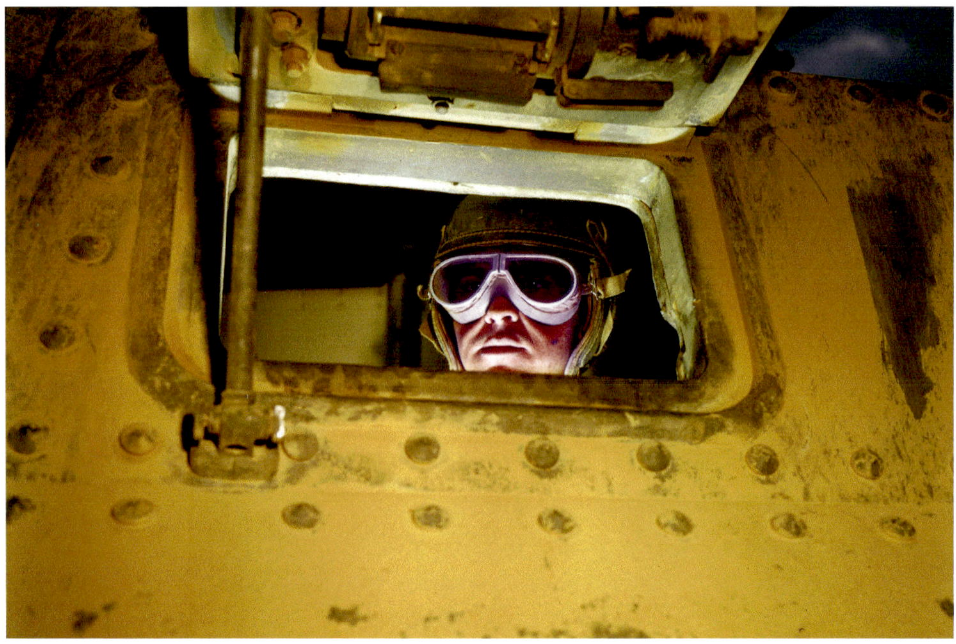

Tank driver, Ft. Knox, Kentucky, June 1942. (*Library of Congress*)

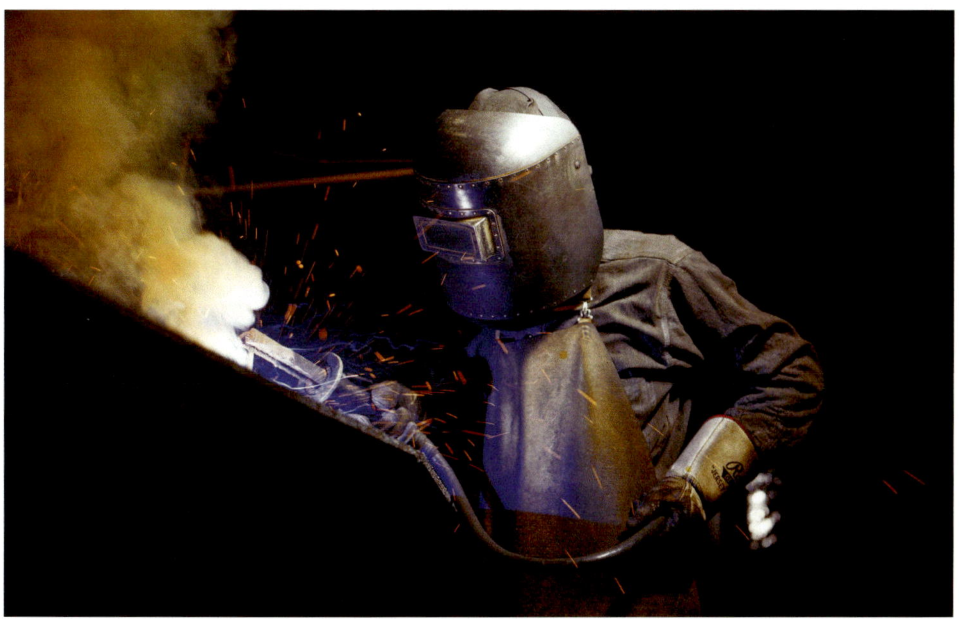

Tank commander, Ft. Knox, Kentucky, June 1942. The photographer assistant is holding a "clip light" (lower right). (*Library of Congress*)

Welder making boilers for a ship, Combustion Engineering Co., Chattanooga, Tennessee. (*Library of Congress*)

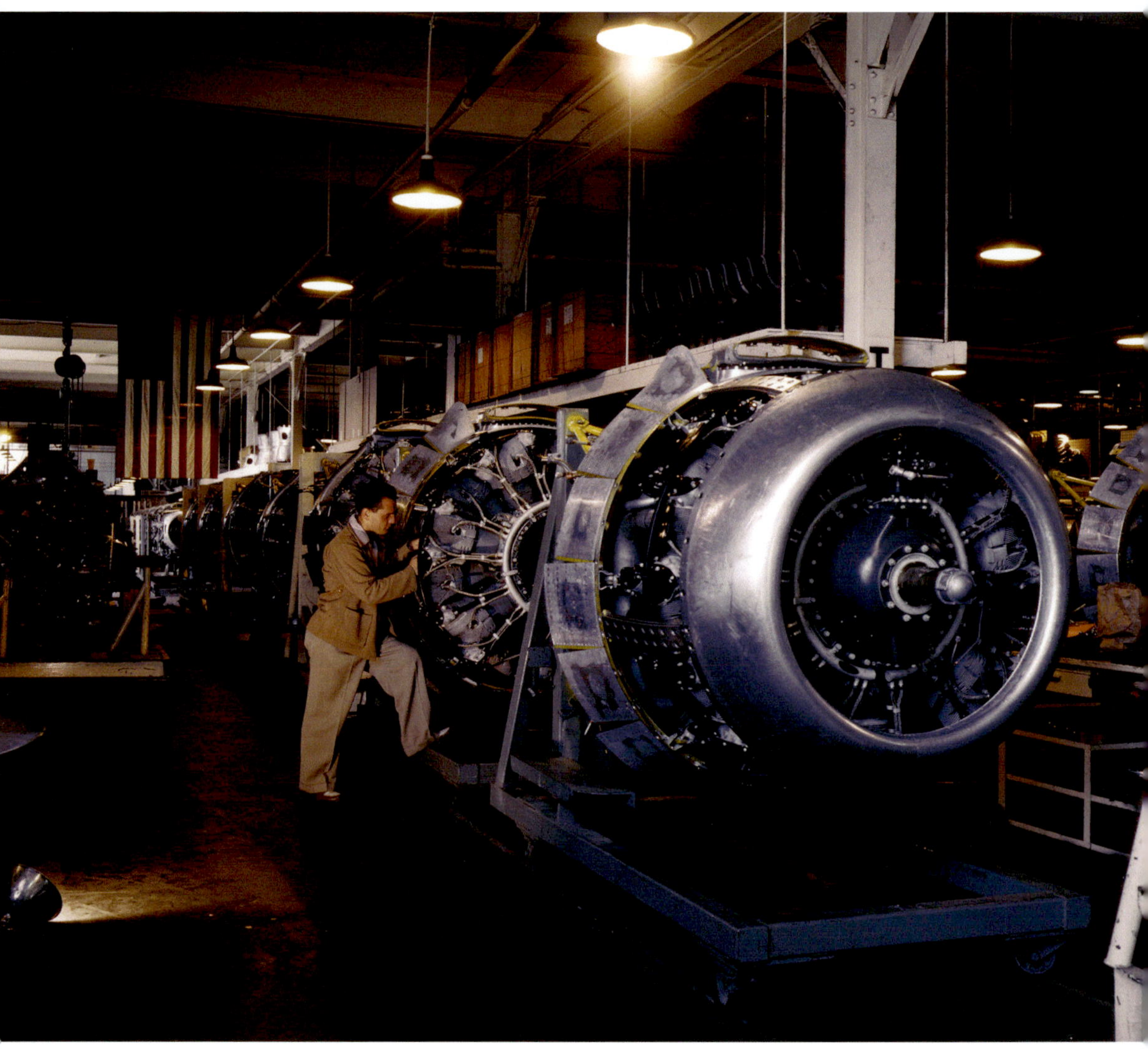

Cowling and control rods are added to motors for North American B-25 bombers as they move down the assembly line, North American Aviation, Inc., Inglewood, California, October 1942. (*Library of Congress*)

Opposite page: Man of the Fort Story, Virginia, coastal defense, March 1942. (*Library of Congress*)

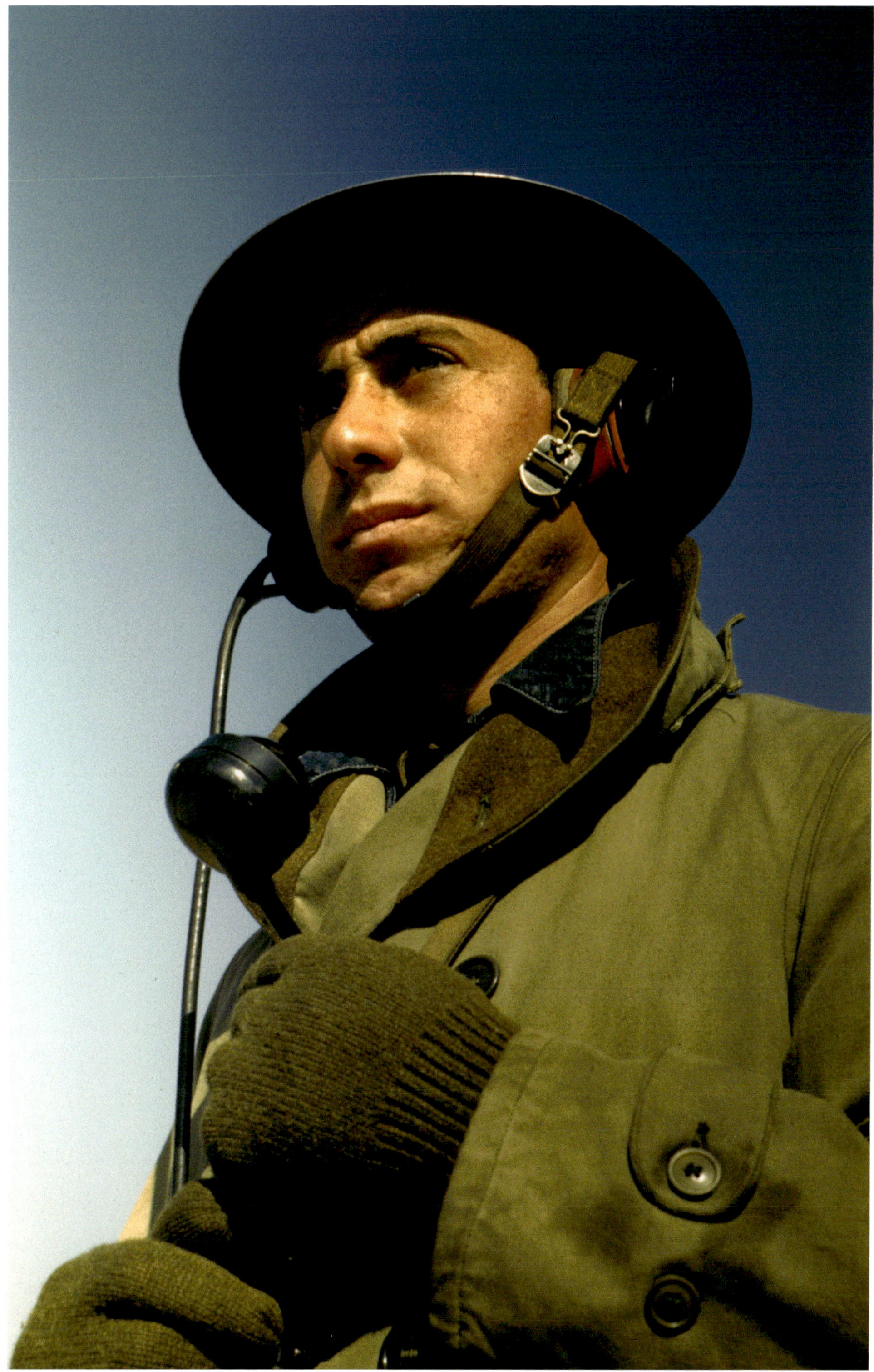

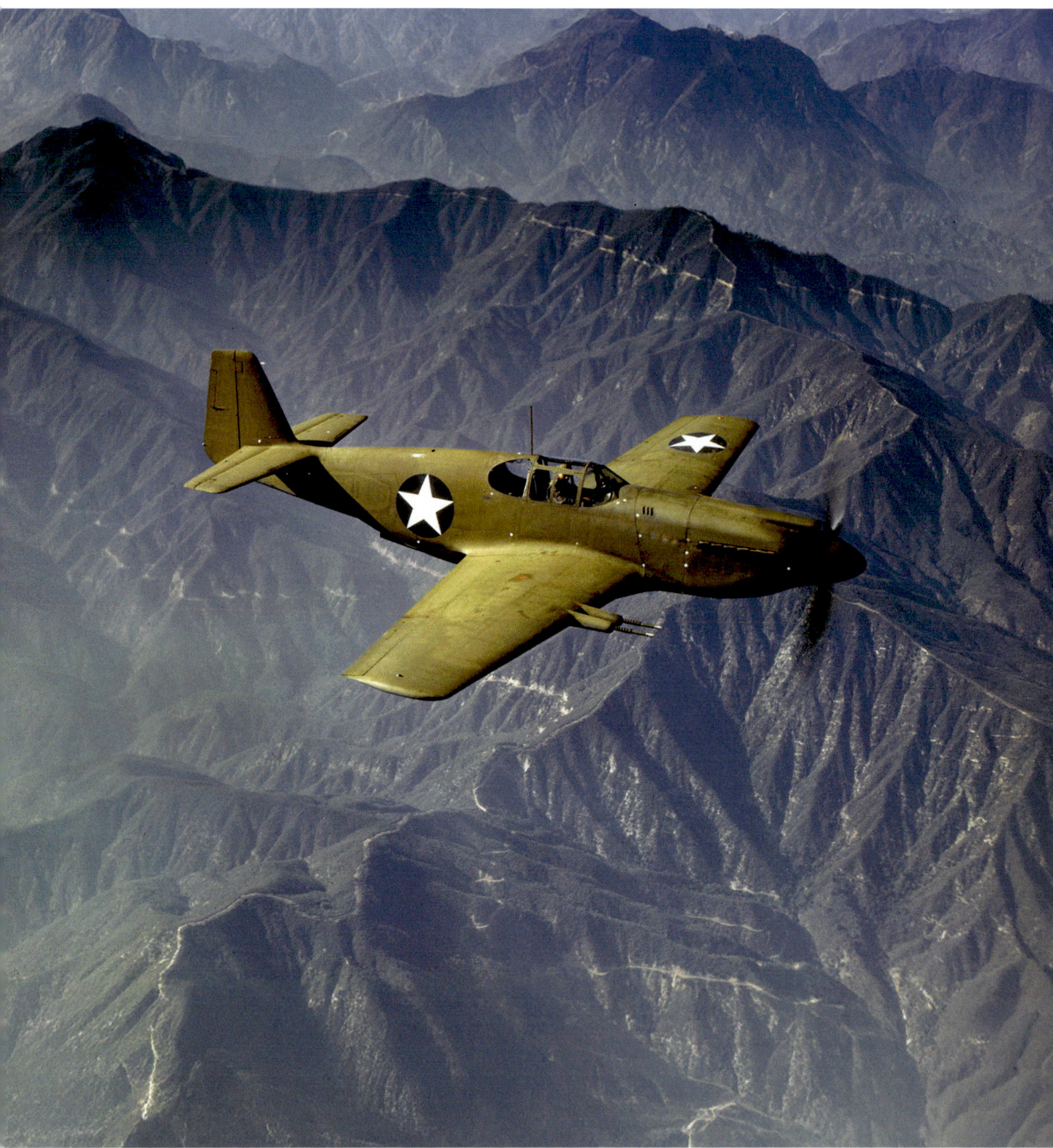

P-51 Mustang fighter in flight, Inglewood, California, October 1942. (*Library of Congress*)

Opposite page: A nose wheel and landing gear assembly for a B-25 bomber under construction in a western aircraft plant, North American Aviation, Inc., California, October 1942. A front section of the plane is shown in the background. (*Library of Congress*)

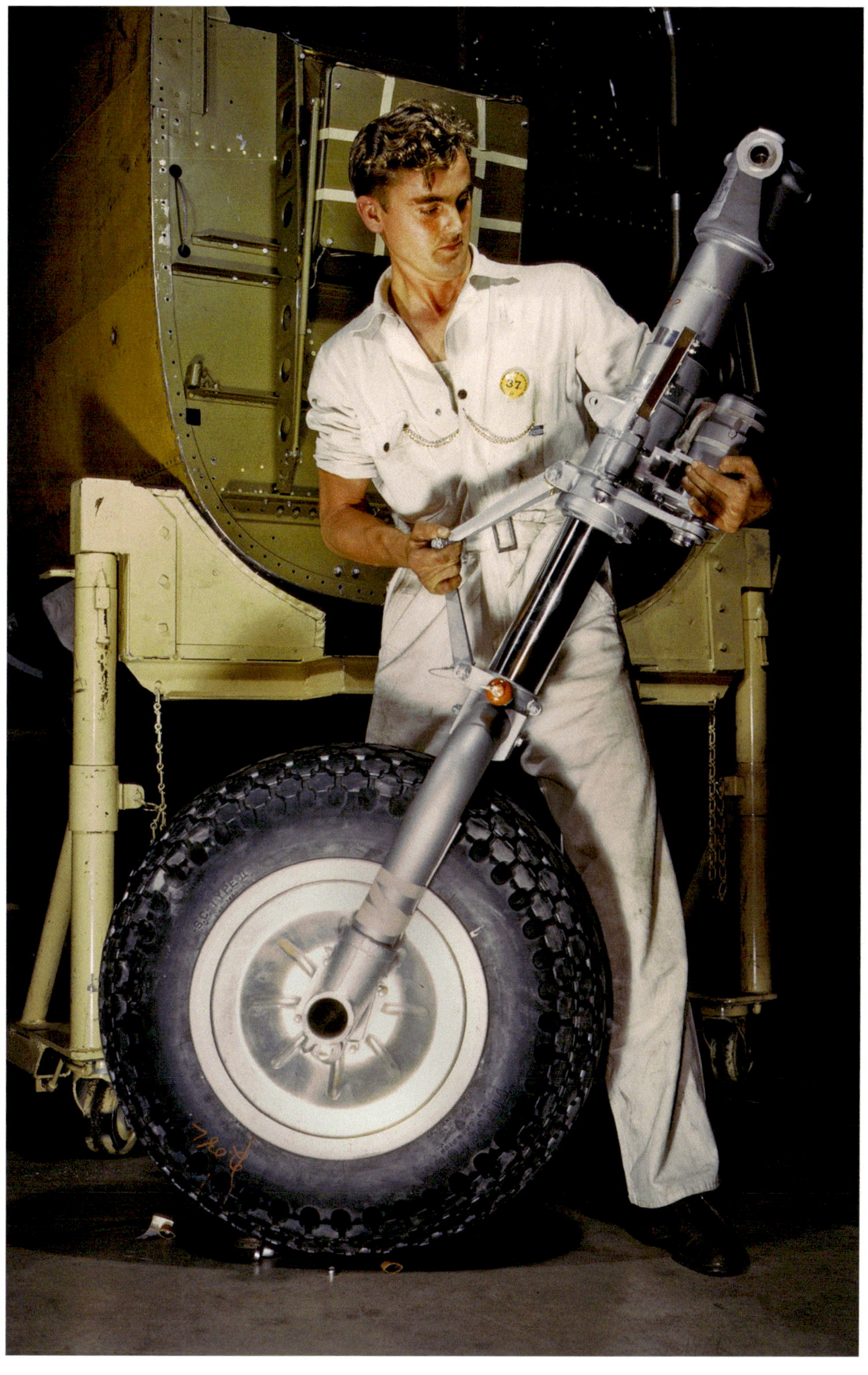

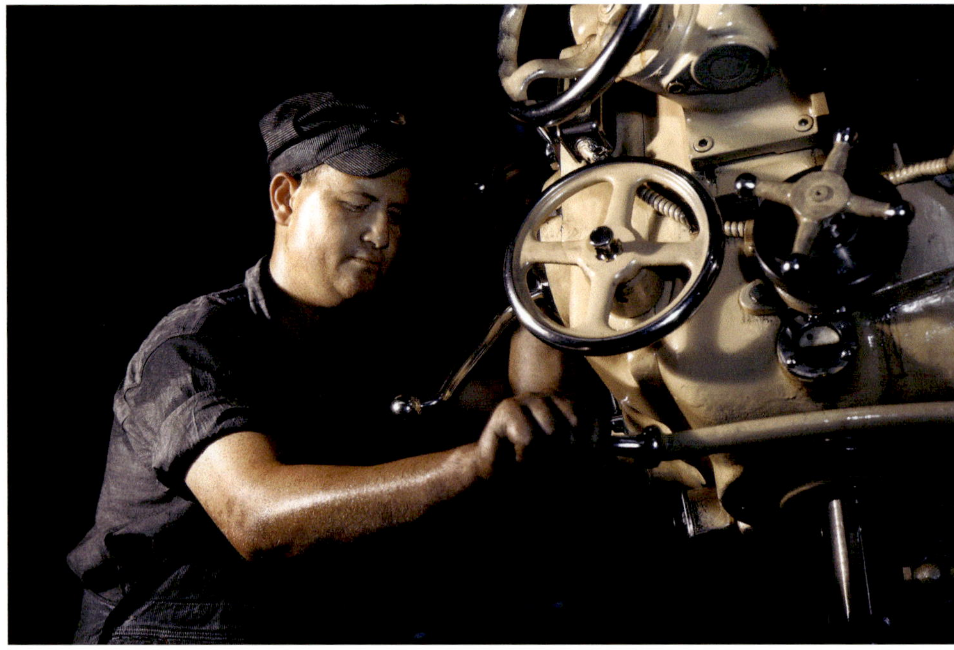

Mechanical operator on boiler parts, Combustion Engineering Co., Chattanooga, Tennessee, June 1942. (*Library of Congress*)

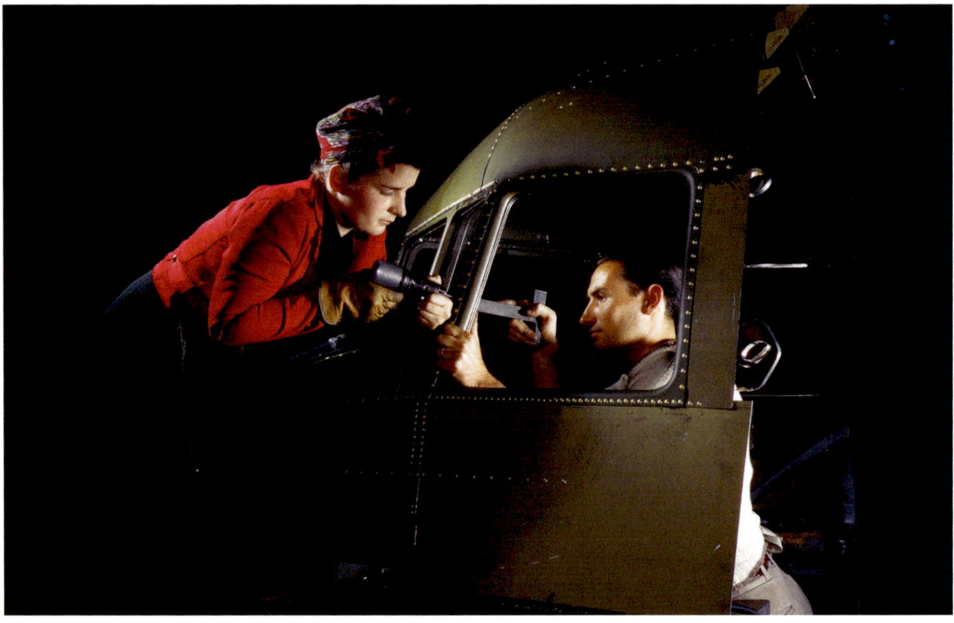

Riveting team working on the cockpit shell of a B-25 (i.e. C-47) bomber at the plant of North American Aviation, Inc., Inglewood (i.e. Douglas Aircraft Company, Long Beach), California, October 1942. (*Library of Congress*)

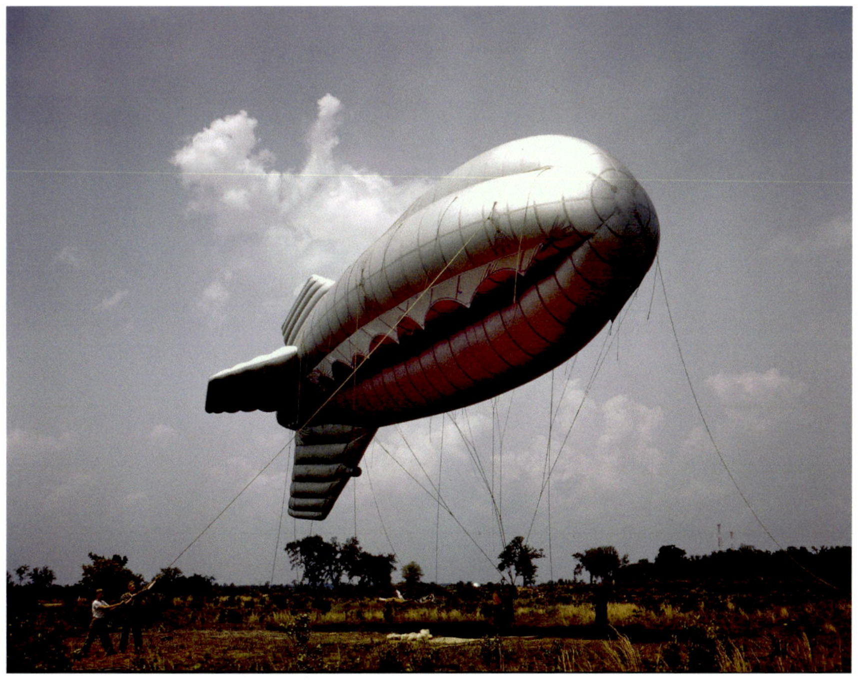

Parris Island, South Carolina, barrage balloon, May 1942. (*Library of Congress*)

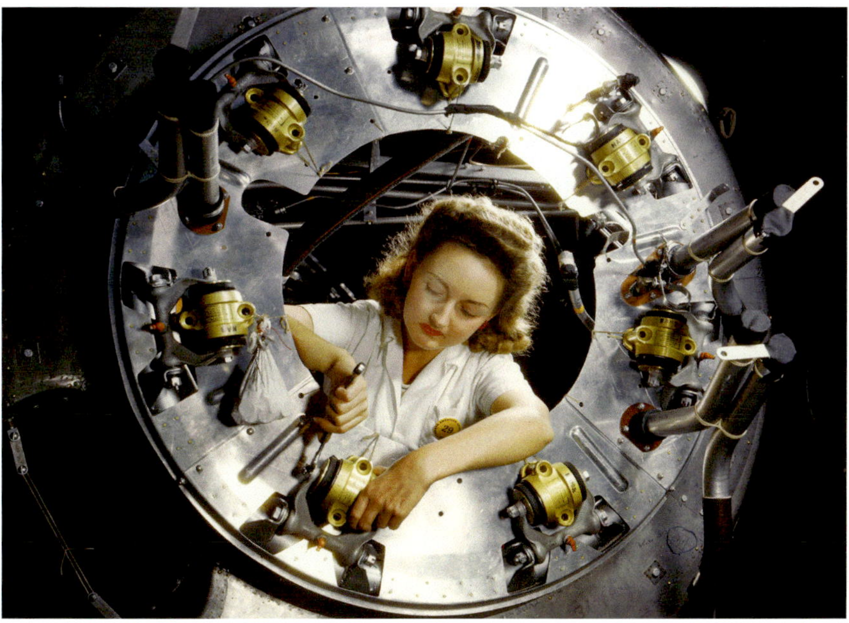

Part of the cowling for one of the motors for a B-25 bomber is assembled in the engine department of North American Aviation, Inc.'s Inglewood, California, plant, October 1942. (*Library of Congress*)

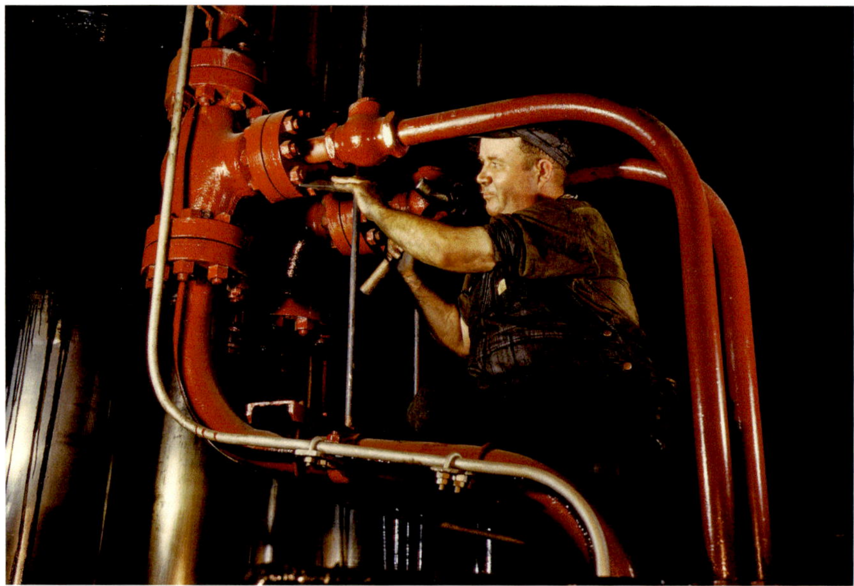

Maintenance man at the Combustion Engineering Co. working at the largest cold steel hydraulic press in the world, Chattanooga, Tennessee, June 1942. This press can shape steel plates several inches in thickness. (*Library of Congress*)

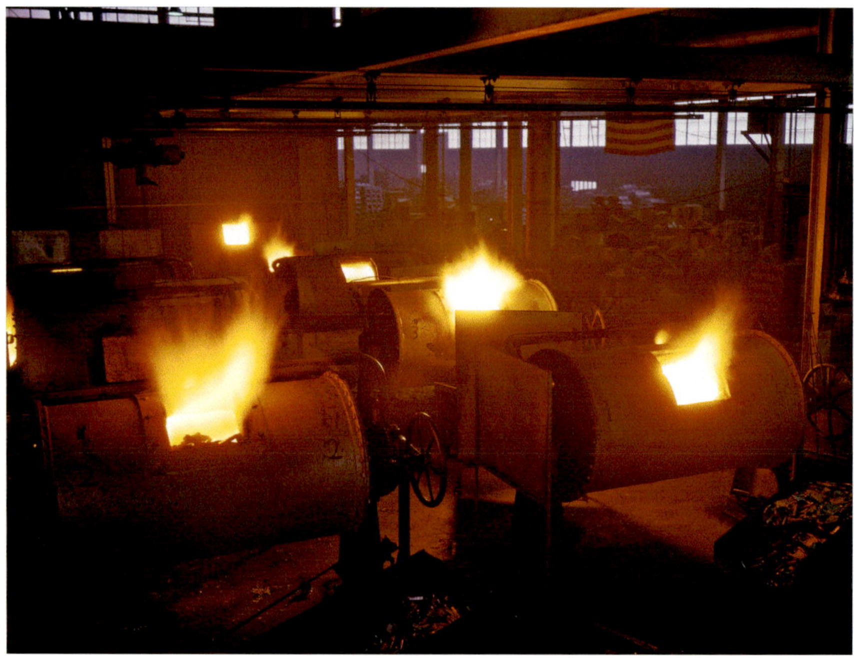

A battery of 1,000- and 2,000-pound furnaces—roaring threats to the Axis. These are rotary, oil-fired melting furnaces at Aluminum Industries Inc., Ohio, February 1942. The destination of the finished aluminum products is kept secret. (*Library of Congress*)

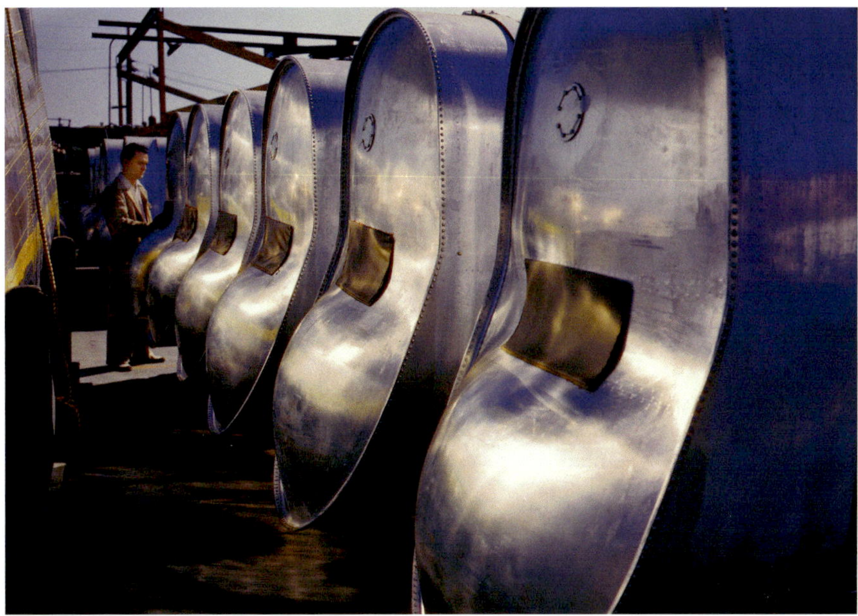

Bomb-bay gasoline tanks for long flights of B-25 bombers await assembly in the plant of North American Aviation, Inc., Inglewood, California, October 1942. (*Library of Congress*)

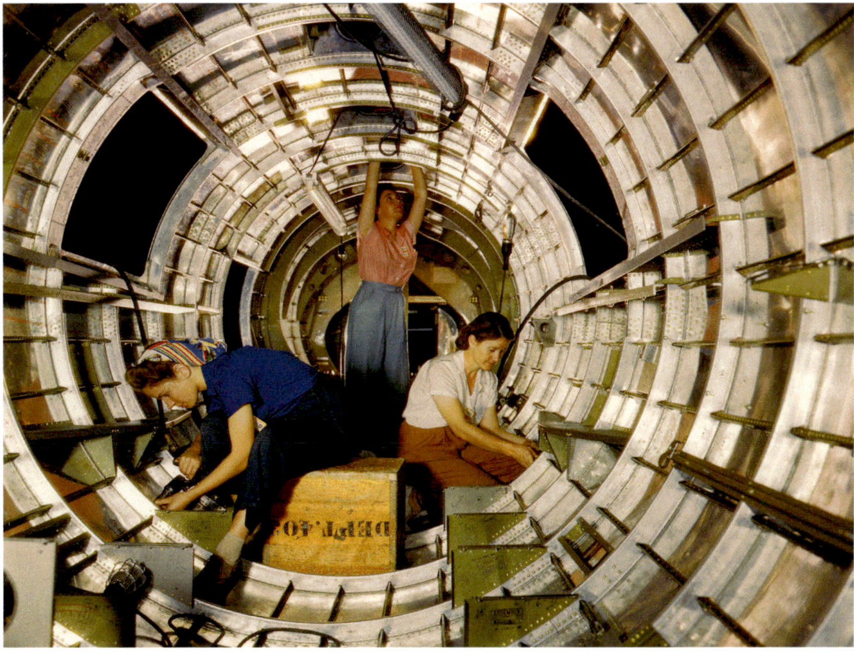

Women workers install fixtures and assemblies to a tail fuselage section of a B-17F bomber at the Douglas Aircraft Company, Long Beach, California, October 1942. (*Library of Congress*)

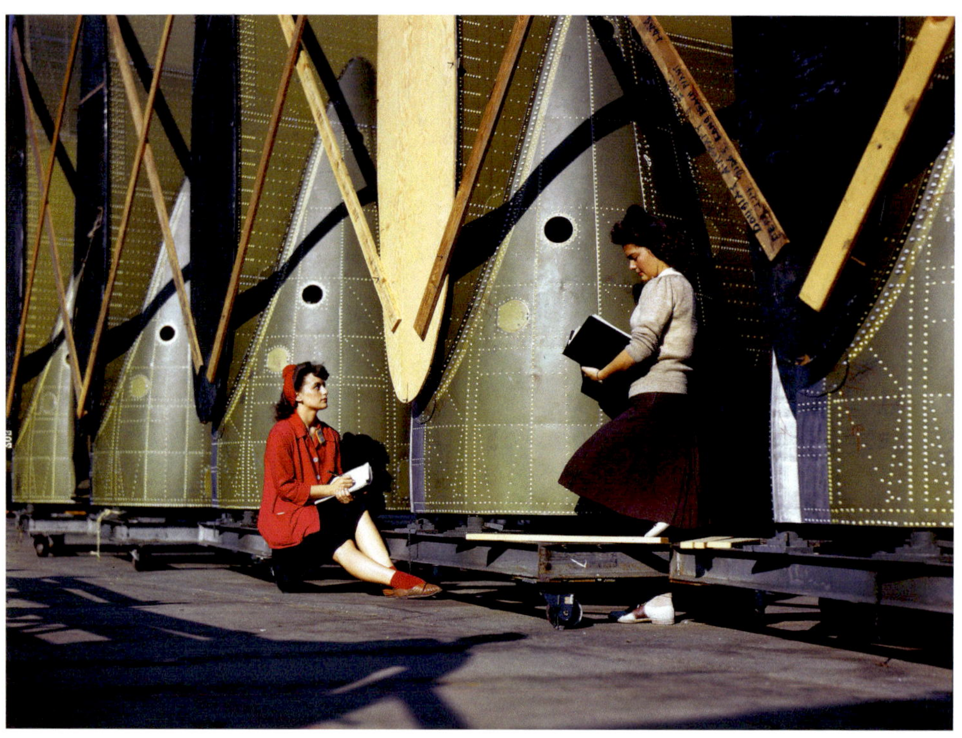

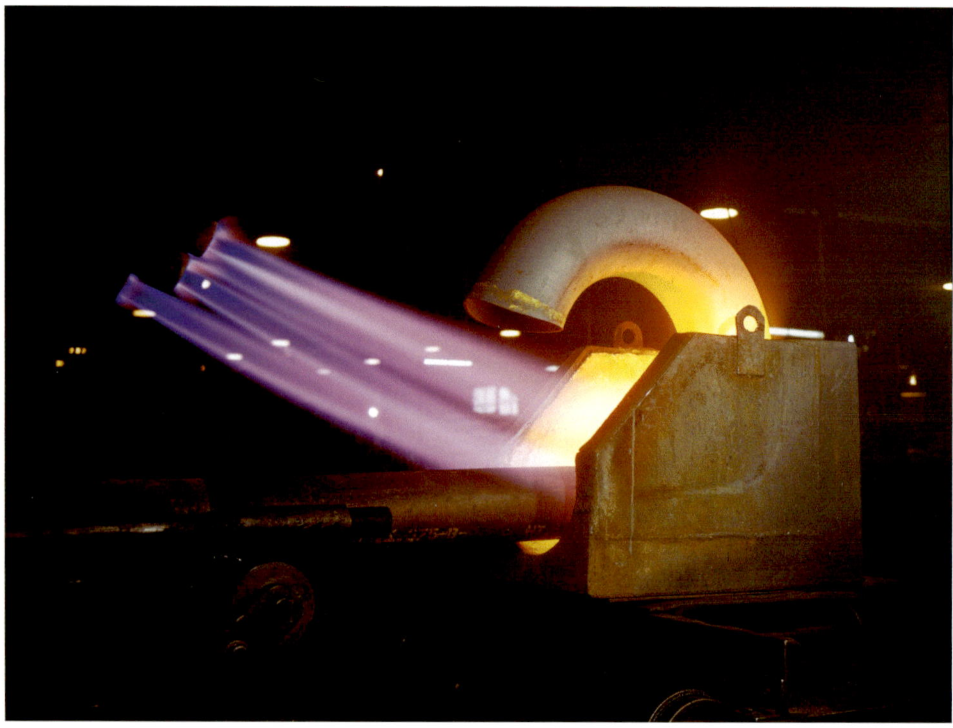

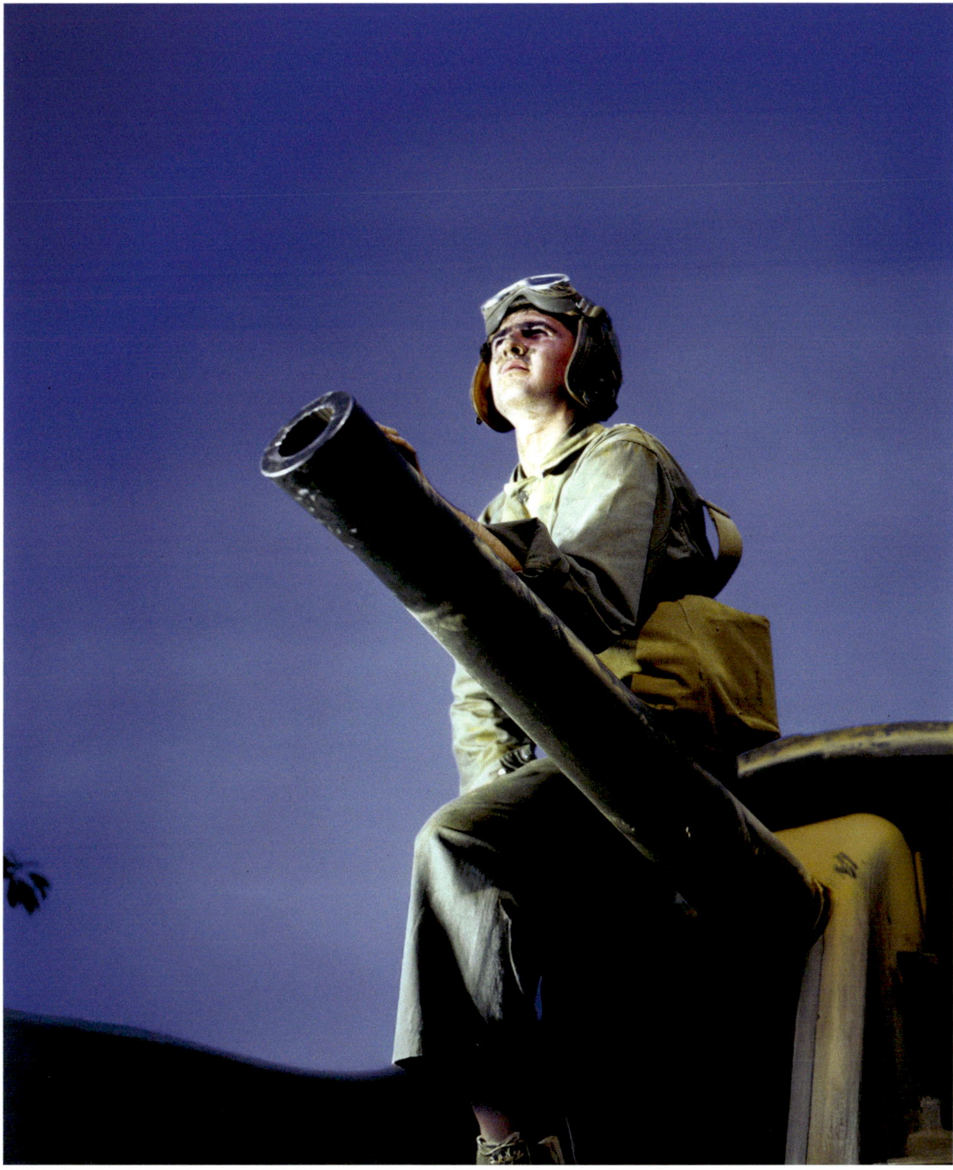

Crewman of an M-3 tank, Ft. Knox, Kentucky, June 1942. (*Library of Congress*)

Opposite above: Female inspectors at the Long Beach, California, plant of Douglas Aircraft Company make a careful check of center wings for C-47 transport planes, October 1942. (*Library of Congress*)

Opposite below: Large pipe elbows for the army are formed at Tube Turns, Inc., by heating lengths of pipe with gas flames and forcing them around a die, Louisville, Kentucky, 1941. (*Library of Congress*)

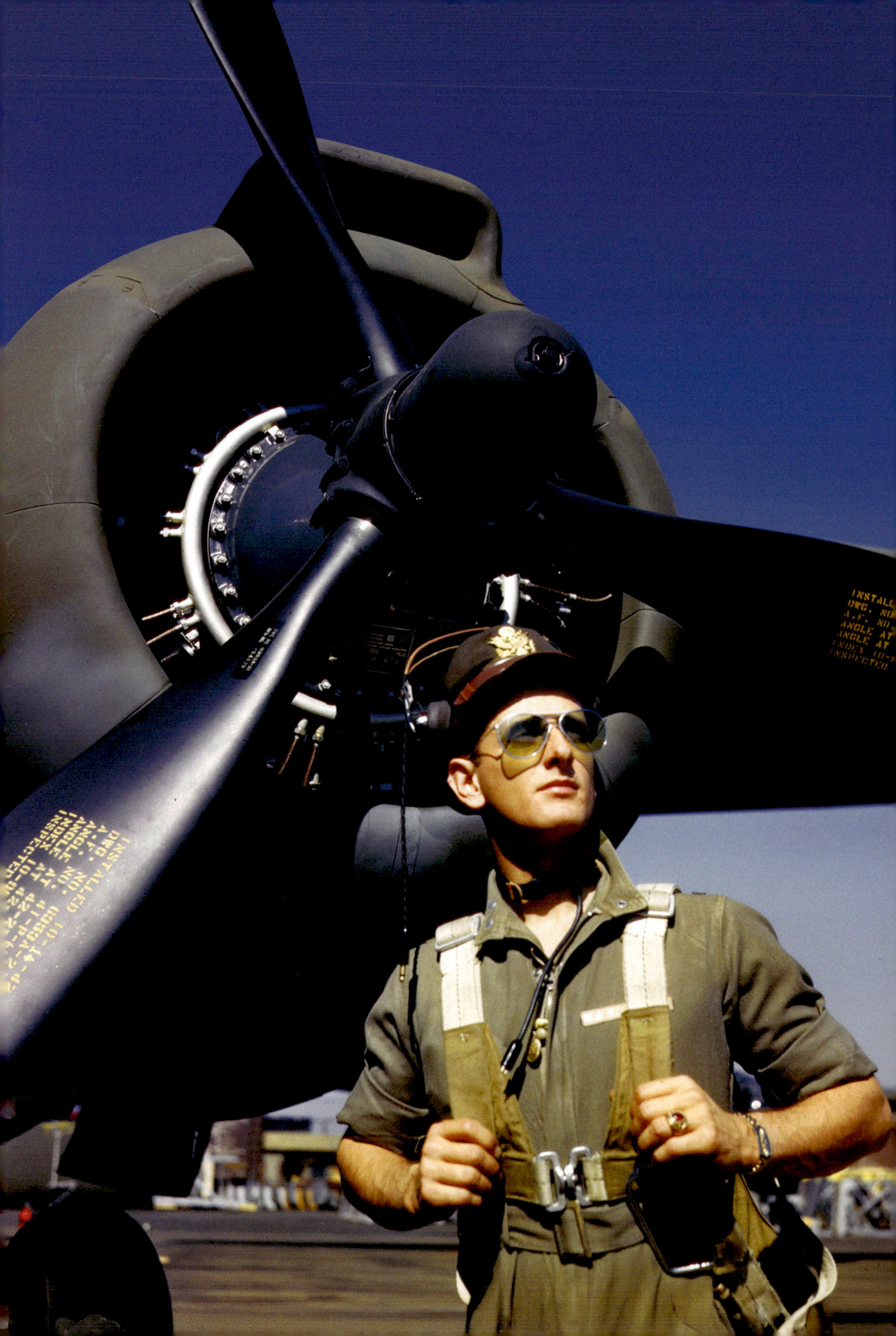
INSTALLED
DWG. NO
A.F. NO
ANGLE AT
ANGLE AT
INDEX 10-
INSPECTED

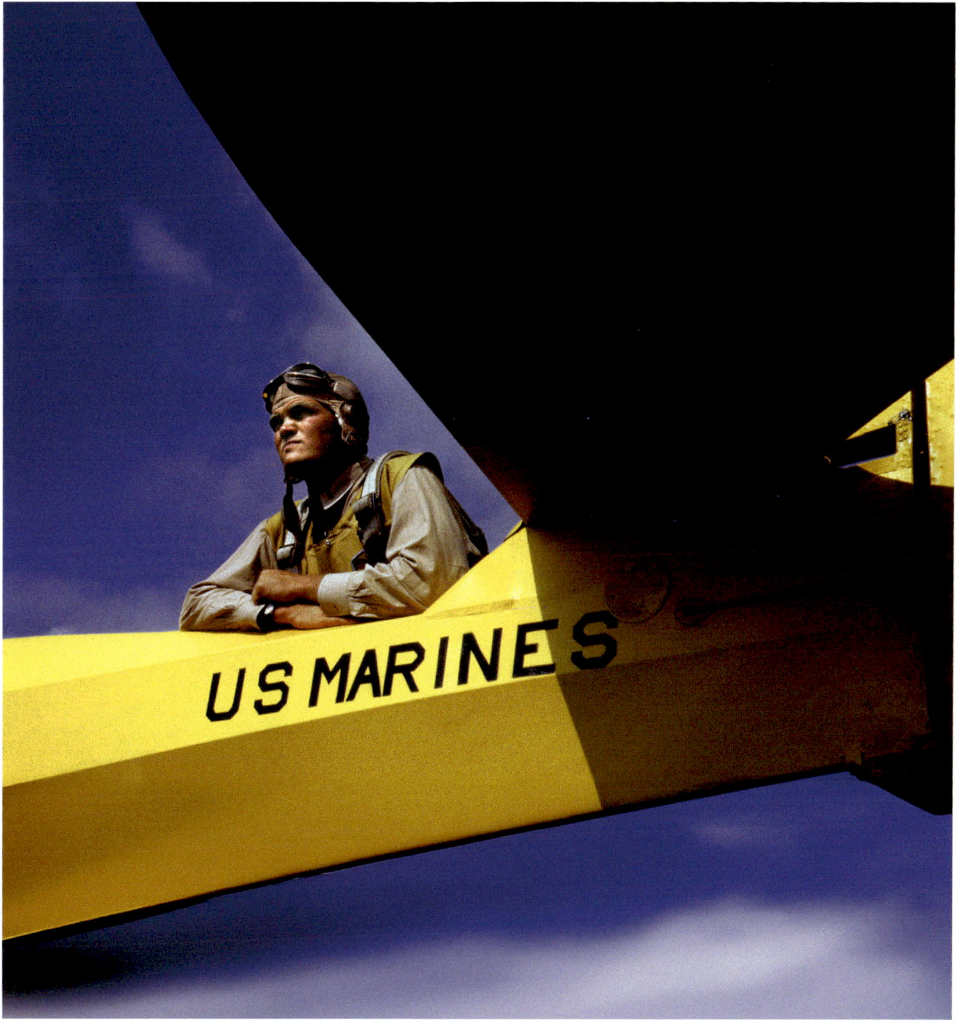

Marine glider pilot in training at Page Field, watching take-offs, Parris Island, South Carolina, May 1942. (*Library of Congress*)

Opposite page: Lieutenant "Mike" Hunter, army pilot assigned to Douglas Aircraft Company, Long Beach, California, October 1942. (*Library of Congress*)

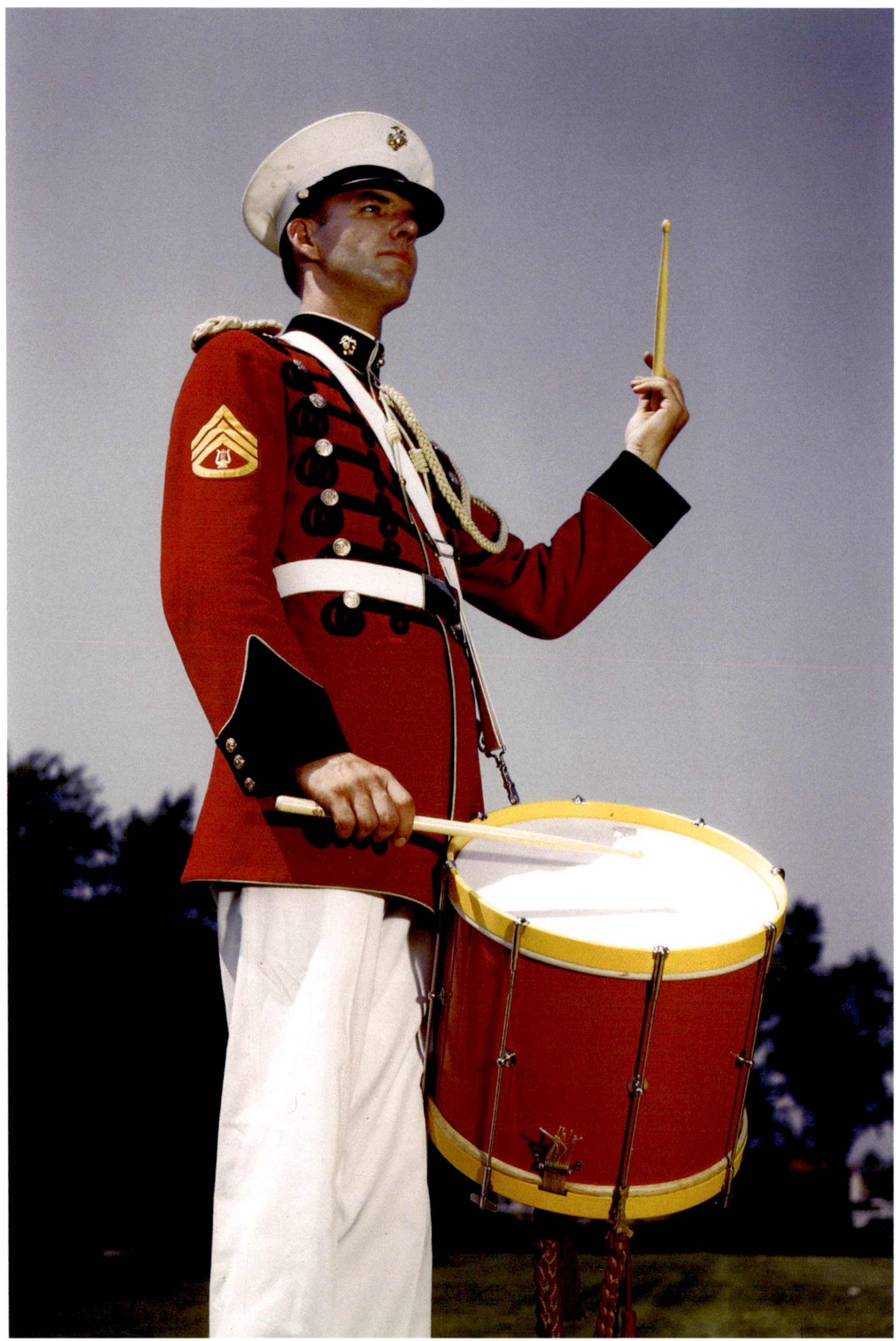

U.S. Marine Band drummer, probably at the Marine Barracks, Washington, D.C., May 1942.
(*Library of Congress*)

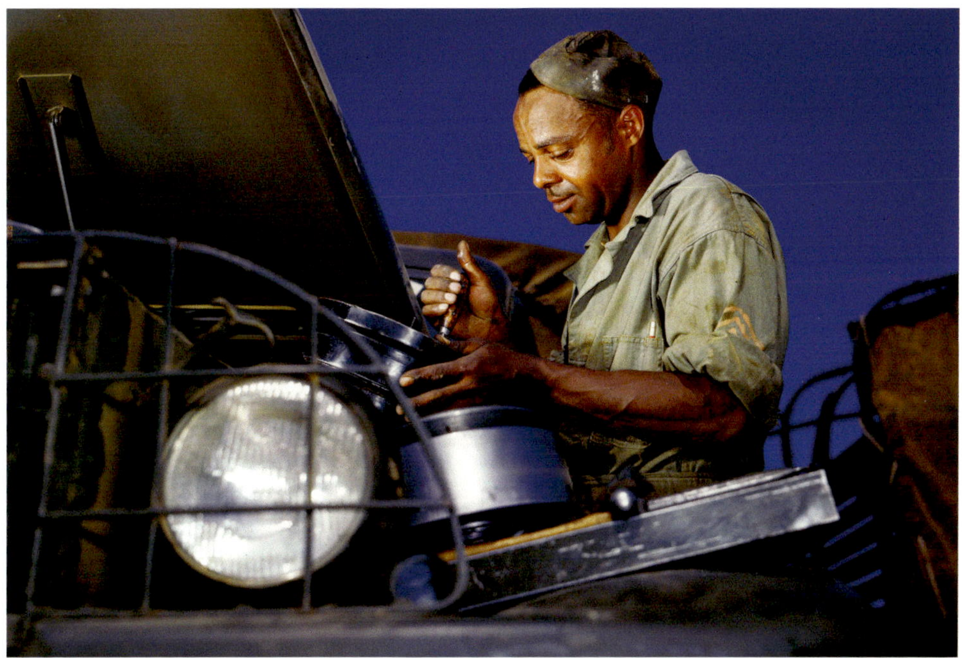

A good job in the air cleaner of an army truck, Fort Knox, Kentucky. This black soldier, who serves as truckdriver and mechanic, plays an important part in keeping army transport fleets in operation, June 1942. (*Library of Congress*)

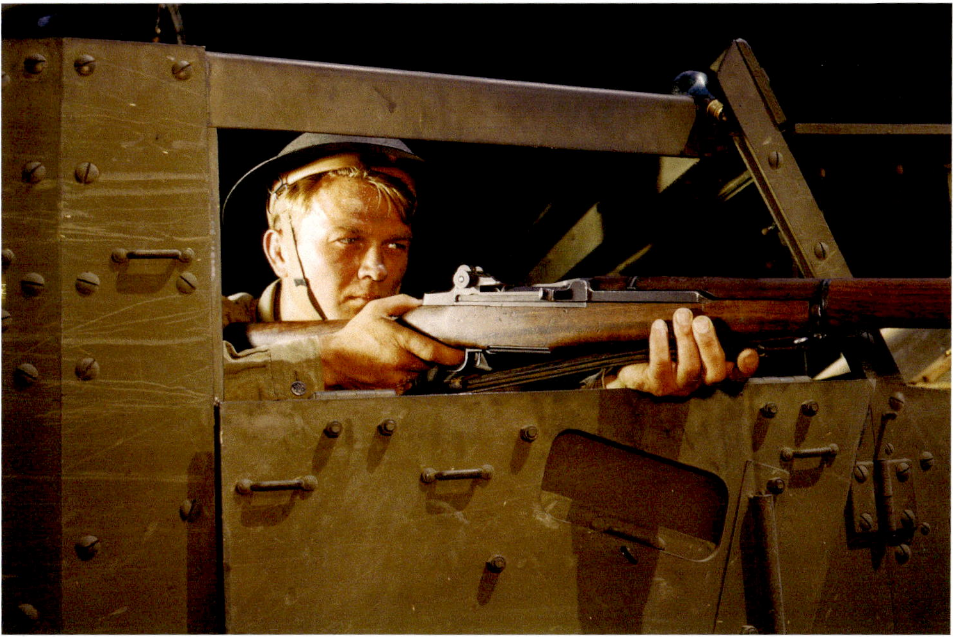

Halftrack infantryman with Garand rifle, Ft. Knox, Kentucky, June 1942. (*Library of Congress*)

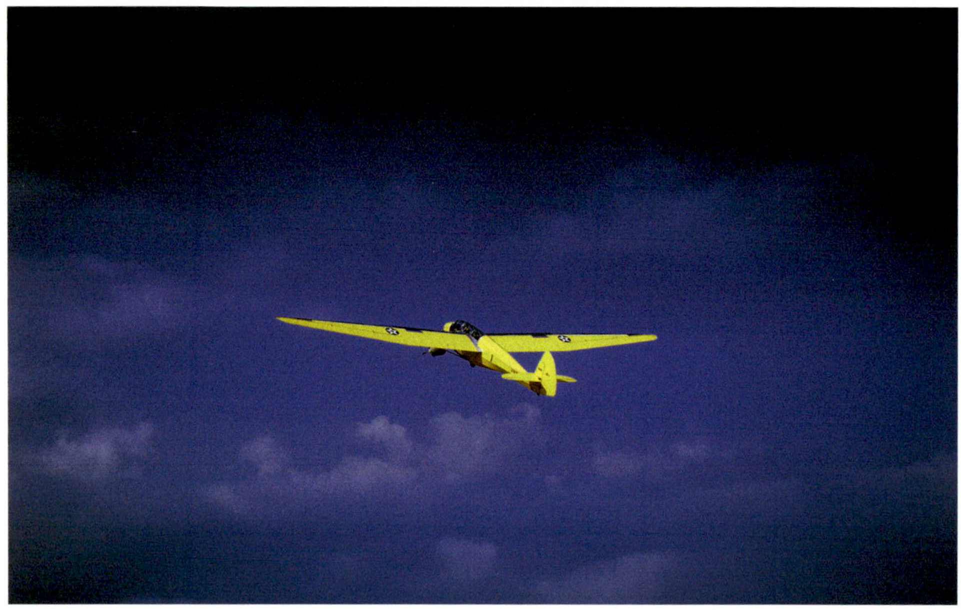

Marine Corps glider in flight out of Parris Island, South Carolina, May 1942. (*Library of Congress*)

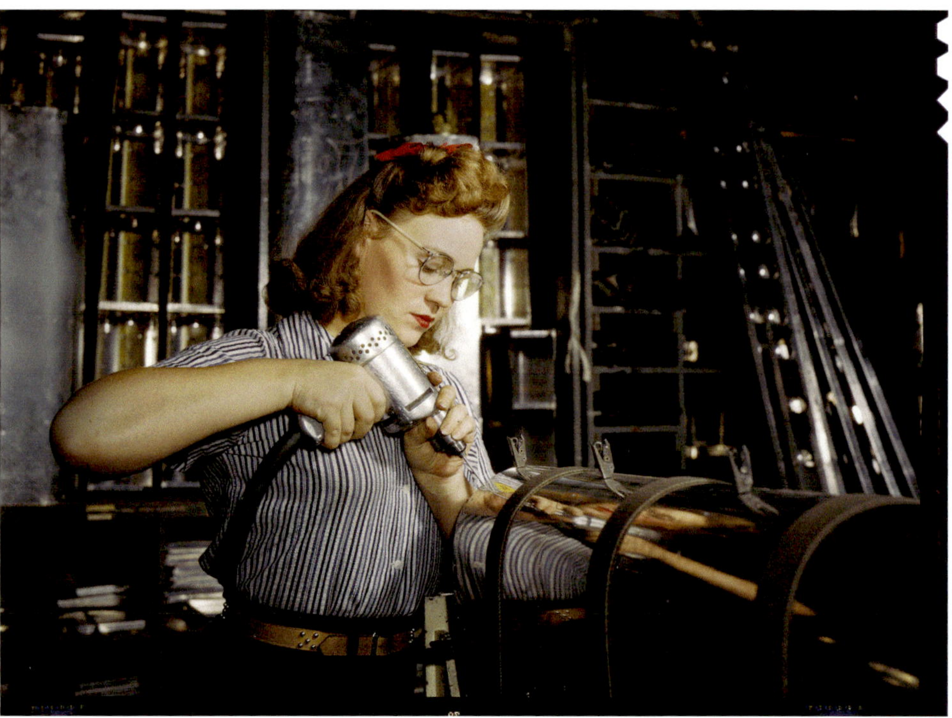

Operating a hand drill at Vultee-Nashville, a woman is working on a Vengeance dive bomber, February 1943. (*Library of Congress*)

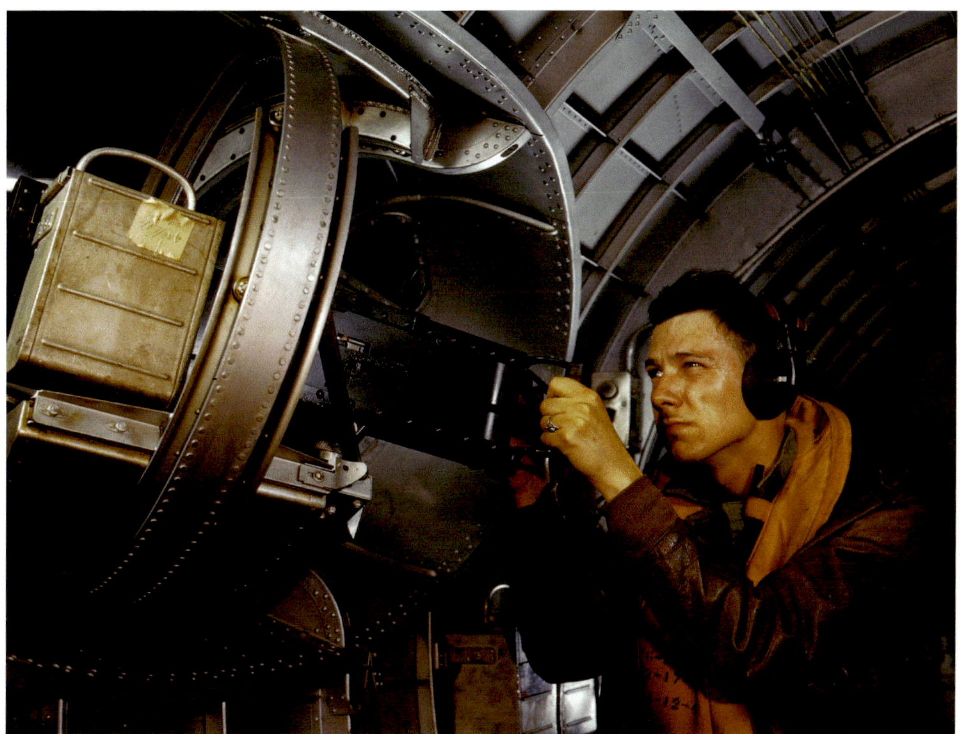

Above: Hitler would like this man to go home and forget about the war. A good American non-com at the side machine gun of a huge YB-17 bomber is a man who knows his business and works hard at it. Langley Air Force Base, Virginia, May 1942. (*Library of Congress*)

Right: An employee in the drill-press section of North American's huge machine shop runs mounting holes in a large dural casting, Inglewood, California, October 1942. This plant produces the battle-tested B-25 ("Billy Mitchell") bomber, used in General Doolittle's raid on Tokyo, and the P-51 ("Mustang") fighter plane which was first brought into prominence by the British raid on Dieppe. (*Library of Congress*)

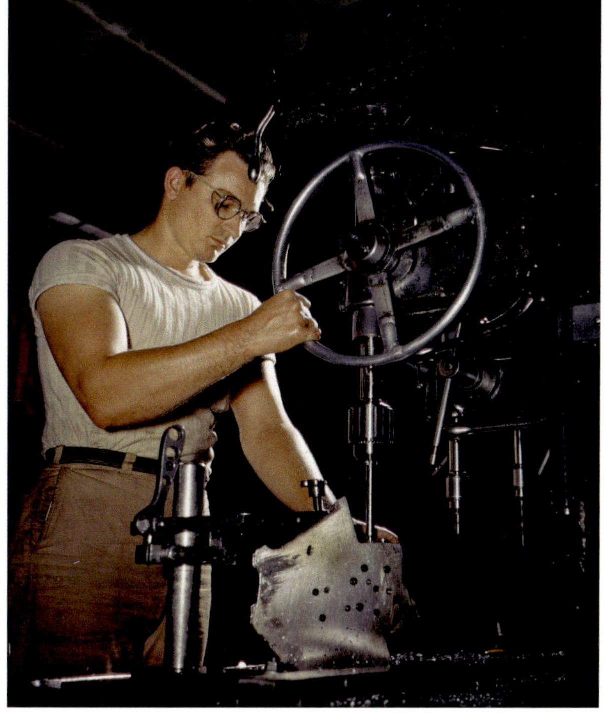

ENDNOTES

Introduction

1 The image also appeared in the April 1942 issue of *Popular Photography*. The slogan was taken from a British World War I song composed in 1914 by Ivor Novello. The lyrics were written by Lena Guilbert Ford. The full title of the song was "Keep the Home-Fires Burning (Till the Boys Come Home)."

2 Lee, M., *Promoting the War Effort: Robert Horton and Federal Propaganda 1938–1946* (Baton Rouge, LA: Louisiana State University Press, 2012), p. 16. Palmer and Land had met at least once prior to the photographer's hire at the U.S. Maritime Commission. Both men had sailed together in 1938 on the *SS Brazil*'s maiden voyage. The ship was owned by the Moore-McCormack Lines. Information from undated Palmer resume, Alfred T. Palmer Papers, hereafter ATP Papers.

3 Lee, *Ibid.*, p. 73.

4 Jowett, G. S. and O'Donnell, V., *Propaganda and Persuasion*, 7th ed. (Los Angeles: Sage Publications, 2019), p. 9.

5 Lee, *op. cit.*, pp. 29, 49; Palmer, A. T., Interview with Macauley, C., June 19, 1988.

6 Lee, *op. cit.*, p. 154.

7 Jowett and O'Donnell, *op. cit.*, pp. 17, 18.

8 Olson, L., *Those Angry Days: Roosevelt, Lindberg, and America's Fight over World War II, 1939–1941* (New York: Random House, 2013), p. xviii.

9 Doenecke, J. D., "Non-Interventionism of the Left: The Keep America Out of War Congress 1938–1941," *Journal of Contemporary History*, vol. 12, no. 2, (1977), pp. 221–236; Berg, A. S., *Lindbergh* (New York: G.P. Putnam, 1988), pp. 386–432.

10 Catton, B., *The War Lords of Washington* (New York: Greenwood Press, 1969), p. 16–18.

11 Olson, *op. cit.*, pp. xiv–xxi. For more on Roosevelt's move toward interventionism, see Simms, B. and Laderman, C., *Hitler's American Gamble: Pearl Harbor and Germany's March to Global War* (New York: Basic Books, 2023), pp. 11–14; Steele, R. W., *Propaganda in an Open Society: The Roosevelt Administration and the Media, 1933–1941* (Westport, CT: Greenwood Press, 1985), pp. 83–84, 88; Winkler, A. M., *The Politics of Propaganda: The Office of War Information 1942–1945* (New Haven, CT: Yale University Press, 1978), p. 20.

12 Lee, *op. cit.*, p. 97; Steele, R. W., "The Great Debate: Roosevelt, the Media, and the Coming of the War, 1940–1941," *Journal of American History*, vol. 71, no. 1, (1984), p. 70; Winkler, 1978, *Ibid.*, pp. 13, 63.

13 Carson, J. C., *Interpreting National Identity in Time of War: Competing Views in United States Office of War Information (OWI) Photography, 1940–1945* (Ph.D. diss., Boston University, 1995), p. 145.

14 "Woman Power," *archives.gov*, Washington, D.C., www.archives.gov/files/education/lessons/images/wwii-womanpower.pdf (accessed April 19, 2023), pp. 3, 7.

15 Wynn, N. A., *The African American Experience during World War II* (New York: Rowman and Littlefield Publishers, 2010), pp. 67–68.

16 "A few facts related to The Arsenal of Democracy and the Four Freedoms exhibits of World War Two," exhibit proposal, ATP Papers.

17 "A few facts," *Ibid.*

18 Palmer, A. T., Interview with Smith, D. and Haller, S., October 25, 1988.

19 Carson, *op. cit.*, p. 47.

20 Palmer, A. T., Interview with Smith, D., November 2, 1988.

21 Steele, 1985, *op. cit.*, p. 142.

22 Quoted in "THE PEOPLE: Smug, Slothful, Asleep?" *Time*, vol. 39, no. 7 (February 16, 1942), p. 11; For more on America's "withdrawal" from taking a leading role in international politics following World War I, see Simms and Laderman, *op. cit.*, pp. 3–4.

23 "THE PEOPLE," *Ibid.*, p. 11.

24 Winkler, 1978, *op. cit.*, pp. 39–41, 54–55, 57.

25 Carson, *op. cit.*, p. 169.

26 Palmer, A. T. to Palmer, A., 1942 (no specific date given). Several strikes occurred at the Ford Motor Company's Willow Run plant. That company's River Rouge Plant also saw a strike. For more, see Baime, A. J., *The Arsenal of Democracy: FDR, Detroit, and an Epic Quest to Arm an America at War* (Boston: Mariner Books, 2015), pp. 115–120, 155–56.

27 Baime, *Ibid.*, p. 156.

28 Rose, K. D., *American Isolationism Between World Wars: The Search for a Nation's Identity* (New York: Routledge, 2021), p. 3.

29 The film debuted in 1935. It was first used as 16-mm motion picture film.

30 Statistics on military enlistments can be found at: Hull, T. J., "The World War II Army Enlistment Records File and Access to Archival Databases," *Prologue Magazine* 38, no. 1, (Spring 2006), available at: www.archives.gov/publications/prologue/2006/spring/aad-ww2.html (accessed June 10, 2023); Dumenil, L., *American Working Women in World War II: A Brief History with Documents* (New York: Bedford/St. Martin's, 2020), p. 8.

31 Broussard, J. C., and Hamilton, J. M., "Covering a Two-Front War: Three African American Correspondents during World War II," *American Journalism*, vol. 22, no. 3, (2005), p. 35; Winkler, 1978, *op. cit.*, pp. 56, 67–68.

32 Winkler, 1978, *Ibid.*, pp. 65–66.

33 For more on Horton and his wartime career, see Lee, *op. cit.*, Palmer cites the 8,000 photographs figure in his interview with Macauley. See: Palmer, A. T., Interview with Macauley, C., June 19, 1988.

34 Palmer, A. T., Interview with Smith, D. and Haller, S., October 25, 1988.

35 Quoted in Hill, J. T., and Liesbrock, H., *Walker Evans: Depth of Field* (New York: Prestel, 2016), p. 310.

36 Marchand, R., *Advertising the American Dream: Making Way for Modernity, 1920–1940* (Berkeley: University of California, 1985), pp. 120, 121, 125, 127.

37 Dumenil, *op. cit.*, p. 8.

38 On praise for Eggleston's work, see Cullinan, N., "Director's Foreword," in *William Eggleston Portraits*, ed. Prodger, P., (New Haven: Yale University Press, 2016), p. 9.

39 Emailed comments from Gennert, J. P. to Cronin, M. M., July 12, 2023.

40 Camhi, L., "Propriety and Provocation: Women, Emigres, and Outliers in American Magazines at Mid-Century," in *Modern Look: Photography and the American Magazine*, ed. Klein, M. (New Haven: Yale University Press, 2020), pp. 126, 127

41 Camhi, *Ibid.*, pp. 126, 127; Heiferman, M., "Astonish Me!: Photography, Graphic Design, and Mid-Century Visual Culture," in *Modern Look: Photography and the American Magazine*, ed. Klein, M. (New Haven: Yale University Press, 2020), pp. 168, 171, 172.

42 Ehrens, S., "Revisiting a Modernist Pioneer," in *Imogen Cunningham: A Retrospective*, by Martineau, P. (Los Angeles: J. Paul Getty Museum, 2020), pp. 44, 46, 47, 48.

43 Swensen, J., "A Strategy of Truth: Andreas Feininger and the Creation of Propaganda for the Office of War Information, 1942," *History of Photography*, vol. 42, no. 1, (2019), pp. 84, 85, 88, 89; Acker, E., *et al.*, *Cult of the Machine: Precisionism and American Art* (New Haven, CT: Yale University Press, 2018); Brock, C., *Charles Sheeler: Across Media* (Berkeley: University of California Press, 2006).

44 Carson, *op. cit.*, p. 35.
45 A detailed assessment of photographic strengths and weaknesses by various federal government departments and the branches of the U.S. military was undertaken by the editors of *U.S. Camera*. See "What About Photography in National Defense?" *U. S. Camera* (August 1941), photocopy in ATP Papers.
46 Lee, *op. cit.*, p. 140; Palmer, A. T., Interview with Macauley, C., June 19, 1988.
47 Frank A. Norick, then the principal museum anthropologist at the Lowie Museum of Anthropology at Berkeley, California, said of Palmer's documentary film footage of Asian nations and Pacific Islanders: "… much of what he captured on film remains a fascinating and accurate anthropological record of the daily and ceremonial lifeways of these Pacific Rim peoples." Norick, F. A., Hayworth, E., Bolinas, California, December 2, 1991, ATP Papers.
48 Palmer recalled that the captain of the Matson Lines SS *Mariposa* criticized the photographer, telling him that he was spending too much time shooting still pictures and motion picture film for Ripley, rather than taking images of the ship and its passengers— the key tasks for which he was hired. Palmer, A. T., Interview with Smith, D. and Haller, S., October 25, 1988.
49 Palmer, A. T., Interview with Smith, D. and Haller, S., October 25, 1988.
50 Haboush Plunkett, S., *Enduring Ideals: Rockwell, Roosevelt, and the Four Freedoms* (New York: Abbeville Press, 2018).
51 Reeves, R., *Infamy: The Shocking Story of the Japanese American Internment in World War II* (New York: Henry Holt, 2016), p. xiii; Daniels, R., *Prisoners without Trial: Japanese Americans in World War II* (New York: Hill and Wang, 2004). Winkler, A. M., *Home Front U.S.A.: America During World War II* (Wheeling, Ill.: Harlan Davidson, 2000), pp. 11, 28-53, 80–83; Michney, T. M., "Constrained Communities: Black Cleveland's Experience with World War II Public Housing," *Journal of Social History*, vol. 40, no. 4, 2007, pp. 933–956; Perrett, G., *Days of Sadness, Years of Triumph: The American People, 1939–1945* (Madison, WI, University of Wisconsin Press, 1985), pp. 240–241.
52 Palmer received a brief mention in both Lee, *op. cit.* and Winkler, 1978, *op cit.*
53 "Salon of Photography," exhibit brochure, Rochester (New York) Museum of Arts and Sciences, 1940, ATP Papers.
54 Museum of Modern Art, "Road to Victory," www.moma.org/calendar/exhibitions/3038 (accessed August 9, 2022). The photographs were displayed but the photographers' names were not attached to their work, thus leaving their visual artistry seen but uncredited.
55 "A few facts related to The Arsenal of Democracy and The Four Freedoms exhibits of World War Two," *op. cit.*, ATP Papers.
56 Carson, *op. cit.*, p. 144.
57 Hurley, F. J., *Portrait of a Decade: Roy Stryker and the Development of Documentary Photography in the Thirties* (New York: Da Capo Press, 1972), p. 13.
58 Niven, P., *Steichen: A Biography* (Fort Washington, PA.: Eastern National, 1997), p. 518.
59 Hambourg, M. M., "The Heart of the Matter," in Hambourg, M. M., and Rosenheim, J. L., eds., *Irving Penn: Centennial* (New Haven, CT: Yale University Press, 2017), pp. 15–18; Friedl, B., "The Hybrid Art of Fashion Photography: American Photographers in Post-World War II Europe," *Amerikastudien*, vol. 52, no. 1, (2007), pp. 47–62.
60 Johnston, P., "The Modernist Fashion: Steichen's Commercial Photography between the Wars," in Brandow, T. and Ewing, W. A., eds., *Edward Steichen: Lives in Photography* (New York: W. W. Norton & Company, 2007), p. 237.
61 Meyer, R., "Photography is Elastic: Weegee's Cockeyed View of Hollywood," *American Art*, vol. 27, no. 2, (2013), p. 33.

Chapter 1

1 An article notes that the family lived "for a time" in Palmer's father's livery stable before the Palmers moved to Long Beach. Cahill, G., "Shadows of the Past," *Pacific Sun*, July 27, 1990, photocopy in ATP Papers.

2   Palmer, A. T., Interview with Macauley, C., June 19, 1988.

3   Palmer, A. T., Interview with Smith, D. and Haller, S., October 25, 1988.

4   Cahill, *op. cit.*; "Alfred T. Palmer," *Marin Independent Journal*, February 5, 1993, clipping in ATP Papers; Palmer, A. T., Interview with Macauley, C., June 19, 1988.

5   Hendricks, C. and Delgaudio, J., "A Vast War Establishment: World War II Comes to Long Beach," *Southern California Quarterly*, vol. 99, no. 4, (2017), pp. 444, 446, 447.

6   Palmer, A. T., Interview with Smith, D. and Haller, S., October 25, 1988.

7   Palmer, A. T., Interview with Macauley, C., June 19, 1988; "Biography of Alfred T. Palmer," ATP Papers. Palmer also was captain of his high school marching band and served as President of the Science Club. For more on these activities, see the Long Beach Polytechnic High School Yearbooks of 1924 and 1925. The 1924 edition of the school's yearbook, the *Caerulea*, praised Palmer's leadership of the marching band, stating: "Capt. Alfred Palmer, assisted by Lieutenants [Don] Gilkerson and [Emory] Diemer, proved himself to be an officer of sterling worth by bringing the marching band up to such a pitch of efficiency that it was remarked upon by the inspecting officer." *Caerulea* 1924, p. 157.

8   All the cruise ships on which Palmer worked also had cargo holds and did joint duty of carrying passengers and cargo.

9   Palmer, A. T., Interview with Smith, D. and Haller, S., October 25, 1988.

10   Palmer, A. T., Interview with Smith, D. and Haller, S., October 25, 1988.

11   For more on the Dollar Line's history, see Goldberg, M. H., *The "Stately President" Liners: American Passenger Liners of the Interwar Years, Part I: The 502's* (Kings Point, N.Y.: American Merchant Marine Museum, 1996), pp. 37–39, 196; Palmer interview (Macauley), ATP Papers.

12   One of Palmer's resumes lists the summer months of 1925 as the period in which he worked for Crandall. The date appears to be incorrect since Palmer graduated from high school that year and immediately went on his first three-month cruise as a cadet with the Dollar Steamship Lines. Undated resume, ATP Papers. His summer in Wyoming most likely took place in 1926.

13   Barrick, K. A., *Harrison R. Crandall: Creating a Vision of Grand Teton National Park* (Layton, UT: Gibbs Smith, 2013), p. 128.

14   Crandall's biographer, Kenneth A. Barrick, does not name which of several art schools in Los Angeles that Crandall attended for several years. Barrick, K. A., "Harrison R. Crandall: Artist, Pioneer and Patron of Grand Teton National Park," *University of Wyoming National Park Service Research Center Annual Report*, vol. 30, (2006), pp. 19–22.

15   Barrick, 2013, *op. cit.*, 2013, p. 128.

16   Barrick, 2013, *Ibid.*, pp. 35, 37, 39, 44–45.

17   Barrick, 2013, *Ibid.*, p. 49.

18   Barrick, 2013, *Ibid.*, pp. 61, 79.

19   Cahill, *op. cit.*; "Biography of Alfred T. Palmer," ATP Papers.

20   Cahill, *Ibid.*

21   Palmer, A. T., Interview with Macauley, C., June 19, 1988.

22   For example, see Palmer, A. T., to Palmer, A., February 16, 1932, ATP Papers.

23   Palmer, A. T., Interview with Macauley, C., June 19, 1988.

24   Petro, D., "Brother, Can you Spare a Dime?: The 1940 Census: Employment and Income," *Prologue*, Spring 2012, www.archives.gov/publications/prologue/2012/spring/1940.html (accessed July 1, 2023).

25   Palmer, A. T., Interview with Macauley, C., June 19, 1988; Palmer billed himself as "The Vagabond Photographer" on his business stationary during the early 1930s.

26   For statistics on magazine readership and circulation see, Sumner, D. E., *The Magazine Century: American Magazines Since 1900* (New York: Peter Lang, 2010), p. 2. Sumner's statistics show that 44,095,000 copies of magazines were printed in the United States in 1920. That number rose to 78,844,000 by 1930.

27   Palmer's images of Shanghai were featured in the following article: Boyden, A., "Changing Shanghai," *National Geographic*, (October 1937), pp. 485–508. Palmer's uncredited images of Brazil appeared in the inaugural, November 23, 1936, issue of *Life*, on pp. 40–45.

28 Palmer, A. T., Interview with Macauley, C., June 19, 1988.

29 Undated resume, ATP Papers; Gennert, J. P. Palmer, Interview with Cronin, M. M., June 9, 2022; Palmer, A. T., Interview with Macauley, C., June 19, 1988.

30 Palmer, A. T., Interview with Smith, D. and Haller, S., October 25, 1988.

31 Palmer, A. T., Interview with Smith, D. and Haller, S., October 25, 1988.

32 Norris, J. D., *Advertising and the Transformation of American Society, 1865–1920* (Westport, CT: Greenwood Press, 1990), p. 168. Johnston, P., *Real Fantasies: Edward Steichen's Advertising Photography* (Berkeley, CA: University of California Press, 1997), p. 1.

33 Johnston, P., "The Modernist Fashion: Steichen's Commercial Photography between the Wars," in *Edward Steichen: Lives in Photography*, eds. Brandow, T. and Ewing, W. A., (New York: FEP Editions, 2007), p. 237. The growing use of flash photography led some photography magazines to publish tutorials on the subject. For example, see Elisofon, E., "Texture, Chiaroscuro, Expression and Form Through Proper Flash Illumination," *U. S. Camera* 1941 annual, pp. 177–205.

34 The home may have been a rental. Palmer and his wife had their Berkeley home built in 1931. Information courtesy of J. P. Gennert.

35 Palmer, A. T., Interview with Macauley, C., June 19, 1988.

36 Palmer, A. T., Interview with Smith, D. and Haller, S., October 25, 1988.

37 Palmer, A. T., Interview with Macauley, C., June 19, 1988.

38 Mall, S., "FreightWaves Classics/Fallen Flags: American President Lines still lives under new ownership (Part 2)," www.freightwaves.com/news/freightwaves-classics-fallen-flags-american-president-lines-still-lives-under-new-ownership-part-2 (accessed August 30, 2022). Originally published September 22, 2021; "Alfred T. Palmer," Office of War Information, Washington, D.C., 1942, ATP Papers.

39 "Biography of Alfred T. Palmer," ATP Papers. (Note: Undated and no author.)

40 Larsen, R., "A lifetime of filming took them on trips around the world," *Marin Independent Journal*, April 14, 1984, photocopied clipping, ATP Papers.

41 Palmer, A. T., Interview with Smith, D. and Haller, S., October 25, 1988.

42 Palmer, A. T., Interview with Smith, D. and Haller, S., October 25, 1988.

43 Palmer, A. T., Interview with Macauley, C., June 19, 1988; French, P., *Bloody Saturday: Shanghai's Darkest Day* (New York: Penguin Books, 2017), pp. 74, 93–95.

44 Palmer, A. T., Interview with Smith, D. and Haller, S., October 25, 1988.

45 A. T. Palmer resume, ATP Papers. The resume is undated, but the last entry is 1947.

46 Palmer, A. T., to Palmer, A., April 27, 1939, ATP Papers.

47 Palmer, A. T., to Palmer, A., *Ibid.*

48 Information from undated OEM resume, ATP Papers.

49 For more on straight photography as an aesthetic, see "Straight Photography," The Alfred Stieglitz Collection, archive.artic.edu/stieglitz/straight-photography/ (Accessed July 9, 2022); Mora, G. and Brannan, B. W., *FSA: The American Vision* (New York: Abrams, 2006), p. 13. For information on early twentieth-century pictorialism, see Gedrim, R. J., "Peinture a la Lumiere: 1898–1907," in Brandow, T. and Ewing, W. A., *Edward Steichen*, pp. 83–85; Johnston, 1997, *op. cit.*, pp. 1, 30–31, 87–88.

50 Norris, *op. cit.*, pp. 167, 168. Pincas, S. and Loiseau, M., *A History of Advertising* (Los Angeles: Taschen, 2008), p. 20; Johnston, 1997, *op. cit.*, pp. 1, 30–31, 87–88.

51 Horton, R. W., to Palmer, A. T., April 25, 1940, ATP Papers.

52 Lacey, J., *The Washington War: FDR's Inner Circle and the Politics of Power that Won World War II* (New York: Bantam Books, 2020), pp. 3–5; Goodwin, D. K., *No Ordinary Time: Franklin and Eleanor Roosevelt: The Home Front in World War II* (New York: Simon and Schuster, 1994), pp. 9, 14.

53 Horton had worked as a journalist for several newspapers and for the Associated Press. He also had hosted a radio show prior to entering public relations work. Lee, M., *Promoting the War Effort: Robert Horton and Federal Propaganda, 1938–1946* (Baton Rouge, LA: Louisiana State University Press, 2021), pp. 28–29.

54 Doenecke, J. D. and Wilz, J. E., *From Isolation to War: 1931–1941*, 3rd edn. (Hoboken, NJ: Wiley-Blackwell, 2015).

55 Palmer, A. T., Interview with Macauley, C., June 19, 1988.

Chapter 2

1 On the America public's disinterest, initially, on not coming the England's aid, see Fleming, T., *The New Dealers' War: Franklin D. Roosevelt and the War within World War II* (New York: Basic Books, 2001), p. 4.

2 Heinrichs, W., *Threshold of War: Franklin D. Roosevelt and American Entry into World War II* (New York: Oxford University Press, 1988), p. 7.

3 Contiguglia, G., "Recruiting Public Opinion: The Posters of World War II," *Colorado Heritage*, (Winter 1995), p. 22.

4 Steele, R. W., *Propaganda in an Open Society: The Roosevelt Administration and the Media, 1933–1941* (Westport, CT: Greenwood Press, 1985), pp. 16–17.

5 Steele, 1985, *Ibid.*

6 Scientific polling companies regularly questioned Americans on their support for the president's policies and published those results. Roosevelt often sought to win the "war" of public opinion against opponents in the U. S. Congress and the opposition media. Daniels, R., *Franklin D. Roosevelt: The War Years, 1939–1944* (Urbana, IL: University of Illinois Press, 2016), p. 158.

7 Steele, 1985, *op. cit.*, pp. x, 8.

8 Baime, A. J., *The Arsenal of Democracy: FDR, Detroit, and an Epic Quest to Arm and America at War* (Boston: Mariner Books, 2015), pp. 66, 67.

9 Reynolds, D., "1940: Fulcrum of the Twentieth Century?" *International Affairs*, vol. 66, no. 2, (1990), p. 334.

10 Daniels, 2016, *op. cit.*, p. 278.

11 Steele, 1985, *op. cit.*, p. 54.

12 Heinrichs, *op. cit.*, p. 7.

13 The laws were meant to keep history from repeating itself by not allowing the economic conditions and naval incidents to reoccur that had drawn the United States into World War I. Reynolds, *op. cit.*, p. 331; Goodwin, D. K., *No Ordinary Time: Franklin & Eleanor Roosevelt: The Home Front in World War II* (New York: Simon & Schuster, 2008), p. 22.

14 Lacey, J., *The Washington War: FDR's Inner Circle and the Politics of Power that Won World War II* (New York: Bantam Books, 2020), p. 22; Dunn, S., *A Blueprint for War: FDR and the Hundred Days that Mobilized America* (New Haven, CT: Yale University Press, 2018), pp. 123–124, 136.

15 Dunn, *Ibid.*, p. 5.

16 Dunn, *Ibid.*

17 On Roosevelt's public pronouncements of neutrality, see Daniels, 2016, *op. cit.*, p. 33.

18 Klingaman, W. K., *The Darkest Year: The American Home Front 1941–1942* (New York: St. Martin's Press, 2019), p. 10.

19 Lacey, *op. cit.*, pp. 14–15, 22-27.

20 Dunn, *op. cit.*, p. 6; Herman, A., *Freedom's Forge: How American Business Produced Victory in World War II* (New York: Random House, 2013), pp. 9–13.

21 Klingaman, *op. cit.*, pp. 14, 19–21.

22 A transcript of the address can be found at: The American Presidency Project, "Fireside Chat," University of California (Santa Barbara), www.presidency.ucsb.edu/documents/fireside-chat-9 (accessed July 19, 2022).

23 Winkler, A. M., *The Politics of Propaganda: The Office of War Information 1942–1945* (New Haven, CT: Yale University Press, 1978), p. 4.

24 Welch, D., *World War II Propaganda: Analyzing the Art of Persuasion during Wartime* (Santa Barbara, CA: ABC-CLIO, 2017), p. xiii.

25 Hamilton, J. N., *Manipulating the Masses: Woodrow Wilson and the Birth of American Propaganda* (Baton Rouge, LA: Louisiana State University Press, 2020), pp. 7, 185.

26 Hamilton, *Ibid.*, pp. 463–467; Axelrod, A., *Selling the Great War: The Making of American Propaganda* (New York: St. Martin's Press, 2009), pp. 211–225; Creel, G., *How We Advertised America: The First Telling of the Amazing Story on the Committee on Public Information that Carried the Gospel of Americanism to Every Corner of the Globe* (New York: Harper and Brothers, 1920).

27 Winkler, 1978, *op. cit.*, p. 3; Hamilton, *Ibid.*, pp. 471, 473–474; Fasce, F., "Advertising America, Constructing the Nation: Rituals of the Homefront During the Great War," *European Contributions to American Studies*, vol. 44, (2000), pp. 161–174; Buitenhuis, P., "The Selling of the Great War," *Canadian Review of American Studies*, vol. 7, no. 2 (1976), pp. 139–150.

28 *American War and Military Operations Casualties: Lists and Statistics*, CRS Report No. RL32492, Version 25, p. 2 (Washington, DC: Congressional Research Service, September 14, 2018), 2, crsreports.congress.gov/product/pdf/RL/RL32492.

29 Dallek, R., *Franklin D. Roosevelt: A Political Life* (New York: Viking, 2017), pp. 12–13.

30 Welch, *op. cit.*, pp. xiii, xiv.

31 Taylor, P. M., *Munitions of the Mind: A History of Propaganda from the Ancient World to the Present Day* (Manchester, UK: Manchester University Press, 1995), p. 210.

32 Welch, *op. cit.*, p. xxii.

33 Steele, 1985, *op. cit.*, pp. 83, 85–86, 87.

34 Winkler, 1978, *op. cit.*, pp. 20–21, 29–31.

35 Carson, J. C., *Interpreting National Identity in Time of War: Competing Views in United States Office of War Information (OWI) Photography, 1940–1945* (Ph.D. diss., Boston University, 1995), pp. 6, 146.

36 Pinkleton, B., "The Campaign of the Committee on Public Information: Its Contributions to the History and Evolution of Public Relations," *Journal of Public Relations Research*, vol. 6, no. 4 (1994), pp. 229–240.

37 Weinberg, S., "What to Tell America: The Writers' Quarrel in the Office of War Information," *Journal of American History*, vol. 55, no. 1 (1968), p. 73.

38 Daniels, 2016, *op. cit.*, p. 279; McMillan, G., "The News Bureau of the OWI—Its Functions and Operations," *Journalism Quarterly*, vol. 20, no. 2, (1943), p. 117; Larson, C., "OWI's Domestic News Bureau: An Account and Appraisal," *Journalism Quarterly*, vol. 26, no. 1 (1949), pp. 3, 7, 9.

39 Broughton, P. S., "Government Agencies and Civilian Morale," *The Annals of the American Academy of Political and Social Science*, vol. 220 (March 1942), p. 171.

40 Quoted in "What About Photography in National Defense," *U.S. Camera* (August 1941), p. 28.

41 Koppes, C. R. and Black, G. D., "Blacks, Loyalty, and Motion-Picture Propaganda in World War II," *Journal of American History*, vol. 73, no. 2 (1986), p. 384; Pinkleton, *op. cit.*, pp. 229–240.

42 Duis, P. R., "Soldiers Without Guns," *Chicago History*, vol. 16, no. 3 (1987–88), pp. 29–30.

43 Winkler, 1978, *op. cit.*, pp. 20–21, 34–35.

44 Carson, *op. cit.*, pp. 1–2.

45 Winkler, 1978, *op. cit.*, p. 70.

46 Blum, J. M., *V was for Victory* (New York: Harvest Books, 1976), p. 8.

47 Lippmann, W., *Public Opinion* (New York: Free Press, 1997), p. 61. The first edition of the book was published in 1922.

48 Heiferman, M., "Astonish Me!: Photography, Graphic Design, and Mid-Century Visual Culture," in Klein, M., (ed.), *Modern Look: Photography and the American Magazine* (New Haven, CT: Yale University Press, 2020), pp. 168, 169.

49 Marchand, R., *Advertising the American Dream: Making Way for Modernity, 1920–1940* (Berkeley, CA: University of California Press, 1985), p. 149.

50 Orbach, B. and Natanson, N., "The Mirror Image: Black Washington in World War II-Era Federal Photography," *Washington History*, vol. 4, no. 1 (1992), p. 6.

51 *U.S. Camera*, *op. cit.*, p. 29.

52 Winkler, 1978, *op. cit.*, pp. 6, 156–157.

53 Palmer, A. T., Interview with Smith, D. and Haller, S., October 25, 1988.

54 Carson, *op. cit.*, p. 26.

55 Carson, *Ibid.*, p. 41.

56 Carson, *Ibid.*, p. 42.

57 Palmer, A. T., Interview with Macauley, C., June 19, 1988.; Carson, *Ibid.*, p. 41.

58 Carson, *Ibid.*, p. 155.

59 Hurley, F. J., *Portrait of a Decade: Roy Stryker and the Development of Documentary Photography in the Thirties* (New York: Da Capo Press, 1972), pp. 158–166.

60 Palmer, A. T., to Palmer, A., September 19, 1938, ATP Papers.

61 Lee, M., *Promoting the War Effort: Robert Horton and Federal Propaganda 1938–1946* (Baton Rouge, LA: Louisiana State University Press, 2012), p. 97; Laurie, C. D., *The Propaganda Warriors: America's Crusade against Nazi Germany* (Lawrence: University of Kansas Press, 1995), p. 57; Winker, 1978, *op. cit.*, p. 22.

62 Carson, *op. cit.*, pp. 78, 79.

63 Rothstein, A., Interview with Doud, R. K., May 25, 1964.

64 The label the "concerned photographer" refers to "photographers who demonstrated in their work a humanitarian impulse to use pictures to educate and change the world, not just to record it." For more, see "Cornell Capa: Concerned Photographer," https://www.icp.org/exhibitions/cornell-capa-concerned-photographer (accessed July 25, 2022); Henri Cartier-Bresson's book, *The Decisive Moment*, was first published in 1952.

65 Roholl, M., "Preparing for Victory: The U. S. Office of War Information Overseas Branch's Illustrated Magazine in the Netherlands and the Foundations for the American Century, 1944–1945," *European Journal of American Studies*, vol. 7, no. 2 (2012), p. 15.

66 Roholl, *Ibid.*, pp. 6, 11–12.

67 Winkler, 1978, *op. cit.*, pp. 62–63.

68 Carson, *op. cit.*, p. 14.

69 Winkler, 1978, *op. cit.*, pp. 156–157.

70 Natanson, N. to Palmer, A. T., undated, ATP Papers.

71 *U S. Camera*, *op. cit.*, p. 29.

72 Stryker, R. to Delano, J., April 30, 1941.

73 Marchand, *op. cit.*, p. 120; Johnston, P., *Real Fantasies: Edward Steichen's Advertising Photography* (Berkeley: University of California Press, 1997), pp. 30–32.

74 Ben Shahn, who also worked as an artist for the OWI, opposed the organization's focus on advertising and positive propaganda. He argued that the federal government should focus instead on educating the public on the evils of Nazism. Greenfeld, H., *Ben Shahn: An Artist's Life* (New York: Random House, 1998), p. 189. Carson, *op. cit.*, pp. 129, 165.

75 Palmer did freelance jobs for advertising agencies prior to World War II, including Lord & Thomas, a San Francisco-based agency. Office for Emergency Management resume, ATP Papers. His pre-war photo albums in the hands of his family reveal Palmer took many images of natural beauty.

76 Becker Ohm, K., "What You See is What You Get: Dorothea Lange and Ansel Adams at Manzanar," *Journalism History*, vol. 4, no. 1 (1977), p. 18.

77 Lee, R. to Stryker, R., December 29, 1941, Stryker Papers.

78 Palmer, A. T., Interview with Macauley, C., June 19, 1988.

79 Stryker, R. to Lange, D., September 16, 1943, Stryker Papers.

80 Orbach and Natanson, *op. cit.*, p. 7.

81 Stryker, R. to Delano, J., Fayetteville, N.C., April 8, 1941, Stryker Papers.

82 Hurley, *op. cit.*, p. 164.

83 Stryker, R. to Delano, J., April 8, 1941, Stryker Papers.

84 The February 19, 1942, shooting script can be found in Stryker, R. and Wood, N., *In This Proud Land: America 1935–1943 as Seen in the FSA Photographs* (Greenwich, CT: New York Graphic Society, 1973), p. 188.

85 Stryker, R. to Delano, J., April 8, 1941, Stryker Papers.

Chapter 3

1 Favreau, M., *Crash: The Great Depression and the Fall and Rise of America* (New York: Little, Brown and Company, 2018), p. 2; On the extent of wartime production, see Perrett, G., *Days of Sadness, Years of Triumph: The American People, 1939–1945* (Madison, WI: University of Wisconsin Press, 1985), pp. 194, 195, 261.

2 The U.S. Maritime Commission was established by the Merchant Marine Act of 1936. Winkler, A. M., *Home Front U. S. A.: America during World War II* (Wheeling, IL.: Harlan Davidson, Inc., 2000), p. 11.

3 Hendrickson, B., "Priming the Flower's Stem: US Maritime Industries Prepare for War," *International Journal of Maritime History*, vol. 18, no. 1 (2006), pp. 132, 135, 136, 137, 138; Foster, M. S., *Henry J. Kaiser: Builder in the Modern American West* (Austin: University of Texas Press, 1989), pp. 69–70.

4 Hendrickson, *Ibid.*, pp. 133, 134, 135.

5 Perrett, *op. cit.*, p. 241.

6 Hendrickson, *op. cit.*, pp. 133, 134.

7 Dumenil, L., *American Working Women in World War II* (Boston, MA: Bedford-St. Martin's, 2020), p. 8.

8 O'Callaghan, T. J., *Ford in the Service of America: Mass Production for the Military During the World Wars* (Jefferson, NC: McFarland & Co., 2009), pp. 36, 45–50.

9 Gilford, S., *Build 'Em by the Mile, Cut 'Em off by the Yard: How Henry J. Kaiser and the Rosies Helped Win World War II* (Richmond, CA: Richmond Museum of History, 2011), pp. 8, 10.

10 Bunker, J., *Heroes in Dungarees: The Story of the American Merchant Marine in World War II* (Annapolis, MD: Naval Institute Press, 1995), p. 15.

11 Foster, *op. cit.*, pp. 71–78; Baime, A. J., *The Arsenal of Democracy: FDR, Detroit, and an Epic Quest to Arm an America at War* (Boston: Mariner Books, 2015), pp. 92–93, 107–108, 242, 248–249.

12 Palmer, A. T., Interview with Macauley, C., June 19, 1988.

13 Palmer, A. T., Interview with Macauley, C., June 19, 1988.

14 Quoted in Lee, M., *Promoting the War Effort: Robert Horton and Federal Propaganda, 1938–1946* (Baton Rouge, LA: Louisiana State University Press, 2021), p. 73.

15 Quoted in Lee, *Ibid.*, pp. 73–74.

16 Quoted in Carson, J. C., *Interpreting National Identity in Time of War: Competing Views in United States Office of War Information (OWI) Photography, 1940–1945* (Ph.D. diss., Boston University, 1995), p. 38.

17 The comments were written on an undated resume created during Palmer's tenure at the Office for Emergency Management. The resume is in Palmer's private papers.

18 Library of Congress records list the states in which Palmer did photographic jobs for the OEM, the OWI, and other federal agencies.

19 Undated Office for Emergency Management resume, ATP Papers.

20 Carson, *op. cit.*, p. 67.

21 Undated Office for Emergency Management resume, ATP Papers.

22 Nelson, W. H. to Brown, R., June 10, 1942, ATP Papers.

23 Carson, *op. cit.*, p. 64.

24 Roholl, M., "Preparing for Victory: The U.S. Office of War Information Overseas Branch's Illustrated Magazine in the Netherlands and the Foundations for the American Century, 1944–1945," *European Journal of American Studies*, vol. 7, no. 2, (2012), pp. 10, 11.

25 Carson, *op. cit.*, p. 156.

26 Nelson, W. H. to Brown, R., June 10, 1942, ATP Papers.

27 Palmer, A. T., Interview with Smith, D. and Haller, S., October 25, 1988.

28 Palmer, A. T., Interview with Smith, D. and Haller, S., October 25, 1988.

29 Quote included in undated Office for Emergency Management resume, ATP Papers.

30 Winkler, A. M., *The Politics of Propaganda: The Office of War Information 1942–1945* (New Haven, CT: Yale University Press, 1978), p. 62.

31 Lee, *op. cit.*, p. 167.

32 Ellis, R., "Getting the Message Out: The Poster Boys of World War II," *Prologue*, vol. 37, no. 2 (2005), p. 25; Contiguglia, G., "Recruiting Public Opinion: The Posters of World War II," *Colorado Heritage*, (Winter 1995), pp. 22, 23.

33 Contiguglia, *Ibid.*, pp. 23, 24.

34 Contiguglia, *Ibid.*, p. 23.

35 Jowett, G. S. and O'Donnell, V., *Propaganda and Persuasion*, 7th edn. (Los Angeles, CA: Sage Publications, 2019), p. 7.

36 "A Few Facts Related to the Arsenal of Democracy and the Four Freedoms exhibits of World War Two," ATP Papers.

37 "Defense Workers," *Survey Graphic*, vol. 30, no. 11 (November 1941), p. 571.

38 Carson, *op. cit.*, pp. 169, 170.

39 Blum, J. M., *V was for Victory* (New York: Harvest Books, 1976), pp. 9–10.

40 Newspapers could not be stopped from covering the overcrowded conditions and commenting on them in editorials. For example, the *Seattle (*Washington) *Times* ran a banner headline in its November 30, 1941, issue that stated, "City Housing Shortage Rapidly Nears Crisis," p. 20. The subhead stated "55,000 'Invade' Seattle from Many States."

41 Mathis-Downs, J. L., *Childersburg* (Charlestown, S.C.: Arcadia Publishing, 2006), p. 9.

42 Unger, P., to Stryker, R., January 1941, Roy Stryker Papers. No specific day of the week was placed on the letter.

43 Delano, J. to Stryker, R., March 20, 1941, Roy Stryker Papers.

44 Delano, J. to Stryker, R., April 9, 1941, Roy Stryker Papers.

45 Miller, R., "From Dustbowl and Dairy Farm to Defense Housing: Understanding the Farm Security Administration Photographs of Bath Iron Works," *Maine History*, vol. 46, no. 1 (2011), pp. 69, 78; Winkler, A. M., *Home Front U.S.A.: America during World War II* (Wheeling, IL: Harlan Davidson, 2000), p. 49.

46 Women's Bureau, "Womanpower Committees During World War II: United States and British Experience" (Washington, D.C.: United States Department of Labor, 1953), p. 3.

47 Dumenil, *op. cit.*, pp. 10–11, 24, 32.

48 For more on the themes that government propagandists used to encourage women to take factory jobs, see Honey, M., "The 'Womanpower' Campaign: Advertising and Recruitment Propaganda during World War II," *Frontiers*, vol. 6, no. 1 (1981), pp. 50–56.

49 Yesil, B., "Who said this is a Man's War? Propaganda, Advertising Discourse and Representations of War Worker Women during the Second World War," *Media History*, vol. 10, no. 2 (2004), pp. 103–104.

50 Honey, 1981, *op. cit.*, p. 51.

51 Rupp, L., *Mobilizing Women for War: German and American Propaganda, 1939–1945* (Princeton, NJ: Princeton University Press, 1978), pp. 51, 52, 68, 73.

52 Kesler-Harris, A., *Out to Work: A History of Wage-Earning Women in the United States* (New York: Oxford University Press, 2003), pp. 108–141.

53 U.S. Bureau of the Census, *Comparative Statistics for the U.S., 1870–1940,* Table XV, p. 92. www2.census.gov/library/publications/decennial/1940/population-occupation/00312147ch2.pdf (accessed August 12, 2022). Page 91 of the same volume reveals that in 1920, almost 52 million women were in the workforce. By 1930, that number had increased to 60.6 million.

54 Lewis, C. and Neville, J., "Images of Rosie: A Content Analysis of Women Workers in American Magazine Ads 1940–1946," *Journalism and Mass Communication Quarterly*, vol. 72, no. 1 (1995), p. 216.

55 Marcellus, J., "These Working Wives: Representation of the 'Two-Job' Woman Between the World Wars," *American* Journalism, vol. 23, no. 3 (2006), pp. 54, 59; Lewis and Neville, *op. cit.*, p. 217; Weiner, L. Y., *From Working Girl to Working Mother: The Female Labor Force in the United States, 1820–1980* (Chapel Hill, NC: University of North Carolina Press, 1985), p. 4.

56 Carson, *op. cit.*, p. 145.

57 Dumenil, *op. cit.*, p. 14.

58 Carson, *op. cit.*, p. 43; Honey, 1981, *op. cit.*, p. 51.

59 Belliveau, R., "These Are Not Normal Times: Masculinity and Femininity in Romance Pulps from the Second World War," *Journal of American Culture*, vol. 44, no. 1 (2021), p. 22.

60 McEuen, M. A., *Making War, Making Women: Femininity and Duty on the American Home Front, 1941–1945* (Athens: University of Georgia Press, 2011), p. 1.

61 Weiner, *op. cit.*, p. 95.

62 Wynn, N. A., *The African American Experience during World War II* (New York: Rowman and Littlefield Publishers, 2010), p. 23.

63 Koppes, C. R. and Black, G. D., "Blacks, Loyalty, and Motion-Picture Propaganda in World War II," *Journal of American History*, vol. 73, no. 2, (1986), p. 383.

64 Finkle, L., "The Conservative Aims of Militant Rhetoric: Black Protest During World War II," *Journal of American History*, vol. 60, no. 3 (1973), p. 692.

65 Koppes and Black, *op. cit.*, p. 387.

66 Winkler, 1978, *op. cit.*, pp. 56-57.

67 Winkler, 1978, *Ibid.*, p. 56.

68 Palmer, A. T., Interview with Macauley, C., June 19, 1988.

69 Winkler, 1978, *op. cit.*, pp. 67, 68.

70 Duis, P. R., "Soldiers Without Guns," *Chicago History*, vol. 16, no. 3, (1987–88), p. 38; Carson, *op. cit.*, p. 47.

71 Palmer, A. T., Interview with Smith, D. and Haller, S., October 25, 1988.

72 Anderson, K. T., "Last Hired, First Fired: Black Women Workers during World War II," *Journal of American History*, vol. 69, no. 1 (1982), pp. 83, 84.

73 Washburn, P. S., "The Black Press: Homefront Clout Hits a Peak in World War II," *American Journalism*, vol. 12, no. 3 (1995), pp. 359–366.

74 Orbach, B. and Natanson, N., "The Mirror Image: Black Washington in World War II-Era Federal Photography," *Washington History*, vol. 4, no. 1, (1992), p. 20.

75 Natanson, N. to Palmer, A. T., undated (but among other early 1990s letters in Palmer's papers. The letter assessed the photographer's career). ATP Papers.

76 Palmer, A. T., to Natanson, N., September 12, 1990, ATP Papers.

Chapter 4

1 Palmer, A. T., Interview with Smith, D. and Haller, S., October 25, 1988.

2 Carson, J. C., *Interpreting National Identity in Time of War: Competing Views in United States Office of War Information (OWI) Photography, 1940–1945* (Ph.D. diss., Boston University, 1995), p. 44.

3 In one letter, Palmer told his wife that he was "staying up all hours of the night" to develop his negatives. Palmer, A. T. to Palmer, A., May 31, 1942, ATP Papers.

4 "Task Force Number One—Building the Arsenal of Democracy," ATP Papers.

5 "Alfred T. Palmer," Office of War Information, Washington, D.C., 1942, ATP Papers.

6 Earle, J. B., "Pictures for Defense," *Popular Photography* (April 1942), p. 20.

7 Klingaman, W. K., *The Darkest Year: The American Home Front 1941–1942* (New York: St. Martin's Press, 2019), pp. 144, 176–177, 222–223.

8 Letters contained in the ATP Papers regularly refer to Alexa's work. The couple also referenced their lifelong business partnership in their interview with C. Macauley. Palmer, A. T., Interview with Macauley, C., June 19, 1988.

9 Palmer, A. T., to Palmer, A., undated (but written in January 1942), ATP Papers.

10 Ewing Krainin Syndicate to Palmer, A. T., December 29, 1942, ATP Papers. The letter accompanying a check for $160 noted that the money "completed the balance of the California Wine Story." An unpublished resume located in Palmer's papers includes the following statement: "During the last year, when not occupied with work for the OEM I have been constantly busy in and around New York City (where I maintain an office and studio) making photographs for advertising agencies and several publications as well as directing the photographic activities of the Good Neighbor Fleet," ATP Papers.

11 Undated resume for the Office for Emergency Management, ATP Papers; Spellacy, A., "Mapping the Metaphor of the Good Neighbor: Geography, Globalism, and Pan-Americanism during the 1940s," *American Studies*, vol. 47, no. 2 (2006), p. 42.

12 Palmer, A. T. to Palmer, A., January 25, 1942, ATP Papers.

13 For one such letter, see Palmer, A. T. to Palmer, A., April 27, 1939. Palmer noted in a 1988 interview that his pre-war income varied considerably. See Palmer, A.T. Interview with Smith, D. and Haller, S. A., October 25, 1988.

14 Palmer, A. T. to Palmer, A., March 22, 1942, ATP Papers.

15 Palmer, A. T. Interview with Smith, D. and Haller, S. A., October 25, 1988.

16 Palmer, A. T. to Palmer, A., January 25, 1942, ATP Papers.

17 Palmer, A. T. to Palmer, A., May 31, 1942, ATP Papers.

18 Palmer, A. T. to Palmer, A., June 4, 1942, ATP Papers.

19 Palmer, A. T. to Palmer, A., June 4, 1942, ATP Papers.

20 Palmer, A. T. to Palmer, A., June 6, 1942, ATP Papers.

21 Nelson, W. M. to Brown, R., June 10, 1942, ATP Papers.

22 Palmer, A. T. to Palmer, A., March 8, 1942, ATP Papers.

23 Palmer, A. T. to Palmer, A., March 15, 1942, ATP Papers.

24 Palmer, A. T. to Palmer, A., undated letter, ATP Papers.

25 Palmer, A. T. to Palmer, A., June 6, 1942, ATP Papers.

26 Palmer, A. T. to Palmer, A., December 12, 1941, ATP Papers.

27 Winkler, A. M. *The Politics of Propaganda: The Office of War Information 1942–1945* (New Haven, CT: Yale University Press, 1978), p. 52; Wendt, P., "The Control of Rubber in World War II," *Southern Economic Journal*, vol. 13, no. 3 (1947), p. 203.

28 Orbach, B. and Natanson, N., "The Mirror Image: Black Washington in World War II-Era Federal Photography," *Washington History*, vol. 4, no. 1 (1992), p. 6.

29 Palmer, A. T. to Palmer, A., March 8, 1942, ATP Papers.

30 Palmer, A. T. to Palmer, A., January 25, 1942, ATP Papers.

31 Palmer, A. T. to Palmer, A., December 12, 1941, ATP Papers.

32 Palmer, A. T. to Palmer, A., December 9, 1941, ATP Papers.

33 Palmer, A. T. to Palmer, A., December 12, 1941, ATP Papers.

34 Palmer, A. T. to Palmer, A., March 1942, ATP Papers.

35 Palmer, A. T. to Palmer, A., December 12, 1941, ATP Papers.

36 Palmer, A. T. to Palmer, A., March 8, 1942, ATP Papers.

37 Palmer, A. T. to Palmer, A., March 15, 1942, ATP Papers.

38 Undated resume for the Office for Emergency Management, ATP Papers.

39 Palmer, A. T. to Palmer, A., undated letter, ATP Papers.

40 Palmer, A. T. to Palmer, A., undated letter, ATP Papers.

41 "Official OEM Photographer Has Hard Time with Police," *Youngstown* (Ohio) *Vindicator*, November 13, 1941. Several of the FSA photographers had run-ins with local police and F.B.I. agents, including Russell Lee, while taking images for the government. Lee, R. to Stryker, R., September 6, 1942, Stryker Papers.

42 "Official OEM Photographer Has Hard Time with Police," *Ibid*. Also see letter from Lee, R. to Stryker, R., telling the latter man that an intermediary was needed for the photographer to do his job of shooting work on the Bonneville and Shasta Dams. Officials, Lee told Stryker, "are a little particular these days about pictures." Lee, R. to Stryker, R., October 7, 1941, Stryker Papers.

43 Earle, J. B. "Pictures for Defense," *Popular Photography* (April 1942), p. 45.

44 Nelson, W. H. to Brown, R., June 10, 1942, ATP Papers.

45 Nelson to Brown, *Ibid*.

46 "Shoots NAA," *Skywriter*, September 25, 1942.

47 "Photographer Visits Peninsula," *Escanaba* (Michigan) *Daily Press*, October 13, 1943, p. 7; "News to Those in Service," *Wakefield* (Michigan) *News*, November 19, 1943, p. 6. The latter newspaper stated that the article would appear in the March 1944 issue of the magazine. It was published in the December 1944 issue. See: Klemmer, H., "Michigan Fights," *National Geographic*, vol. 86., no. 6, (December 1944), pp. 676–715.

48 Dunathan, C., "Picture Story," *Escanaba* (Michigan) *Daily Press*, October 8, 1943, p. 4. Dunathan expressed equal pleasure with *National Geographic*'s choice of the writer for the article, Harvey Klemmer, a former reporter for the *Detroit News*.

49 Palmer, A. T., Interview with Macauley, C., June 19, 1988.

50 Carson, *op. cit.*, p. 17.

51 "Notice of Resignation," Roy Stryker Papers. Stryker's resignation was dated October 2, 1943.

52 Palmer, A. T., Interview with Macauley, C., June 19, 1988; Lee, M., *Promoting the War Effort: Robert Horton and Federal Propaganda, 1938–1946* (Baton Rouge, LA: Louisiana State University Press, 2021), p. 184.

53 Hendrickson, B., "Priming the Flower's Stem: US Maritime Industries Prepare for War," *International Journal of Maritime History*, vol. 18, no. 1 (2006), p. 131.

54 Butler, J. A., *Sailing on Friday: The Perilous Voyage of America's Merchant Marine* (Washington, D.C.: Brassey's, 1997), p. 193; Bunker, J., *Heroes in Dungarees: The Story of the American Merchant Marine in World War II* (Annapolis, MD: Naval Institute Press, 1995), p. xii.

55 Palmer, A. T., Interview with Macauley, C., June 19, 1988.

56 Butler, *op. cit.*, p. 165.

57 Palmer, A. T., Interview with Macauley, C., June 19, 1988.; "ADM. EMORY LAND, LED SHIP AGENCY," *New York Times*, November 28, 1971, p. 72.

58 Leahy, W. D, Admiral to Land, E. S., Vice Admiral, October 10, 1944, ATP Papers.

59 Land, E. S., Vice Admiral, to Palmer, A. T., January 16, 1945, ATP Papers.

60 Cahill, G., "Shadows of the Past," *Pacific Sun*, July 27, 1990.

61 Herman, A., *Douglas MacArthur: American Warrior* (New York: Random House, 2017), pp. 542–549, 562, 564, 570–577; Morrison, S. E., *The Liberation of the Philippines: Luzon, Mindanao, the Visayas, 1944–1945* (Annapolis, MD: Naval Institute Press, 2012); Manchester, W., *American Caesar: Douglas MacArthur, 1880–1964* (New York: Back Bay Books, 2008), pp. 381, 391–394, 386, 389, 428–430.

62 A Palmer, A. T. to Palmer, A., January 30, 1945, ATP Papers. A letter from Alfred written three days earlier told Alexa that the trip was delayed because neither the film he needed, nor his passport had arrived in Oakland. Palmer, A. T. to Palmer, A., January 27, 1945, ATP Papers.

63 Palmer, A. T. to Palmer, A., March 10, 1945, ATP Papers.

64 Palmer, A. T. to Palmer, A., March 22, 1945, ATP Papers.

65 Palmer, A. T. to Palmer, A., March 23, 1945, ATP Papers.

66 For more on the history of the camp, the mass starvation that occurred, and the liberation of the camp on February 3, 1945, see Wilkinson, R., *Surviving a Japanese Internment Camp: Life and Liberation at Santo Tomas, Manila, in World War II* (Jefferson, NC: McFarland, 2014); Holland, R. B., *100 Miles to Freedom: The Epic Story of the Rescue of Santo Tomas and the Liberation of Manila: 1943–1945* (Nashville: Turner Publishing, 2011).

67 Cahill, *op. cit.*

Chapter 5

1 Pincas, S. and Loiseau, M., *A History of Advertising* (Los Angeles, CA: Taschen, 2008), p. 75.

2 "Salon of Photography," Rochester (New York) Museum of Arts and Sciences, 1940).

3 Palmer, A. T. to Palmer, A., January 27, 1945, ATP Papers.

4 Marchand, R., *Advertising the American Dream: Making Way for Modernity, 1920–1940* (Berkeley, CA: University of California Press, 1985), pp. 127, 140.

5 Murphy, J., "Charles Sheeler (1883–1965)," in *Heilbrunn Timeline of Art History*, New York: The Metropolitan Museum of Art, 2000, www.metmuseum.org/toah/hd/shee/hd_shee.htm (Accessed July 3, 2023).

6 Johnston, P., *Real Fantasies: Edward Steichen's Advertising Photography* (Berkeley, CA: University of California Press, 1997), pp. 238–240.

7 Quote reprinted in undated resume produced for the Office of Emergency Management, ATP Papers.

8 Evans, N. to Gilmore, O., December 14, 1942, ATP Papers.

9 Carson, J. C., *Interpreting National Identity in Time of War: Competing Views in United States Office of War Information (OWI) Photography, 1940–1945* (Ph.D. diss., Boston University, 1995), p. 164.

10 Prodger, P., *William Eggleston Portraits* (New Haven, CT: Yale University Press, 2016), p. 19. On Adams' darkroom techniques, see Adams, A., *The Print*, (New York: Little, Brown, 1995).

11 For more on the B-17, see Doyle, D., *B-17 Flying Fortress, Vol. 1: Boeing's Model 299 through B-17D in World War II* (Atglen, PA: Schiffer Military History, 2020) and Doyle, D., *B-17 Flying Fortress, Vol. 2: Boeing's B-17E through B-17H in World War II* (Atglen, PA: Schiffer Military History, 2021). On the number of B-17s that were shot down during the war, see "History of the Boeing B-17," *Together We Fly*, www.eaa.org/eaa/events-and-experiences/aluminum-overcast-eaa-b-17-bomber-tour/b-17-history-with-boeing-and-eaa (accessed June 25, 2023).

12 Norton, M. B. and Sheriff, C., *et al.*, *A People and A Nation: A History of the United States, Vol. 2: Since 1865*, 8th edition (Belmont, CA: Wadsworth, 2005), p. 746.

Epilogue

1 Palmer, A. T. to Palmer, A., January 27, 1945, ATP Papers.
2 Palmer, A. T. to Palmer, A., May 24, 1945, ATP Papers.
3 Palmer, A. T., Interview with Macauley, C., June 19, 1988.
4 Palmer, A. T., Interview with Macauley, C., June 19, 1988.
5 Undated resume, *op. cit.*, ATP Papers.
6 Report written by Rudy, J., of the public relations office of the National Federation of American Shipping, ATP Papers.
7 "Task Force Number One—Building the Arsenal of Democracy," ATP Papers.

BIBLIOGRAPHY

Primary Sources

Julia Palmer Gennert, interviewed by Mary M. Cronin, June 9, 2022.
Alfred T. Palmer Papers, privately held.
Alfred T. Palmer, interviewed by C. Cameron Macauley for the National Maritime Museum Park, San Francisco, June 19, 1988, transcript.
Alfred T. Palmer, interviewed by Douglas Smith and Stephen A. Haller for the National Maritime Museum Park, San Francisco, October 25, 1988, transcript.
Alfred T. Palmer, interviewed by Douglas Smith for the National Maritime Museum Park, San Francisco, November 2, 1988, transcript.
Arthur Rothstein, interviewed by Richard K. Doud for the Smithsonian Archives of American Art, Washington, D.C., May 25, 1964, transcript.
Roy Emerson Stryker Papers, Roy Stryker Papers, Series 1 (Correspondence 1941–1945), Reel 3. Microfilm. Originals held at Archives and Special Collections, Ekstrom Library, University of Louisville, Louisville, KY.
Roy Emerson Stryker, interviewed by Richard K. Doud for the Smithsonian Archives of American Art, Washington, D.C., October 17, 1963, transcript.

Secondary Sources

Acker, E., *et al.*, *Cult of the Machine: Precisionism and American Art* (New Haven, CT: Yale University Press, 2018).
Adams, A., *The Print* (New York: Little, Brown, 1995).
"ADM. EMORY LAND, LED SHIP AGENCY," *New York Times*, November 28, 1971.
"Alfred Palmer," *San Francisco Chronicle*, February 2, 1993, clipping in ATP Papers.
"Alfred T. Palmer," *Marin Independent Journal*, February 5, 1993, clipping in ATP Papers.
American Presidency Project, The, "Fireside Chat," University of California (Santa Barbara), www.presidency.ucsb.edu/documents/fireside-chat-9 (accessed July 19, 2022).
American War and Military Operations Casualties: Lists and Statistics, CRS Report No. RL32492, Version 25, p. 2 (Washington, DC: Congressional Research Service, September 14, 2018), crsreports.congress.gov/product/pdf/RL/RL32492 (accessed December 3, 2022).
Anderson, K. T., "Last Hired, First Fired: Black Women Workers during World War II," *Journal of American History*, vol. 69, no. 1, (1982).
Axelrod, A., *Selling the Great War: The Making of American Propaganda* (New York: St. Martin's Press, 2009).
Baime, A. J., *The Arsenal of Democracy: FDR, Detroit, and an Epic Quest to Arm an America at War* (Boston, MA: Mariner Books, 2015).
Barrick, K. A., *Harrison R. Crandall: Creating a Vision of Grand Teton National Park* (Layton, UT: Gibbs Smith, 2013).

Barrick, K. A., "Harrison R. Crandall: Artist, Pioneer and Patron of Grand Teton National Park," *University of Wyoming National Park Service Research Center Annual Report*, vol. 30, (2006).

Belliveau, R., "'These Are Not Normal Times:' Masculinity and Femininity in Romance Pulps from the Second World War," *Journal of American Culture*, vol. 44, no. 1, (2021).

Berg, A. S., *Lindbergh* (New York: G.P. Putnam), 1988.

Blum, J. M., *V was for Victory* (New York: Harvest Books, 1976).

Boyden, A., "Changing Shanghai," *National Geographic*, vol. 72, no. 4, (October 1937).

Brannan, B. W. and Mora, G., *FSA: The American Vision* (New York: Abrams, 2006).

Brock, C., *Charles Sheeler: Across Media* (Berkeley, CA: University of California Press, 2006).

Broughton, P. S., "Government Agencies and Civilian Morale," *The Annals of the American Academy of Political and Social Science*, vol. 220, (March 1942).

Broussard, J. C. and Hamilton, J. M., "Covering a Two-Front War: Three African American Correspondents during World War II," *American Journalism*, vol. 22, no. 3, (2005).

Buitenhuis, P., "The Selling of the Great War," *Canadian Review of American Studies*, vol. 7, no. 2, (1976).

Bunker, J., *Heroes in Dungarees: The Story of the American Merchant Marine in World War II* (Annapolis, MD: Naval Institute Press, 1995).

Butler, J., *Sailing on Friday: The Perilous Voyage of America's Merchant Marine* (Washington, D.C.: Brassey's, 1997).

Cahill, G., "Shadows of the Past," *Pacific Sun*, July 27, 1990, photocopy in ATP Papers.

Camhi, L., "Propriety and Provocation: Women, Emigres, and Outliers in American Magazines at Mid-Century," in Klein, M., (ed.), *Modern Look: Photography and the American Magazine* (New Haven, CT: Yale University Press, 2020).

Carson, J. C., *Interpreting National Identity in Time of War: Competing Views in United States Office of War Information (OWI) Photography, 1940–1945* (Ph.D. diss., Boston University, 1995).

Cartier-Bresson, H., *The Decisive Moment* (Gottingen, Germany: Steidl, 2015).

Catton, B., *The War Lords of Washington* (New York: Greenwood Press, 1969).

"City Housing Shortage Rapidly Nears Crisis," *Seattle* (Washington) *Times*, November 30, 1941.

Contiguglia, G., "Recruiting Public Opinion: The Posters of World War II," *Colorado Heritage* (Winter 1995).

"Cornell Capa: Concerned Photographer," www.icp.org/exhibitions/cornell-capa-concerned-photographer (accessed May 20, 2023).

Creel, G., *How We Advertised America: The First Telling of the Amazing Story on the Committee on Public Information that Carried the Gospel of Americanism to Every Corner of the Globe* (New York: Harper and Brothers, 1920).

Cullinan, N., "Director's Foreword," in Prodger, P., (ed.), *William Eggleston Portraits* (New Haven, CT: Yale University Press, 2016).

Dallek, R., *Franklin D. Roosevelt: A Political Life* (New York: Viking, 2017).

Daniels, R., *Prisoners without Trial: Japanese Americans in World War II* (New York: Hill and Wang, 2004).

Daniels, R., *Franklin D. Roosevelt: The War Years, 1939–1945* (Chicago, IL: University of Illinois Press, 2016).

"Defense Workers," *Survey Graphic*, vol. 30, no. 11 (November 1941).

Doenecke, J. D., "Non-Interventionism of the Left: The Keep America Out of War Congress 1938–1941," *Journal of Contemporary History*, vol. 12, no. 2 (1977).

Doenecke, J. D. and Wilz, J. E., *From Isolation to War: 1931–1941*, 3rd edn. (Hoboken, NJ: Wiley-Blackwell, 2015).

Doyle, D., *B-17 Flying Fortress, Vol. 1: Boeing's Model 299 through B-17D in World War II* (Atglen, PA: Schiffer Military History, 2020).

Doyle, D., *B-17 Flying Fortress, Vol. 2: Boeing's B-17E through B-17H in World War II* (Atglen, PA: Schiffer Military History, 2021).

Duis, P. R., "Soldiers Without Guns," *Chicago History*, vol. 16, no. 3 (1987–88).

Dumenil, L., *American Working Women in World War II* (Boston, MA: Bedford-St. Martin's, 2020).

Dunn, S., *A Blueprint for War: FDR and the Hundred Days that Mobilized America* (New Haven, CT: Yale University Press, 2018).

Earle, J. B., "Pictures for Defense," *Popular Photography* (April 1942).

Ehrens, S., "Revisiting a Modernist Pioneer," in Martineau, P. (ed.), *Imogen Cunningham: A Retrospective*, (Los Angeles: J. Paul Getty Museum, 2020).

Ellis, R., "Getting the Message Out: The Poster Boys of World War II," *Prologue*, vol. 37, no. 2 (2005).

Elisofon, E., "Texture, Chiaroscuro, Expression and Form Through Proper Flash Illumination," *U. S. Camera* (1941 annual).

Farnham, B. R., *Roosevelt and the Munich Crisis: A Study of Political Decision-Making* (Princeton, NJ: Princeton University Press, 1997).

Fasce, F., "Advertising America, Constructing the Nation: Rituals of the Homefront During the Great War," *European Contributions to American Studies*, vol. 44 (2000).

Favreau, M., *Crash: The Great Depression and the Fall and Rise of America* (New York: Little, Brown and Company, 2018).

Finkle, L., "The Conservative Aims of Militant Rhetoric: Black Protest During World War II," *Journal of American History*, vol. 60, no. 3 (1973).

"Fireside Chat," The American Presidency Project, www.presidency.ucsb.edu/documents/fireside-chat-9 (accessed November 11, 2022).

Fleming, T., *The New Dealers' War: Franklin D. Roosevelt and the War within World War II* (New York: Basic Books, 2001).

Foster, M. S., *Henry J. Kaiser: Builder in the Modern American West* (Austin, TX: University of Texas Press, 1989).

French, P., *Bloody Saturday: Shanghai's Darkest Day* (New York: Penguin Books, 2017).

Friedl, B., "The Hybrid Art of Fashion Photography: American Photographers in Post-World War II Europe," *Amerikastudien*, vol. 52, no. 1 (2007).

Gedrim, R. J., "Peinture a la Lumiere: 1898–1907," in Brandow, T. and Ewing, W. A. (eds.), *Edward Steichen: Lives in Photography* (New York: W. W. Norton, 2008).

Gilford, S., *Build 'Em by the Mile, Cut 'Em off by the Yard: How Henry J. Kaiser and the Rosies Helped Win World War II* (Richmond, CA: Richmond Museum of History, 2011).

Goldberg, M. H., *The "Stately President" Liners: American Passenger Liners of the Interwar Years* Part I (Kings Point, NY: American Merchant Marine Museum, 1996).

Goodwin, D. K., *No Ordinary Time: Franklin & Eleanor Roosevelt: The Home Front in World War II* (New York: Simon & Schuster, 2008).

Greenfeld, H., *Ben Shahn: An Artist's Life* (New York: Random House, 1998).

Hambourg, M. M., "The Heart of the Matter," in Hambourg, M. M. and Rosenheim, J. L. (eds.), *Irving Penn: Centennial* (New Haven, CT: Yale University Press, 2017).

Hamilton, J. M., *Manipulating the Masses: Woodrow Wilson and the Birth of American Propaganda* (Baton Rouge, LA: Louisiana State University Press, 2020).

Heiferman, M., "Astonish Me!: Photography, Graphic Design, and Mid-Century Visual Culture," in Klein, M. (ed.), *Modern Look: Photography and the American Magazine* (New Haven, CT: Yale University Press, 2020).

Heinrichs, W., *Threshold of War: Franklin D. Roosevelt and American Entry into World War II* (New York: Oxford University Press, 1988).

Hendricks, C. and Delgaudio, J., "A Vast War Establishment: World War II Comes to Long Beach," *Southern California Quarterly*, vol. 99, no. 4 (2017).

Hendrickson, B., "Priming the Flower's Stem: U. S. Maritime Industries Prepare for War," *International Journal of Maritime History*, vol. 18, no. 1 (2006).

Herman, A., *Douglas MacArthur: American Warrior* (New York: Random House: 2017).

Herman, A., *Freedom's Forge: How American Business Produced Victory in World War II* (New York: Random House, 2013).

Hill, J. T. and Liesbrock, H., *Walker Evans: Depth of Field* (New York: Prestel), 2016.

"History of the Boeing B-17," *Together We Fly*, www.eaa.org/eaa/events-and-experiences/aluminum-overcast-eaa-b-17-bomber-tour/b-17-history-with-boeing-and-eaa (accessed June 25, 2023).

Holland, R. B., *100 Miles to Freedom: The Epic Story of the Rescue of Santo Tomas and the Liberation of Manila: 1943–1945* (Nashville, TN: Turner Publishing, 2011).

Honey, M., "The 'Womanpower' Campaign: Advertising and Recruitment Propaganda during World War II," *Frontiers: A Journal of Women Studies*, vol. 6, no. 1–2 (1980).

Honey, M., *Creating Rosie the Riveter: Class, Gender, and Propaganda during World War II* (Amherst, MA: University of Massachusetts Press, 1984).

Hull, T. J., "The World War II Army Enlistment Records File and Access to Archival Databases," *Prologue Magazine* 38, no. 1, Spring 2006, available at: www.archives.gov/publications/prologue/2006/spring/aad-ww2.html (accessed June 10, 2023).

Hurley, F. J., *Portrait of a Decade: Roy Stryker and the Development of Documentary Photography in the Thirties* (New York: Da Capo Press, 1972).

Johnston, P., *Real Fantasies: Edward Steichen's Advertising Photography* (Berkeley, CA: University of California Press, 1997).

Johnston, P., "The Modernist Fashion: Steichen's Commercial Photography Between the Wars," in Brandow, T. and Ewing, W. A., *Edward Steichen: Lives in Photography* (New York: W.W. Norton, 2007).

Jowett, G. S. and O'Donnell, V., *Propaganda and Persuasion*, 7th edn. (Los Angeles: Sage Publications, 2019).

Kessler-Harris, A., *Out to Work: A History of Wage-Earning Women in the United States* (New York: Oxford University Press, 2003).

Klemmer, H., "Michigan Fights," *National Geographic*, vol 86, no. 6 (December 1944).

Klingaman, W. K., *The Darkest Year: The American Home Front 1941–1942* (New York: St. Martin's Press, 2019).

Koppes, C. R. and Black, G, D., "Blacks, Loyalty, and Motion-Picture Propaganda in World War II," *Journal of American History*, vol. 73, no. 2 (1986).

Lacey, J., *The Washington War: FDR's Inner Circle and the Politics of Power That Won World War II* (New York: Bantam Books, 2020).

Larsen, R., "A lifetime of filming took them on trips around the world," *Marin Independent Journal*, April 14, 1984, clipping in ATP Papers.

Larson, C., "OWI's Domestic News Bureau: An Account and Appraisal," *Journalism Quarterly*, vol. 26, no. 1 (1949).

Laurie, C. D., *The Propaganda Warriors: America's Crusade against Nazi Germany* (Lawrence, KS: University of Kansas Press, 1995).

Lee, M., *Promoting the War Effort: Robert Horton and Federal Propaganda, 1938–1946* (Baton Rouge, LA: Louisiana State University Press, 2021).

Leibbrand, C., *et al.*, "The Great Migration and Residential Segregation in American Cities during the Twentieth Century," *Social Science History*, vol. 44, no. 1 (2020).

Lewis, C. and Neville, J., "Images of Rosie: A Content Analysis of Women Workers in American Magazine Ads 1940–1946," *Journalism and Mass Communication Quarterly*, vol. 72, no. 1 (1995).

Lippmann, W., *Public Opinion* (New York: Free Press, 1997).

McEuen, M. A., *Making War, Making Women: Femininity and Duty on the American Home Front, 1941–1945* (Athens, GA: University of Georgia Press, 2011).

McMillan, G., "The News Bureau of the OWI—Its Functions and Operations," *Journalism Quarterly*, vol. 20, no. 2 (1943).

Mall, Scott. "FreightWaves Classics/Fallen Flags: American President Lines still lives under new ownership (Part 2)," FreightWaves, www.freightwaves.com/news/freightwaves-classics-fallen-flags-american-president-lines-still-lives-under-new-ownership-part-2. (Accessed November 12, 2022).

Manchester, W., *American Caesar: Douglas MacArthur, 1880–1964* (New York: Back Bay Books, 2008).

Marcellus, J., "These Working Wives: Representation of the 'Two-Job' Woman Between the World Wars," *American Journalism*, vol. 23, no. 3 (2006).

Marchand, R., *Advertising the American Dream: Making Way for Modernity, 1920–1940* (Berkeley, CA: University of California Press, 1985).

Mathis-Downs, J. L., *Childersburg* (Charlestown, S.C.: Arcadia Publishing, 2006).

Mendelson, A., "Slice-of-Life Moments as Visual 'Truth': Norman Rockwell, Feature Photography, and American Values in Pictorial Journalism," *Journalism History*, vol. 29, no. 4 (2004).

Meyer, R., "Photography is Elastic: Weegee's Cockeyed View of Hollywood," *America Art*, vol. 27, no. 2 (2013).

Michney, T. M., "Constrained Communities: Black Cleveland's Experience with World War II Public Housing," *Journal of Social History*, vol. 40, no. 4 (2007).

Miller, R., "From Dustbowl and Dairy Farm to Defense Housing: Understanding the Farm Security Administration Photographs of Bath Iron Works," *Maine History*, vol. 46, no. 1 (2011).

Morrison, S. E., *The Liberation of the Philippines: Luzon, Mindanao, the Visayas, 1944–1945* (Annapolis, MD: Naval Institute Press, 2012).

Murphy, J., "Charles Sheeler (1883–1965)," In *Heilbrunn Timeline of Art History*. New York: The Metropolitan Museum of Art, 2000, www.metmuseum.org/toah/hd/shee/hd_shee.htm. (Accessed July 3, 2023).

"News to Those in Service," *Wakefield* (Michigan) *News*, November 19, 1943.

Niven, P., *Steichen: A Biography* (Fort Washington, PA: Eastern National, 1997).

Norris, J. D., *Advertising and the Transformation of American Society, 1865–1920* (Westport, CT: Greenwood Press, 1990).

Norton, M. B. and Sheriff, C., *et al.*, *A People and A Nation: A History of the United States, Vol. 2: Since 1865*, 8th edition (Belmont, CA: Wadsworth, 2005).

O'Callaghan, T. J., *Ford in the Service of America: Mass Production for the Military During the World Wars* (Jefferson, NC: McFarland & Co., 2009).

"Official OEM Photographer Has Hard Time with Police," *Youngstown* (Ohio) *Vindicator*, November 13, 1941.

Ohm, K. B., "What You See is What You Get: Dorothea Lange and Ansel Adams at Manzanar," *Journalism History*, vol. 4, no. 1 (1977).

Olson, L., *Those Angry Days: Roosevelt, Lindbergh, and America's Fight Over World War II* (New York, Random House, 2014).

Orbach, B. and Natanson, N., "The Mirror Image: Black Washington in World War II-Era Federal Photography," *Washington History*, vol. 4, no. 1 (1992).

"THE PEOPLE: Smug, Slothful, Asleep?" *Time*, February 16, 1942.

Petro, D., "Brother, Can you Spare a Dime?: The 1940 Census: Employment and Income," *Prologue* (Spring 2012), www.archives.gov/publications/prologue/2012/spring/1940.html. (Accessed March 21, 2023).

Perrett, G., *Days of Sadness, Years of Triumph: The American People, 1939–1945* (Madison, WI: University of Wisconsin Press, 1985).

"Photographer Visits Peninsula," *Escanaba* (Michigan) *Daily Press*, October 13, 1943.

"Picture Story," *Escanaba* (Michigan) *Press*, October 8, 1943.

Pincas, S. and Loiseau, M., *A History of Advertising* (Los Angeles: Taschen, 2008).

Pinkleton, B., "The Campaign of the Committee on Public Information: Its Contributions to the History and Evolution of Public Relations," *Journal of Public Relations Research*, vol. 6, no. 4 (1994).

Plunkett, S. H., *Enduring Ideals: Rockwell, Roosevelt, and the Four Freedoms* (New York: Abbeville Press, 2018).

Prodger, P. *William Eggleston Portraits*, (New Haven, CT: Yale University Press, 2016).

Reeves, R., *Infamy: The Shocking Story of the Japanese American Internment in World War II* (New York: Henry Holt, 2013).

Reynolds, D., "1940: Fulcrum of the Twentieth Century?" *International Affairs* 66, no. 2 (1990).

Richman-Abdou, K., "Precisionism: The Modern American Style Sparked by Industrialization," My Modern Met, mymodernmet.com/precisionism/. (Accessed May 15, 2023).

"Road to Victory," Museum of Modern Art, www.moma.org/calendar/exhibitions/3038. (Accessed August 9, 2022).

Roholl, M., "Preparing for Victory: The U. S. Office of War Information Overseas Branch's Illustrated Magazine in the Netherlands and the Foundations for the American Century, 1944–1945," *European Journal of American Studies*, vol. 7, no. 2 (2012).

Rose, K. D., *American Isolationism Between World Wars: The Search for a Nation's Identity* (New York: Routledge, 2021).

Rupp, L. J., *Mobilizing Women for War: German and American Propaganda, 1939–1945* (Princeton, NJ: Princeton University Press, 1978).

"Salon of Photography," Rochester (New York) Museum of Arts and Sciences, 1940.

"Shoots NAA," *Skywriter*, September 25, 1942.

Simms, B. and Laderman, C., *Hitler's American Gamble: Pearl Harbor and Germany's March to Global War* (New York: Basic Books, 2023).

Spellacy, A., "Mapping the Metaphor of the Good Neighbor: Geography, Globalism, and Pan-Americanism during the 1940s," *American Studies*, vol. 47, no. 2 (2006).

Steele, R. W., "The Great Debate: Roosevelt, the Media, and the Coming of the War, 1940–1941," *Journal of American History*, vol. 71, no. 1 (1984).

Steele, R. W., *Propaganda in an Open Society: The Roosevelt Administration and the Media, 1933–1941* (Westport, CT: Greenwood Press, 1985).

"Straight Photography," The Alfred Stieglitz Collection, 2016, archive.artic.edu/stieglitz/straight-photography/. (Accessed November 22, 2022).

Stryker, R. E., "The FSA Collection of Photographs," Stryker, R. E. and Wood, N. (eds.), *In This Proud Land: America 1935–1943 as seen in the FSA Photographs* (Greenwich, CT: New York Graphic Society, 1973).

Sumner, D. E., *The Magazine Century: American Magazines Since 1900* (New York: Peter Lang, 2010).

Swensen, J., "A Strategy of Truth: Andreas Feininger and the Creation of Propaganda for the Office of War Information, 1942," *History of Photography*, vol. 43, no. 1 (2019).

Taylor, P. M., *Munitions of the Mind: A History of Propaganda from the Ancient World to the Present Day* (Manchester, UK: Manchester University Press, 1995).

U.S. Bureau of the Census, *Comparative Statistics for the U.S., 1870–1940*, Table XV, 92, www2.census.gov/library/publications/decennial/1940/population-occupation/00312147ch2.pdf. (Accessed July 14, 2023).

Vogt, G. L., "When Posters Went to War: How America's Best Commercial Artists Helped Win World War I," *Wisconsin Magazine of History*, vol. 84, no. 2 (December 2000).

Washburn, P. S., "The Black Press: Homefront Clout Hits a Peak in World War II," *American Journalism*, vol. 12, no. 3 (1995).

Weinberg, S., "What to Tell America: The Writers' Quarrel in the Office of War Information," *Journal of American History*, vol. 55, no. 1 (1968).

Weiner, L. Y., *From Working Girl to Working Mother: The Female Labor Force in the United States, 1820–1980* (Chapel Hill, NC: University of North Carolina Press, 1985).

Welch, D., *World War II Propaganda: Analyzing the Art of Persuasion during Wartime* (Santa Barbara, CA: ABC-CLIO, 2017).

Wendt, P., "The Control of Rubber in World War II," *Southern Economic Journal*, vol. 13, no. 3 (1947).

"What About Photography in National Defense?" *U.S. Camera*, (August 1941).

Wilkinson, R., *Surviving a Japanese Internment Camp: Life and Liberation at Santo Tomas, Manilla, in World War II* (Jefferson, NC: McFarland, 2014).

Winkler, A. M., *The Politics of Propaganda: The Office of War Information 1942–1945* (New Haven, CT: Yale University Press, 1978).

Winkler, A. M., *Home Front U.S.A.: America during World War II* (Wheeling, IL: Harlan Davidson, 2000).

Winton, A. G., "The Bauhaus, 1919–1933," The Met Museum, www.metmuseum.org/toah/hd/bauh/hd_bauh.htm. (Accessed September 3, 2023).

Witkowski, T. H., "World War II Poster Campaigns: Preaching Frugality to American Consumers," *Journal of Advertising*, vol. 32, no. 1 (2003).

"Woman Power," archives.gov, Washington, D.C., www.archives.gov/files/education/lessons/images/wwii-womanpower.pdf. (Accessed April 19, 2023).

Women's Bureau, "Womanpower Committees During World War II: United States and British Experience" (Washington, D. C.: United States Department of Labor, 1953).

Wood, N., "Portrait of Stryker," in Stryker, R. E. and Wood, N. (eds.), *In This Proud Land: America 1935–1943 as seen in the FSA Photographs* (Greenwich, CT: New York Graphic Society, 1973).

Wynn, N. A., *The African American Experience during World War II* (New York: Rowman and Littlefield Publishers, 2010).

Yesil, B., "Who said this is a Man's War? Propaganda, Advertising Discourse and Representations of War Worker Women during the Second World War," Media History, vol. 10, no. 2 (2004).